Practical Data Science Environments with Python and R

Build and Manage Streamlined Workflows with Python and R for Real-World Insights and Analysis

Astha Puri

Rohan Mathur

www.orangeava.com

First Published: January 2026

Published By: Orange Education Pvt Ltd, AVA®

Address: 9, Daryaganj, Delhi, 110002, India

275 New North Road Islington Suite 1314 London,

N1 7AA, United Kingdom

ISBN (PBK): 978-93-49887-55-8

ISBN (E-BOOK): 978-93-49887-39-8

Scan the QR code to explore our entire catalogue

www.orangeava.com

Dedicated To

Every Beginner Who Opened Their First Notebook,

Wrote Their First Line of Code,

Or

Were Felt Overwhelmed by Their First Dataset,

This Book is for You.

About the Authors

Astha Puri is a senior data science leader at a Fortune 10 healthcare organization, where she builds large-scale recommendation systems that shape millions of user journeys each day. With over nine years of experience, she has honed her expertise in machine learning, personalization, and applied AI through roles at Oracle, Twilio, and CVS Health.

Beyond her industry work, Astha is a founding board member and Vice President of "Women Who Do Data". She mentors emerging talent and frequently speaks at national conferences, championing greater representation and opportunity in data and AI. She earned her M.S. in Data Science from the University of Minnesota, and her B. Tech from VIT University.

Rohan Mathur is a Senior Software Engineer in Nvidia's autonomous vehicles division, specializing in large-scale data analytics, machine learning, and fleet data strategies. His work helps shape the data systems that power perception and decision-making for next-generation autonomous driving.

With eight years of experience across Nvidia, Pandora Music, PayPal, and Mu Sigma, Rohan has built and led data science and analytics solutions spanning autonomous vehicles, fintech, streaming, and consulting. His expertise spans analytics engineering, machine learning, experimentation, and visual storytelling. He holds an M.S. from UCLA and a B. Tech from VIT University.

About the Technical Reviewer

Madhuri Jha has over 12 years of experience in the IT industry, with expertise spanning cloud platforms, automation, containerization, and programming. She is known for delivering dynamic workshops and courses tailored to diverse skill levels, from beginners to experienced professionals. Her technical strengths include AWS, Terraform, Ansible, Docker, Kubernetes, Python, and Java. She has also worked extensively on projects involving cloud computing, data analytics, and ETL pipelines using Pandas, Power BI, Spark, and Airflow.

Madhuri is a co-author of several Udemy courses, including *PostgreSQL for Beginners*, *Automation with Ansible*, and *Unlocking Python for Beginners*. With a strong background in corporate training, she has conducted programs for numerous clients covering Python, Java, Linux, Cloud, Ansible, Docker, Kubernetes, Git, JIRA, Terraform, and SQL.

Currently, Madhuri works as a **Senior DevOps Specialist at Thinknyx Technologies**, where she manages projects across cloud and DevOps domains and delivers training in cloud technologies and programming. She is also engaged in projects involving Artificial Intelligence (AI), Machine Learning (ML), and Generative AI (GenAI), with a passion for enabling organizations to harness these technologies for innovation and growth.

Acknowledgments

Writing this book has been a truly collaborative effort. We are deeply grateful to the professors, mentors, and colleagues who have guided us throughout our journeys, and helped shape our understanding of data science in practice.

To our families in India - your love traveled every distance. Thank you for your unwavering encouragement from afar. It grounded us through long stretches of research, writing, and revision.

We also extend our appreciation to the global data science community. Their open-source contributions, shared research, and thoughtful discussions continue to elevate the field, and inspire learners everywhere.

Finally, to every student, beginner, and aspiring data scientist who opens this book: Thank you! Your curiosity and determination are the reasons we wrote it, and we hope it serves as a meaningful step on your learning journey.

Preface

Data science today powers everything- from healthcare and finance to entertainment, retail, and autonomous vehicles. But for someone just beginning, the field can feel overwhelming. You may wonder which language to learn first, how to set up your environment, how to work with real data, and which tools professionals actually use. This book was created to make those first steps simple, practical, and encouraging.

This book has been written as a hands-on guide. Instead of focusing on heavy theory, it walks you through the real workflows that data scientists use every day. You will learn by installing tools, writing codes, exploring datasets, creating visualizations, building your first machine learning models, and understanding how these pieces fit together.

The book is structured to follow the natural learning path of a beginner stepping into data science. It begins in Chapter 1 with an introduction to what data science is, and how it shapes decision-making across different industries. Chapter 2 then compares the major programming languages and tools used in the field, helping you to understand when and why each one matters. In Chapter 3, you will learn how to set up your environment by installing Python, R, Jupyter, and RStudio on your own computer.

Building on this foundation, Chapters 4 and 5 guide you through working with real-world data, teaching you how to import, clean, organize, and wrangle messy datasets so that they become usable. Chapter 6 shifts the focus to visualization, showing how to turn raw numbers into clear, insightful graphics. With your data skills in place, Chapters 7 and 8 provide an approachable introduction to machine learning, walking you step-by-step through common algorithms, and how to implement them.

Since collaboration is essential in data work, Chapter 9 introduces Git and GitHub for version control and teamwork. Chapter 10 then bridges your technical skills with real workplace practices, covering topics like documentation, security, reproducibility, and effective project structure. Finally, Chapter 11 looks ahead to the future, preparing you for emerging areas such as cloud environments, large-scale data pipelines, AI-assisted development, and long-term career growth in the data science field.

Throughout the book, you will work with real datasets, see side-by-side examples in Python and R, and follow screenshots that make each step easy to repeat.

Hence, whether you are a student, a working professional, or simply someone curious about data, this book will give you a solid, practical foundation. By the end, you will have the skills to set up your environment, analyze data, build simple models, and contribute meaningfully to data projects.

Thus, welcome to your data science journey, and let us get started!

Get a Free eBook

We hope you are enjoying your recently purchased book! Your feedback is incredibly valuable to us, and to all other readers looking for great books.

If you found this book helpful or enjoyable, we would truly appreciate it, if you could take a moment to leave a short review with a 5 star rating on Amazon. It helps us grow, and lets other readers discover our books.

As a thank you, we would love to send you a free digital copy of this book, and a **30%** discount code on your next cart value on our official websites:

www.orangeava.com

www.orangeava.in (For Indian Subcontinent)

☑ **Here's how:**

Leave a review for the book on Amazon.

Take a screenshot of your review, and send an email to **info@orangeava.com** (it can be just the confirmation screen).

Once, we receive your screenshot, we will send you the digital file, within 24 hours.

Thank you so much for your support – it means a lot to us!

Downloading the code bundles and colored images

Please follow the links or scan the QR codes to download the
Code Bundles and Images of the book:

https://github.com/ava-orange-education/Practical-Data-Science-Environments-with-Python-and-R

The code bundles and images of the book are also hosted on
https://rebrand.ly/f69ikr7

In case there's an update to the code, it will be updated on the existing GitHub repository.

Errata

We take immense pride in our work at **Orange Education Pvt Ltd,** and follow best practices to ensure the accuracy of our content to provide an indulging reading experience to our subscribers. Our readers are our mirrors, and we use their inputs to reflect and improve upon human errors, if any, that may have occurred during the publishing processes involved. To let us maintain the quality and help us reach out to any readers who might be having difficulties due to any unforeseen errors, please write to us at :

errata@orangeava.com

Your support, suggestions, and feedback are highly appreciated.

DID YOU KNOW

Did you know that Orange Education Pvt Ltd offers eBook versions of every book published, with PDF and ePub files available? You can upgrade to the eBook version at **www.orangeava.com** and as a print book customer, you are entitled to a discount on the eBook copy. Get in touch with us at: **info@orangeava.com** for more details.

At **www.orangeava.com**, you can also read a collection of free technical articles, sign up for a range of free newsletters, and receive exclusive discounts and offers on Print Books and eBooks.

PIRACY

If you come across any illegal copies of our works in any form on the internet, we would be grateful if you would provide us with the location address or website name. Please contact us at **info@orangeava.com** with a link to the material.

ARE YOU INTERESTED IN AUTHORING WITH US?

If there is a topic that you have expertise in, and you are interested in either writing or contributing to a book, please write to us at **business@orangeava.com**. We are on a journey to help developers and tech professionals to gain insights on the present technological advancements and innovations happening across the globe and build a community that believes Knowledge is best acquired by sharing and learning with others. Please reach out to us to learn what our audience demands and how you can be part of this educational reform. We also welcome ideas from tech experts and help them build learning and development content for their domains.

REVIEWS

Please leave a review. Once you have read and used this book, why not leave a review on the site that you purchased it from? Potential readers can then see and use your unbiased opinion to make purchase decisions. We at Orange Education would love to know what you think about our products, and our authors can learn from your feedback. Thank you!

For more information about Orange Education, please visit **www.orangeava.com**.

Table of Contents

Chapter 1
An Overview of Data Science

Introduction

Data science has become a cornerstone of modern decision-making, shaping how organizations innovate, compete, and create value in an increasingly data-driven world. From predicting customer behavior to optimizing healthcare outcomes and powering intelligent systems, data science bridges raw data and actionable insight. The reader will be introduced to data science and analytics as well as a comparison of the different disciplines within data careers. They will deep dive into the skills that are required to grow and evolve as a seasoned professional in the field of data science. In this chapter, we will explore the applications of data in various industries and also understand the broad workflow that is used in the process.

Structure

This chapter will address the following topics:

- Introduction to Data Science and Analytics
- Importance and Applications
- Data Science Workflow: From Data Collection to Deployment

Introduction to Data Science and Analytics

Data science is an interdisciplinary field that leverages statistical, computational, and domain-specific knowledge to extract insights and knowledge from both structured and unstructured data. Over the past decade, data science has transformed from a niche area into a cornerstone of modern technological and business practices.

Data science integrates techniques and theories from various disciplines like statistics, computer science, and information theory to analyze and interpret complex data. This data could be structured like a table in Excel, unstructured like tweets on X, comments on Meta, images on Pinterest, or videos on YouTube. By utilizing algorithms, data mining, machine learning, and big data analytics, we can extract actionable insights from vast amounts of data. These insights drive decision-making, optimize processes, and create new opportunities for innovation.

Data analytics is a subset of data science and is focused specifically on examining raw data to find trends and answer business questions. It involves various processes like data cleaning, transformation, and modeling, that discover useful information, develop insights, and support decision-making.

Data science and data analytics are closely related yet distinct fields, while differing primarily in scope and focus. Data science aims to extract insights and make predictions using algorithms, machine learning, and various theoretical elements of statistics, computer science, and mathematics. In contrast, data analytics has a narrower focus and emphasizes interpreting existing data to provide actionable insights, which often involves summarizing historical data to understand past events. Data science aims to provide predictive and prescriptive insights by building models that forecast future trends and recommend actions, driving innovation and development. In contrast, data analytics primarily provides descriptive insights to support decision-making, improve operational efficiency, and help with diagnostic analytics.

Apart from data scientist and data analyst, there are other roles such as that of a data engineer, which is similar to the former two but focuses more on designing, building, and maintaining data pipelines. The core skills of SQL and a deep understanding of Python is a subject overlap in the career profiles of a data engineer and a data scientist. All these other allied roles in the data domain are critical as they determine the success of a project as well as an organization.

Comparing the Three Disciplines

Aspect	Data Science	Data Analytics	Data Engineering
Primary Focus	Predictive modeling	Descriptive analysis	Data infrastructure
Time Orientation	Future	Past and Present	Ongoing
Key Tools	Python, R, TensorFlow	SQL, Tableau, Excel	Hadoop, Spark, AWS
Output	Predictive models	Reports and dashboards	Data pipelines

***Figure 1.1**: Key Differences in Data Science, Data Analytics, and Data Engineering*

This chapter provides an overview of data science, its importance, and its myriad applications across different industries. Towards the end, we will walk you through some tips to help you make the most out of this book.

Requisite Skills Needed in Data Science

Data science requires a blend of technical skills, domain knowledge, and soft skills. Mastering this combination of skills enables practitioners to move beyond executing tasks to solving meaningful, real-world problems. Technical expertise allows data scientists to work efficiently with complex datasets, while domain knowledge ensures that insights are relevant and actionable within a specific business or industry context. Equally important, strong soft skills, such as communication, critical thinking, and collaboration, help translate analytical results into decisions that stakeholders can understand and trust. Together, these skills support continuous professional growth and distinguish effective data scientists from those who only focus on tools and techniques. These components are explained as follows:

Technical Skills

- **Programming**: Proficiency in programming languages like Python and R is essential for any aspiring data science professional. Python, in particular, is favored for its compatibility with other engineering tools, ease of use, and extensive libraries (for example, Pandas, NumPy, Scikit-learn). R on the other hand has been a favorite language in economics, forecasting, and medical analysis. Its English-like syntax makes it easier to use as well. Both these languages help with data cleaning, transformation, and exploratory data analysis (EDA). Tools like Pandas in Python or dplyr in R are commonly used for these tasks. Knowledge of SQL for database querying is crucial, as accessing and manipulating data stored in relational databases is a common task.
- **Mathematics and Statistics**: A solid understanding of statistical concepts, probability, linear algebra, and calculus is important for understanding the backend workings of machine learning algorithms.
- **Machine Learning**: Familiarity with machine learning algorithms and techniques is essential for building predictive models. Understanding different types of models and their evaluations is also important to know the right tools to apply to the right set of problems. .
- **Data Visualization**: The ability to create compelling visualizations to communicate findings effectively is a significant one. Tools like Matplotlib, Seaborn, and Tableau help in creating insightful graphs and dashboards. These also communicate the technical insights to business audiences in a better way.

- **Big Data Technologies**: Knowledge of big data tools and frameworks like Hadoop, Spark, and cloud platforms (AWS, Google Cloud, Azure) is becoming increasingly valuable as the amount of data and its users scale up.

Domain Knowledge

Understanding the specific context in which data is being analyzed is crucial. This can involve knowledge of business processes, market trends, or industry-specific challenges. Domain expertise helps users frame the right questions, select appropriate methods, and interpret results meaningfully. As data scientists, it is essential to collaborate with business partners and stakeholders from the get-go. Having the appropriate domain knowledge and business context is crucial for building and tuning model performance effectively in order to ensure that it is usable when deployed in production.

Soft Skills

- **Problem-Solving Methodology**: A Data Scientist must be adept at breaking down complex problems into manageable parts and devising solutions. This often involves critical thinking and creativity. In data science, the problem often begins with ambiguity. Breaking the big ambiguous problem into small chunks of actionable.
- **Collaboration**: Data science is rarely a solo endeavor, as successful solutions require input from multiple functions across an organization. Working closely with business partners and product managers helps ensure that problems are well-defined and aligned with strategic goals, while collaboration with data engineers and platform teams enables scalable and reliable data pipelines. Engagement with analysts, sales, and support teams provides operational context and real-world feedback, allowing data scientists to build solutions that are practical, actionable, and widely adopted.
- **Curiosity and Continuous Learning**: The field of Data Science is dynamic as it is currently witnessing constant advancements in techniques, tools, and technologies. A successful data scientist is always open to learning, staying updated with the latest trends, and continuously improving their skill set. Without this quality, it is very easy to be left behind and become obsolete in this fast-evolving field.

  Data Science has evolved significantly from its roots in statistics and computer science to become a multidisciplinary field that drives decision-making and innovation across industries. It requires a balanced combination of technical expertise, domain knowledge, and soft skills. As the field continues to grow and evolve, the demand for skilled data scientists who can harness the power of data will remain strong, which makes it an exciting and rewarding career path.

- **Communication**: The ability to explain technical concepts and analytical findings to non-technical stakeholders is a vital skill for any data science professional. Effective communication ensures that insights lead to actionable decisions. Without it, models may never make it to production and, therefore, will fail to have a real-world impact.

Importance of Data Science

Businesses, academics, and researchers from across the world have all embraced data science for better visualization, analysis, and productivity. We will now dive into why mastering this field is critical to success and growth in today's world and you can use it to gain a clear edge in your career.

Decision Making

Data Science enables organizations to make informed decisions. By analyzing historical data and identifying trends, companies can forecast future events, optimize operations, and adapt strategies to meet market demands. For example, a retailer might use data science to predict inventory needs, while a financial institution could assess risk more accurately.

Competitive Advantage

In today's data-driven economy, the ability to leverage data effectively is a significant competitive advantage. Companies that excel in data science can outpace their competitors by understanding customer behavior, improving product offerings, and enhancing customer experiences. For instance, Amazon uses data science to analyze customer behavior and preferences, and generate highly personalized product recommendations as a consequence. This enhances customer satisfaction and increases sales and customer loyalty by providing a tailored shopping experience.

Continuous Improvement

Building a data-driven culture can bring about improvement in processes and products, while revealing inefficiencies within processes and suggesting novel product features. For example, predictive analytics can forecast equipment failures in manufacturing, allowing for preemptive maintenance that reduces downtime. In retail, customer segmentation models help tailor marketing strategies to different customer groups, enhancing customer satisfaction and sales. Additionally, anomaly detection algorithms can monitor financial transactions in real time to prevent fraud, thereby ensuring operational integrity and efficiency.

Innovation

Data Science fosters innovation by uncovering new opportunities and even creating entirely new business models. For example, the healthcare industry utilizes data science to develop predictive models for patient outcomes, which can lead to better treatment plans and innovations in patient care. One practical result has been IBM Watson's usage to analyze medical literature and identify existing drugs that could potentially be repurposed for treating different diseases. Enabling real-time data processing, advanced ML algorithms for object detection, path planning, and decision-making has led to the creation of autonomous vehicles. For example, companies like Tesla and Waymo use data science to analyze sensor data from LIDAR, cameras and radar, which allows vehicles to navigate safely and efficiently without human intervention. As stated on https://waymo.com/waymo-driver/

> *"Driving situations can involve hundreds of objects, each with their own unique behaviors and intentions. The Waymo Driver takes the information it gathers in real time, as well as the experience it has built up over its 20+ million miles of real world driving and 20+ billion miles in simulation, to anticipate what other road users might do. It understands how a car moves differently than a cyclist, pedestrian, or other object, and then predicts the many possible paths that the other road users may take, all in the blink of an eye."*

Societal Impact

Data science has profound implications for society beyond business applications. It helps address critical issues like climate change, public health, and urban planning. For instance, data-driven models can predict the spread of diseases, thus allowing for timely interventions and resource allocation. Similarly, analyzing environmental data can inform policies to combat climate change. With the help of data science communities and philanthropic funds, farmers in sub-Saharan Africa can identify crop yields, pests, and diseases helping them with food security and income growth.

Applications of Data Science

Data science has applications across almost all industries. Businesses apply data science and analytics to gain competitive edge against competition, while creating new products and improving their respective efficiencies. Here, we will discuss how data science is used in some of the major industries.

Healthcare

In healthcare, data science is revolutionizing patient care and medical research. Predictive analytics can forecast disease outbreaks, while personalized medicine tailors treatments as per individual genetic profiles. ML algorithms can be useful in diagnosing diseases from medical imaging, and data-driven approaches improve hospital management and patient care workflows.

Cardiovascular medicine doctors and scientists at Mayo Clinic are currently combining AI with clinical practice for better care. For example, in emergency rooms, when people come in with an intracerebral hemorrhage, they get a CT scan, which is examined by a computer trained to analyze CT data. This method has been shown to reduce the time of diagnosis and limit brain damage.

You can find more by going to the links provided at the end of this chapter.

Finance

The finance industry uses data science for fraud detection, risk management, and investment strategies. Algorithms can analyze transaction patterns to detect fraudulent activities in real time. Predictive models assess credit risk and market trends, enabling better decision-making for loans and investments. High-frequency trading relies on data-driven models to execute trades at optimal times.

Retail

Retailers leverage data science to enhance customer experiences, optimize inventory, and drive sales. Customer segmentation and recommendation systems personalize shopping experiences, which increases customer satisfaction and loyalty. Sales forecasting and demand planning reduce stockouts and overstock situations, thereby improving operational efficiency.

When you visit a website like Amazon to shop for clothes, home improvement, gadgets, and so on, the recommendation shelves you see employ data science. Here is an example of some digital shelves:

Figure 1.2: *Digital Recommendation Shelves on Amazon*

Transportation

Data science plays a crucial role in optimizing transportation systems and logistics. Ride-sharing companies like Uber and Lyft use data-driven algorithms to match riders with drivers efficiently. These apps have to optimize the interface for multiple features like rider preferences, driver preferences, calculating the distance between rider and driver, the distance to destination, and so on. Predictive maintenance models in the automotive industry anticipate vehicle failures, thus reducing downtime and improving safety. Traffic management systems analyze real-time data to alleviate congestion and improve urban mobility.

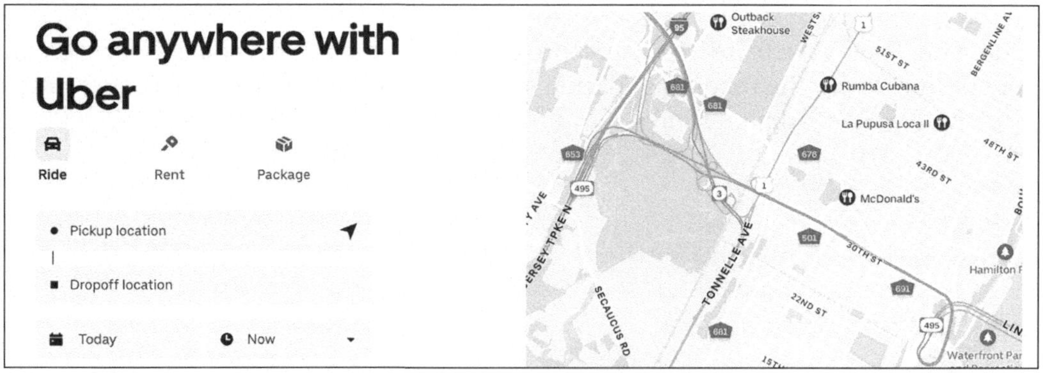

Figure 1.3: *Data Collected by Uber from Users to Run Optimization Algorithms.*
Source: www.uber.com

Marketing

In marketing, data science helps professionals tailor campaigns for target audiences more effectively. Companies can design personalized marketing strategies that resonate with their customers by analyzing consumer behavior and preferences. Sentiment analysis on social media data provides insights into public perception, allowing brands to manage their reputation proactively.

Duolingo does a great job at marketing to keep you on your streak of practice. Here is an example of personalized targeting used by the app:

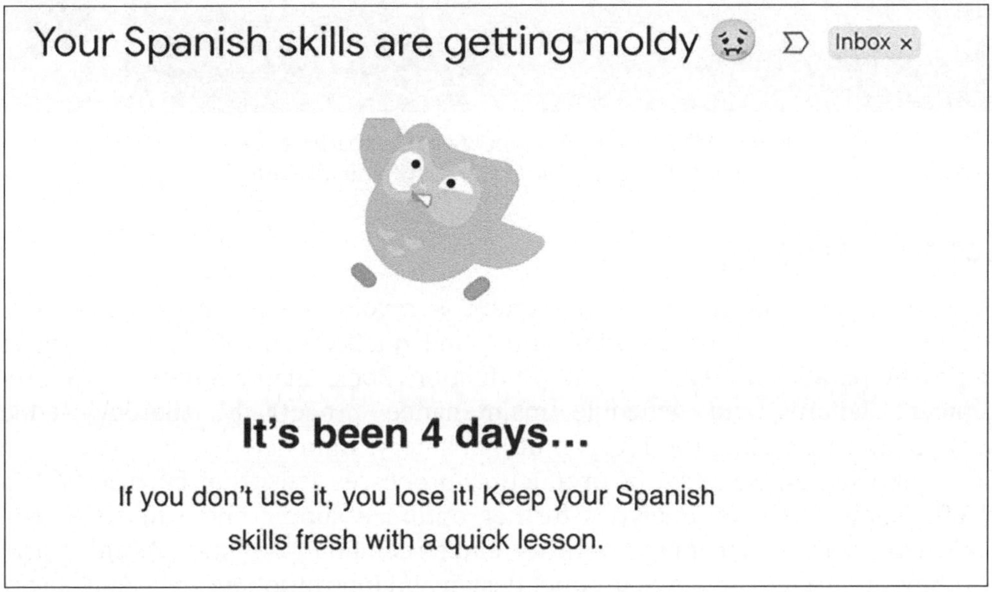

Figure 1.4: *An Alert from Duolingo Reminding the User to Revisit Their Practice*

Sports

Data science is now transforming sports by enhancing player performance and strategy. Teams use data analytics to evaluate player statistics, optimize game strategies, and prevent injuries. Fans can also benefit from personalized experiences through predictive ticketing and customized content, which enriches their engagement with their favorite sports.

For example: The F1 team, Oracle Red Bull Racing, uses data science on Oracle Cloud to power race strategy, engine development, sim racing, fan engagement, and more. By running Monte Carlo simulations on OCI during the championship run, Oracle Red Bull Racing increased the number of simulations that they ran by 25% to improve the accuracy of their predictions and sharpen their decision-making. Further, OCI significantly reduced the cost of these simulations, enabling the team to cost-effectively improve performance on the track.

Figure 1.5: *Cloud Environments in Competitive Sports.*
Source: https://www.oracle.com/redbullracing/

Manufacturing

In the manufacturing sector, data science is revolutionizing operations through predictive analytics, process optimization, and quality control. By analyzing large volumes of data from sensors and production lines, manufacturers can predict equipment failures and schedule maintenance proactively, thereby reducing downtime and extending the lifespan of machinery. Data science also enables real-time monitoring and control of production processes, ensuring consistent quality and efficiency. Advanced analytics further optimize supply chain management by forecasting demand, managing inventory, and streamlining logistics. Additionally, ML algorithms are used to enhance product design and innovation by analyzing customer feedback and market trends. Overall, data science empowers manufacturers to increase productivity, reduce costs, and maintain a competitive edge in the market.

Entertainment

In the entertainment industry, platforms like Netflix and Spotify use data science extensively to enhance user experience and content delivery. Both companies leverage machine learning algorithms to analyze vast amounts of user data, such as viewing or listening history, search queries, and interaction patterns, to provide personalized recommendations. By predicting what content users are likely to enjoy, these companies improve customer satisfaction and engagement.

***Figure 1.6**: Recommendation Shelves on www.Netflix.com*

Additionally, data science aids in content creation decisions by analyzing trends and preferences to invest in original programming or curate playlists that are more likely to succeed. This data-driven approach has been a significant factor in their ability to retain and grow their subscriber bases.

***Figure 1.7:** Recommendation Shelves on Spotify*

Data science is a powerful tool that harnesses the potential of data to drive decision-making, foster innovation, and address complex challenges. Its applications span various industries that have benefitted immensely from the actionable insights that can be extracted from vast amounts of data. As the volume of data continues to grow, the importance and impact of Data Science will only increase, thereby shaping the future of technology, business, and society.

By understanding the fundamentals and recognizing the transformative potential of Data Science, organizations and individuals can better navigate the data-driven landscape, thus making informed decisions that lead to sustainable growth and societal advancement.

The Data Science Workflow: From Collection to Deployment

A structured data science workflow ensures that projects are executed systematically, leading to reliable and actionable insights. Here is a detailed overview of the steps involved in a typical data science workflow, from problem definition to decision-making:

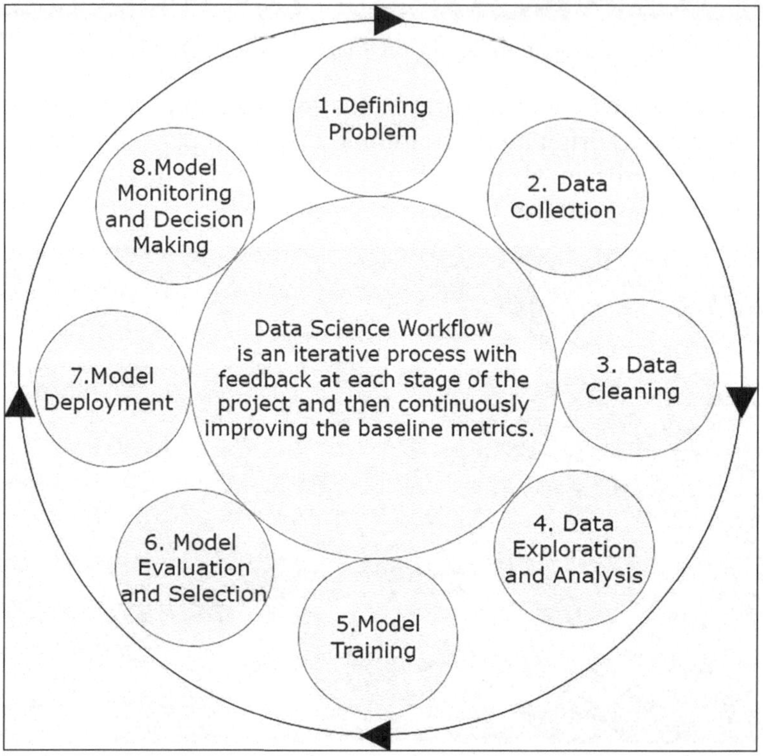

***Figure 1.8**: Explaining the Process Flow of a Data Science Workflow*

1. **Definition Problem:** It is critical to understand to the problems we are trying to solve before diving into data science-powered solutions. Understanding the problem, asking the right questions to clarify the scope, and then framing a hypothesis are essential before diving into data analysis. By knowing what questions to ask, data scientists can focus on analyses that will provide the most valuable insights. For example, in healthcare, understanding patient care workflows helps in identifying key metrics for improving treatment outcomes. This is also where contextual relevance comes into play. Domain knowledge is instrumental in understanding the business environment and the specific challenges faced by a certain industry. This knowledge allows data scientists

to frame questions that are relevant and impactful. While analyzing the results, domain knowledge can help in developing analytics into an actionable solution relevant to the specific problem.

2. **Data Collection:** Data collection is the first step where you begin coding and utilizing various data science tools. The goal is to gather relevant data which starts with identifying the data sources. Sources can include databases, web scraping, APIs, sensors, surveys, and external datasets. Next is understanding the data acquisition methods. For example, you can use SQL queries for databases, scraping tools for web data, or API requests for external services. Another critical aspect is data integration which combines data from different sources, while ensuring consistency and completeness.

3. **Data Cleaning:** The objective of data cleaning is to prepare the data for analysis by removing inaccuracies and inconsistencies. At this stage, you might be looking at various inconsistencies and cater to problems like handling missing data, removing duplicates, outlier detection, and data transformation. To handle missing values you need to first identify them and then decide on a strategy (for example, imputation, deletion) to address them. Duplicate records and outliers are removed to avoid skewing the analysis and distorting results. You might also need to convert data into a suitable format, which includes normalization, scaling, or encoding categorical variables.

4. **Data Exploration and Analysis:** The goal of data exploration and analysis is to understand the data through descriptive statistics and visualizations to inform subsequent steps. This could include calculating descriptive statistics like mean, median, and standard deviation to get a sense of the data distribution. Often a data scientist would want to create visualizations (histograms, scatter plots, box plots) to identify trending patterns and compare relationships.

   For specific ML problems, results from basic data exploration could present a case where feature engineering might be required. **Feature engineering** refers to creating new features or modifying existing ones to improve model performance. At this stage, a data scientist would also look into feature selection. This can be done with techniques like correlation analysis, mutual information, or recursive feature elimination.

5. **Model Training:** Not all data science problems are solved by building an ML solution; however, a data scientist might know when an ML solution is needed and which ML techniques can be applied to tackle the problem. At this stage, the data scientist identifies the set of models to train and thus prepares the data by splitting it into training and validation sets to ensure the model can generalize well to unseen data. The high-level goal is to train the model on the training set by adjusting parameters to minimize the loss function. Model

evaluation on the validation set is performed to tune hyperparameters and prevent overfitting.

6. **Model Evaluation and Selection**: On a high level, the goal will be to choose an appropriate model that performs well on the validation set and address the problem at hand. Model evaluation is performed by analyzing performance metrics relevant to the problem (for example, accuracy, precision, recall for classification, and RMSE, MAE for regression). Selecting a model is not just based on evaluation criteria, but also on the principles of explainability. There are many cases when humans would need to explain why models are selecting certain classes and which features can influence the model. For instance, in a credit risk model, understanding the impact of income, credit score, and debt-to-income ratio can guide officials whether to approve a loan or deny them. There can also be cases of bias in the model such as when it can reject a specific race of individuals, thus contributing to an ethical violation.

7. **Model Deployment:** More often than not, the goal of an ML model is to be integrated into a production environment where it can be used for predictions. There is a decision to be made on choosing an appropriate environment for deployment, such as cloud services (AWS, Azure, GCP), on-premises servers, or edge devices. This stage is technically collaborative with engineering as model deployment should not adversely affect the system's performance.

8. **Model Monitoring and Decision Making**: Based on the goal of an ML model, a data scientist would need to ensure that the insights can solve the problem. Often, analyzing model insights is pivotal to drive decision-making and innovation. For example, a real-time ML model that identifies fraudsters while creating an account at a website can prevent future losses. The insight from the attributes of fraudsters can help product teams develop deterrent features and instill policy changes. A data scientist must also ensure the deployed model remains accurate and stays relevant over time. This is where performance monitoring and building a feedback loop come in, along with considerations like scalability and fault tolerance. Moreover, it should be ensured that the model infrastructure can scale with increasing data volume and request load.

   Periodically, a data scientist would also need to retrain the model with new data to maintain its accuracy and relevance. There might arise a need for building an API (RESTful or GraphQL) to expose the model's endpoints for other processes. This is where software engineering principles are required, as the API would need to handle requests, input validation, and authentication.

The data science workflow is a comprehensive process that transforms raw data into actionable insights and deploys predictive models in production environments. By following these steps diligently, data scientists can ensure that their models are accurate, robust, and capable of providing valuable predictions that drive decision-making and innovation.

Conclusion

Data science and analytics are not fancy methodologies reserved for specialized roles, but are the essential foundational building blocks that must be integrated at the core of any business to ensure success in today's data-driven era. In this chapter, we explored the critical importance of data science across various industries, highlighting how it drives decision-making, optimizes operations, and creates competitive advantages. We also discussed the key skills required to thrive in this field, from statistical analysis to machine learning and data visualization.

In the upcoming chapter, we will learn about the practical aspects of data science. We will delve into the essential tools and environments you need to get build your data systems. The next chapters will provide you with the knowledge and resources about various tools and languages in data science.

CHAPTER 2

Comparing Programming Languages and Various Environments

Introduction

A wide range of programming languages and development environments are available for data science and analytics, each offering distinct strengths and trade-offs. Choosing the right tools can significantly influence the efficiency, scalability, and maintainability of data-driven solutions, particularly as projects grow in complexity. Languages such as Python, R, and SQL have emerged as industry standards due to their strong ecosystems, versatility, and widespread adoption across domains. This chapter introduces these core languages and the essential environments required to effectively initiate, develop, and manage data science projects.

Structure

This chapter will address the following topics:

- Popular Programming Languages in Data Science and Analytics
- Diving into Python, R, and SQL
- Essential Development Environments in Python and R
- Understanding Notebooks in Data Science
- Local versus Cloud Environments

Popular and Relevant Programming Languages in Data Science and Analytics

Data science has evolved significantly over the decades as a field. Several environments and programming languages have laid the foundation for modern data science. These early environments and languages were pivotal to data analysis, statistical computing, and data management.

Early Languages and Environment in Data Science

The evolution of data science and analytics spanned many years. Before the modern open-source languages and environments, the industry was niche and primarily driven by proprietary environments and languages.

- **FORTRAN (Formula Translation):** FORTRAN, which was developed in the 1950s by IBM, was one of the first high-level programming languages. It was designed for numeric computation and scientific computing. FORTRAN was widely used in areas requiring intensive numerical computations, such as engineering, physics, and applied mathematics. It was essential for early data analysis and modeling.
- **COBOL (Common Business-Oriented Language):** Developed in the late 1950s and early 1960s, COBOL was designed for business data processing and was extensively used in finance, business, and administrative systems for companies and governments. It handled large volumes of data exceptionally well and was integral to early data processing tasks.
- **SAS (Statistical Analysis System):** SAS, which was developed in the 1970s, is a software suite for advanced analytics, business intelligence, and data management. Later, SAS became a leading tool for statistical analysis in various industries, particularly in finance, healthcare, and market research. It provided robust data handling capabilities and comprehensive statistical functions. It was the go-to tool and language of choice where data security and privacy were critical.
- **SPSS (Statistical Package for the Social Sciences):** Developed in the late 1960s, SPSS was designed for data analysis in social science disciplines. SPSS became popular in academia and research for its ease of use and comprehensive statistical analysis capabilities. It allowed researchers to perform complex statistical analyses with minimal programming.
- **MATLAB (Matrix Laboratory):** Developed in the late 1970s and early 1980s, MATLAB is a high-level language and interactive environment for numerical

computation, visualization, and programming. MATLAB is widely used in engineering, physics, finance, and other fields for data analysis, algorithm development, and modeling. Its powerful matrix computations and visualization capabilities made it a valuable tool for data scientists.

- **S (Programming Language):** Developed at Bell Laboratories in the mid-1970s, S was designed for data analysis and statistical computing. S provided a flexible environment for data analysis, which later influenced the development of R. It was used in academic and research settings for statistical analysis and data visualization.
- **SQL (Structured Query Language):** SQL, developed in the 1970s at IBM, is a standardized language for managing and manipulating relational databases. SQL became the standard language for Database Management Systems (DBMS). It was essential for data retrieval, manipulation, and management in various areas, such business and scientific research.

  It still remains the most important language in industrial settings and is often used as the first step in any data science project to fetch and filter relevant data.
- **MINITAB:** Developed in the 1970s, MINITAB is a statistical software package used for data analysis. MINITAB was widely used in quality improvement and Six Sigma projects. It provided an easy-to-use interface for performing statistical analyses, which made it popular in education and industry.

There have been numerous other environments that are still used in niche domains. These early environments and languages laid the groundwork for further innovations in data science. They provided the necessary computational and analytical capabilities to handle data-intensive tasks. As technology evolved, these environments influenced the development of more advanced and specialized languages and environments that now form the backbone of modern data science.

Modern Prominent Languages in Data Science

Data science and analytics have evolved into critical domains for businesses and researchers alike. As data science has matured, the tools used to collect, process, and analyze data have also evolved to support larger datasets, more complex models, and faster iteration. The choice of programming language depends on the use case, team skills, and compatibility with other tools. Among the plethora of languages available, Python, R, and SQL stand out as the most popular and relevant in the field.

Python has garnered immense popularity due to its simplicity, versatility, and a robust ecosystem of libraries tailored for data science, such as Pandas, NumPy, Matplotlib, and Scikit-Learn. It is widely used for data manipulation, statistical analysis, machine learning, and visualization.

R is another powerful language specifically designed for statistical computing and graphics. It is favored in academia and among statisticians for its extensive range of packages and tools for data analysis like ggplot2, dplyr, and caret.

SQL (Structured Query Language) remains the go-to language for managing and querying relational databases. It is crucial for extracting, manipulating, and analyzing data stored in database systems.

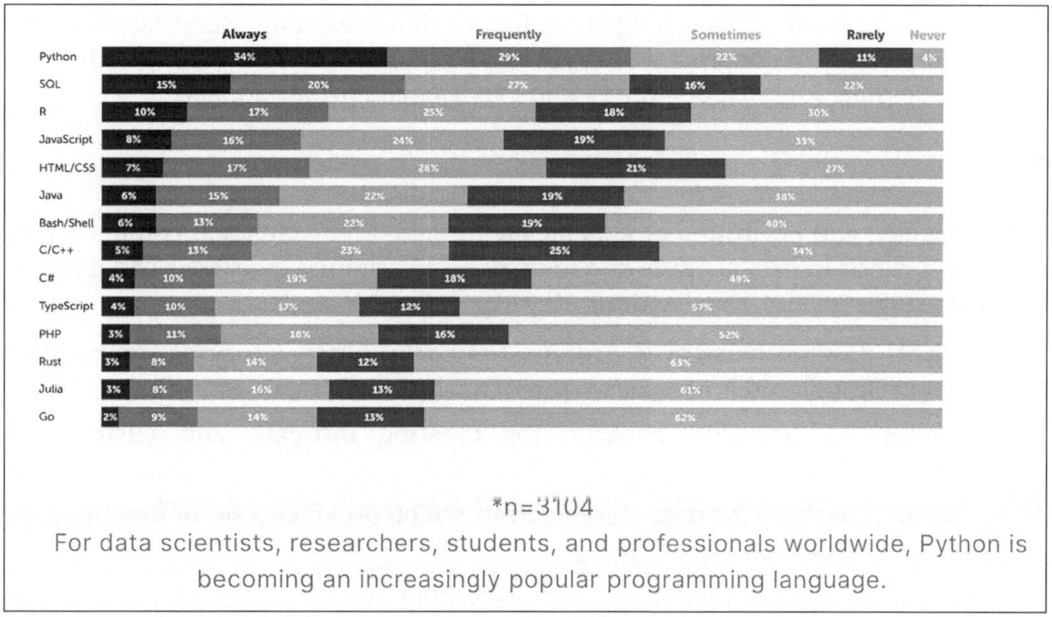

***Figure 2.1**: Survey Results by Anaconda. Source: https://www.anaconda.com/resources/whitepapers/state-of-data-science-2021*

Anaconda, the maker of a data science distribution of Python, conducted a survey in 2021, which concluded that Python could soon be the most popular programming language and surpass SQL.

Diving into Python, R, and SQL

Let us dive in and start exploring these languages in detail:

Python

Python is a high-level, interpreted language known for its readability and comprehensive standard library. In data science, it provides an extensive collection of libraries that support various stages of the data analysis pipeline:

- **Pandas**: Essential for data manipulation and analysis

- **NumPy**: Fundamental for numerical computations
- **Matplotlib and Seaborn**: Used for data visualization
- **Scikit-Learn**: A go-to library for machine learning

Python's versatility allows it to integrate seamlessly with web applications, automate tasks, and develop machine learning models, thereby making it a staple in data science. It is widely used in industries for its versatility and integration capabilities. It is one of the most chosen languages for machine learning, deep learning, and production-level code deployment. Python's simple syntax and extensive libraries make it accessible for both beginners and experienced professionals.

R

R is a language and environment specifically designed for statistical computing and graphics. It excels in data analysis due to its rich ecosystem of packages and its ability to produce high-quality visualizations. Key aspects of R include:

- **CRAN (Comprehensive R Archive Network)**: A repository of thousands of packages tailored for various types of analysis
- **ggplot2**: A powerful package for creating intricate and customizable visualizations
- **dplyr**: A package for data manipulation, which provides a set of functions that simplify complex operations

People in marketing, risk modeling, and forecasting extensively use R for its strong community support, functionality, and syntax.

SQL

SQL is a standard language used to interact with relational databases. It is essential for data extraction, transformation, and loading (ETL) processes. Key features of SQL include:

- **Data Querying**: The ability to retrieve specific data from large datasets using `SELECT` statements
- **Data Manipulation**: Inserting, updating, and deleting data within a database
- **Data Definition**: Creating and modifying database structures like tables and indexes

SQL's declarative nature allows users to specify what they want to do with the data without defining how to do it, thereby making it efficient for database management and data wrangling tasks.

As you advance in the field, you will typically use SQL or a similar query language to retrieve data from databases. Ad-hoc analyses in industry are often performed using SQL. Users often obtain results from a SQL query and perform quick analyses in Google Sheets or MS Excel, or upload the CSV file to Python or R for further study.

Here we provide a side-by-side comparison of the two languages that would help you decide which language to choose:

User Friendliness	Easy to learn but needs an understanding of basic Python before diving into data science libraries	English-like syntax can be simpler for someone just starting the data science journey
	Familiarity for anyone coming from any programming background	The unique syntax can be difficult for people with a programming background
	Range of special libraries compatibility with other tools	Has a range of specialized statistical functions
Usage	Can be customized for various tasks	The availability of statistical functions makes it more efficient for certain tasks
Data Manipulation	Offers pandas for data manipulation	Offers dplyr for data manipulation
Visualization	Offers matplotlib and seaborn for charts and visuals	Offers ggplot2 for creating charts and visuals
Machine Learning	Has an edge with ML libraries like Scikit-Learn, TensorFlow, and Keras	Less commonly used in production by it offers ML packages like caret and randomForest

Community Support	Python's community is vast, covering a wide range of domains beyond data science, such as web development, automation, and machine learning. Its extensive documentation and numerous open-source libraries make it highly accessible for beginners and professionals alike.	While R's overall community is smaller than Python's, it has a strong and specialized presence in academic research, statistics, and data analysis. It is widely used in fields like bioinformatics, finance, and social sciences, where statistical computing and visualization are essential.

***Table 2.1**: Comparison of Python and R*

As you can see from the table, both languages have their own pros and cons. Ultimately, the choice of language is very dependent on the type of business and their use cases, as well as the stage of development.

Essential Development Environments in Python and R

As you start writing code in your language of choice, it is important to understand the differences between command-line interfaces (CLI), text editors, and Integrated Development Environments (IDEs).

CLI and text editors can be used for scripting and quick tasks, while IDEs enhance coding productivity by offering features like a code editor, compiler, debugger, build automation tools, intelligent code completion, and a Graphical User Interface (GUI) to write programs all in one place.

Python IDEs

- **PyCharm:** This is one of the most commonly used IDEs developed by JetBrains. It consists of auto-complete suggestions and refactoring capabilities that make debugging easy. It is also simple to navigate and has an intuitive UI. PyCharm has an integrated terminal that manages the application's virtual environments. Users have the option to use its community version or the professional version.

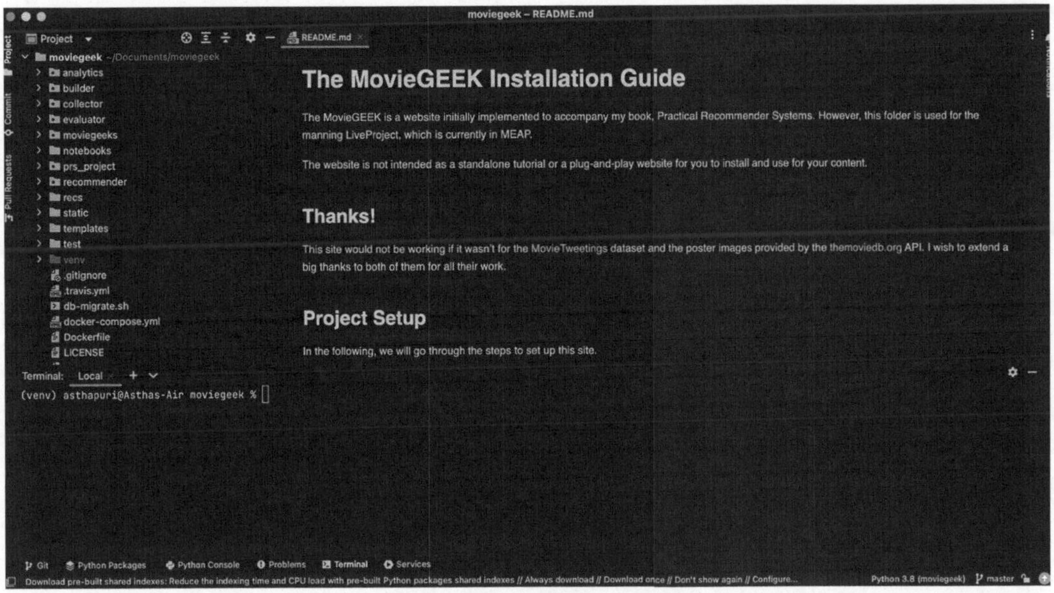

Figure 2.2: *PyCharm IDE*

- **Jupyter Notebooks**: This is an open-source web application where you can create, execute, and share your analysis. Jupyter Notebooks are extremely popular among data scientists because it has both text and code cells, which allow users to weave a story and communicate insights in a data-driven way. Originally developed as part of the IPython project, Jupyter later evolved to support multiple programming languages like R, via the Jupyter kernel system.

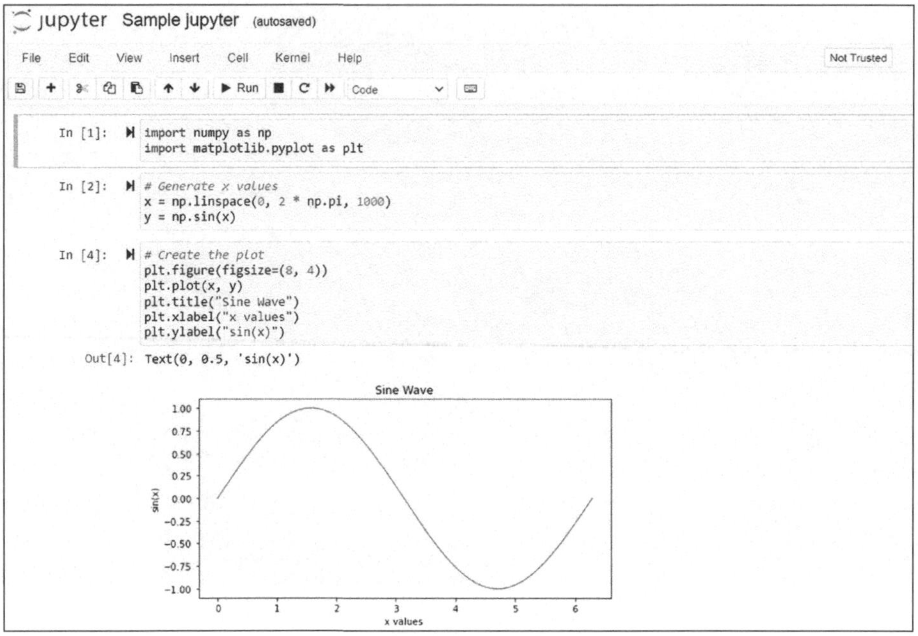

***Figure 2.3**: Sample Jupyter Notebook*

- **Spyder**: This is another open-source IDE. It comes with the Anaconda distribution which is popular for data science. It is well-suited for scientific computing and data analysis due to its built-in variable explorer, interactive console.

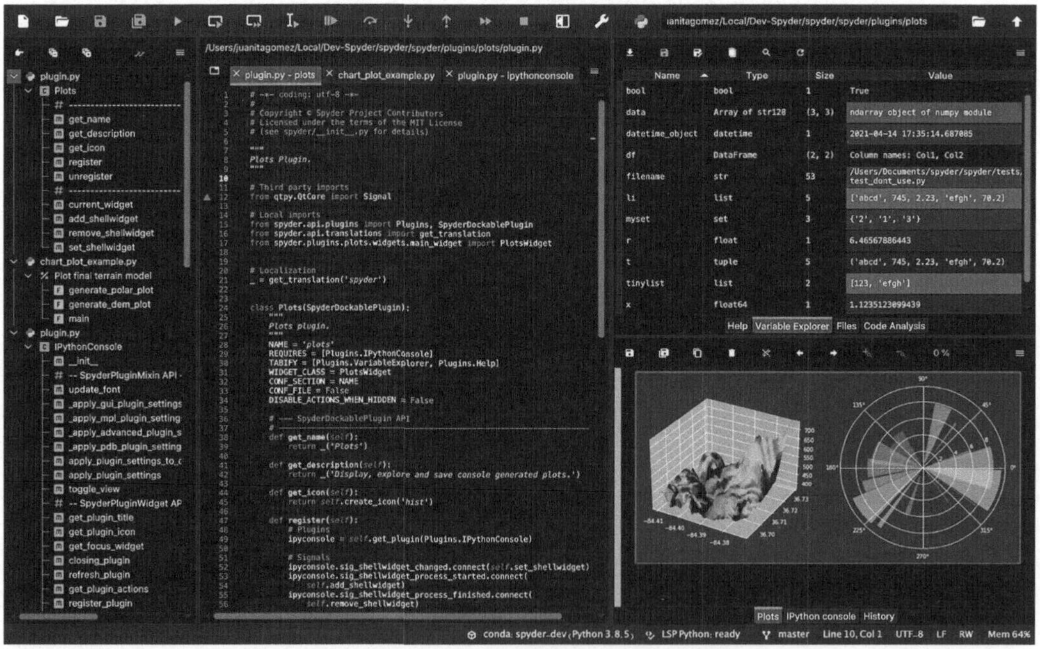

***Figure 2.4**: Spyder IDE. Source: https://github.com/spyder-ide/spyder?tab=readme-ov-file*

- **Visual Studio Code (VS Code):** This is an open-source IDE developed by Microsoft. It facilitates easy navigation between code and its output. It also has a large extension store, which makes it highly versatile in terms of functionality.

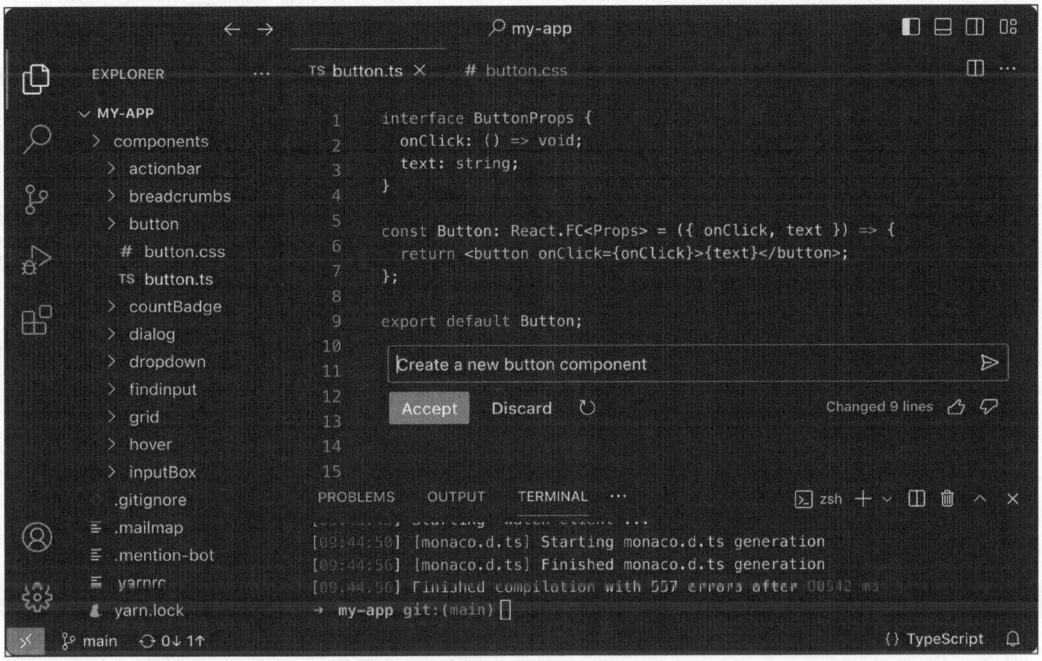

Figure 2.5: *Visual Studio Code. Source: https://code.visualstudio.com/*

R IDEs

- **RStudio**: RStudio is the most prominent IDE for R. It offers a user-friendly interface with tools for plotting, history, debugging, and workspace management. While other options like Jupyter Notebooks and VS Code exist, RStudio remains the most popular among R developers. It can seamlessly integrate with the R compiler, and has features like autocomplete, as well as the ability to create R Markdown documents.

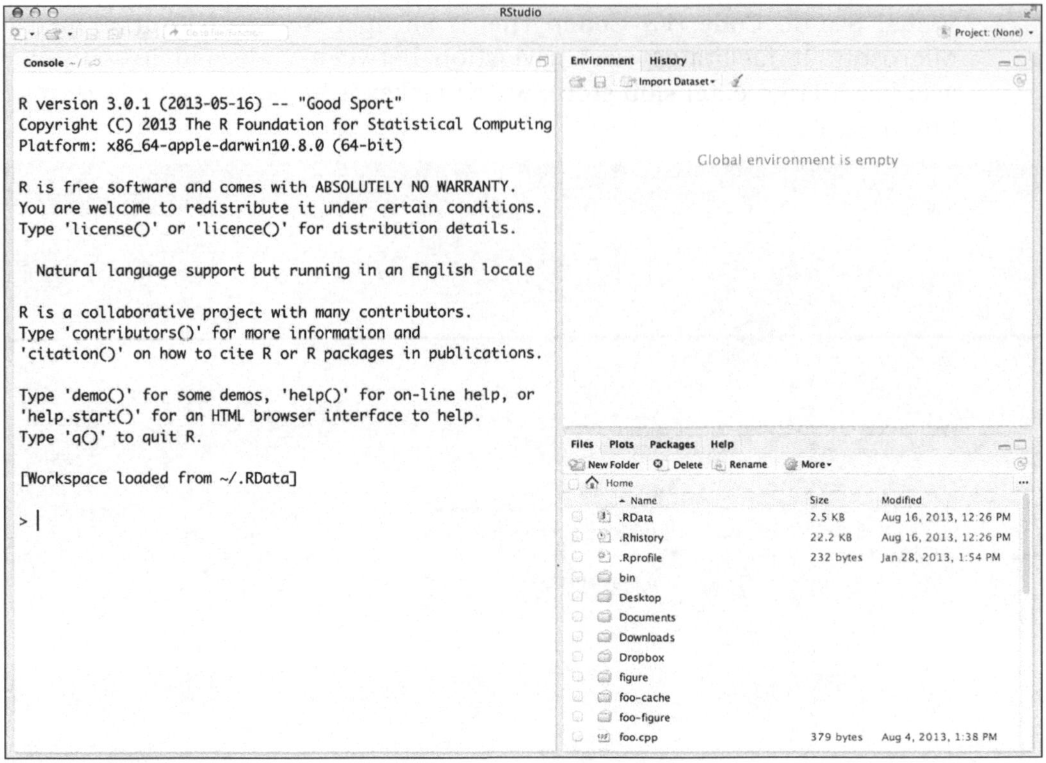

Figure 2.6: *Rstudio IDE. Source: https://rstudio-education.github.io/hopr/starting.html*

Since notebooks are extensively used by data scientists, it is useful to learn about them. Let us dive into the concept.

Understanding Notebooks in Data Science

In data science, notebooks are interactive, web-based documents that combine code, text, and visualizations, and present them in a consolidated manner. They are popular because they facilitate data analysis, exploration, and communication of results intuitively. Hence, notebooks become the means to document insights, assumptions, and mathematical formulations as rich text. Users can see images, HTML, and LaTeX next to the code chunk in a notebook. They are an effective means to collaborate on projects, and provide teams a shared space to work on certain chunks of code blocks as well as combine results effectively.

Popular Notebook Platforms

The choice of a programming tool depends on the project and the collaboration scope. There are other ways to execute code, such as using GUI or via a terminal, but notebooks have made data science presentable and widespread in businesses. We have listed some popular Notebook platforms as follows:

- **Jupyter Notebooks**: Originally a part of the IPython project, Jupyter Notebooks support multiple programming languages and have extensive libraries for data analysis and visualization.
- **R Notebook**: Integrated within RStudio, R Notebook is inherently an R Markdown notebook that combines R code with Markdown text. It supports a wide range of output formats including HTML, PDF, and Word. In later chapters, we will closely witness how to work with R Markdown and create a notebook.

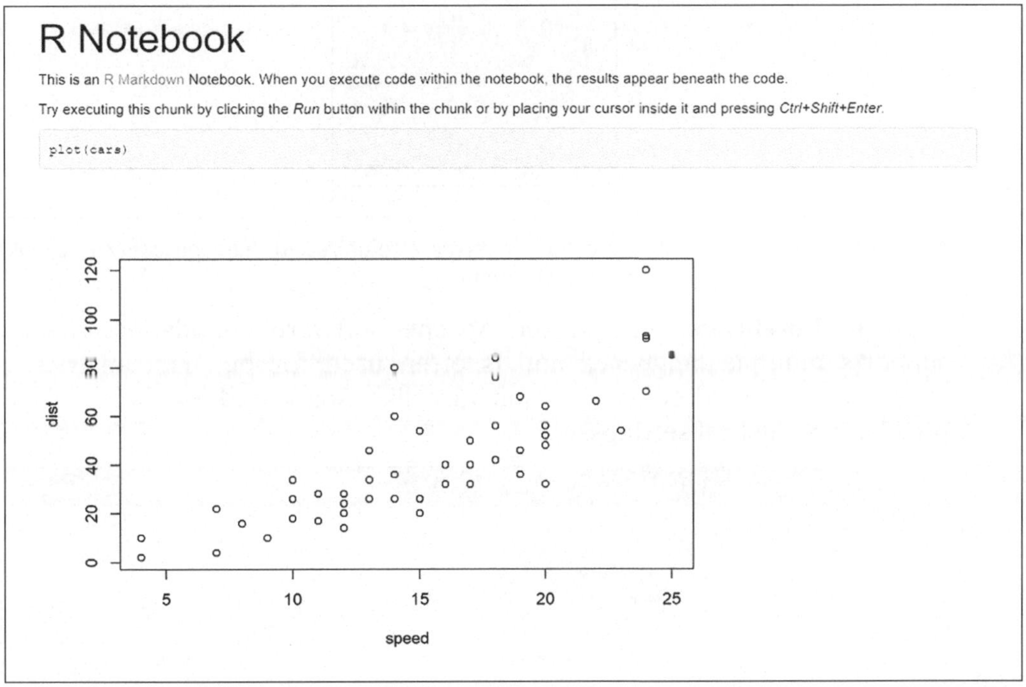

***Figure 2.7**: Sample R Notebook*

- **Google Colab**: This is a cloud-based Jupyter Notebook environment provided by Google, which is particularly popular for its ease of use and integration with Google Drive. Another advantage of Google Colab is that it uses cloud resources for execution instead of local memory and compute resources.

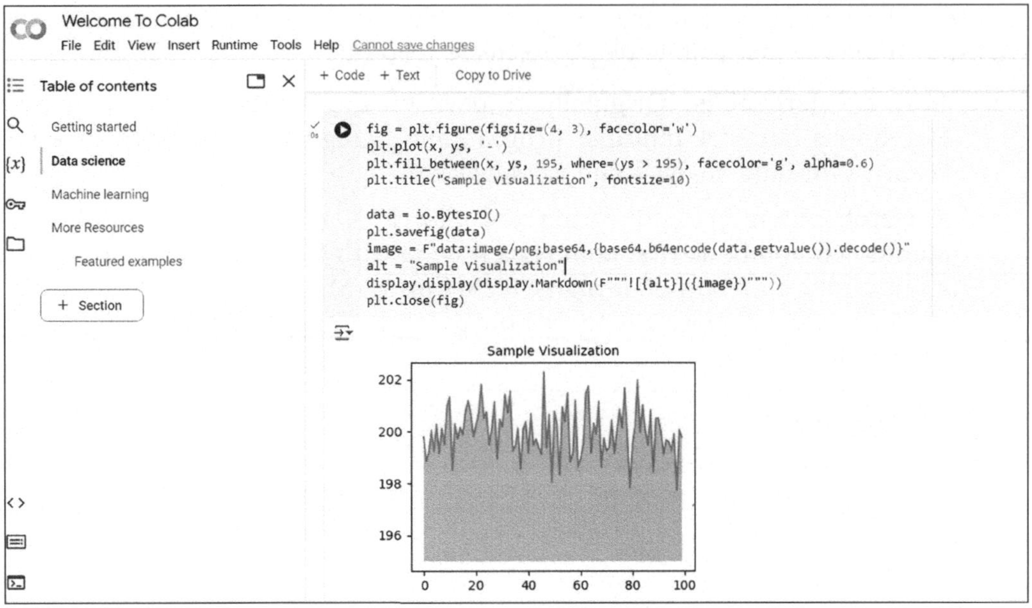

Figure 2.8: *Sample Google Colab Notebook. Source: https://colab.research.google.com/notebooks/intro.ipynb*

- **Zeppelin Notebooks**: Part of the Apache Software Foundation, Zeppelin supports multiple languages and is often used for big data analysis. Its integration with other Apache software like Spark and Hadoop makes it popular in industrial settings.

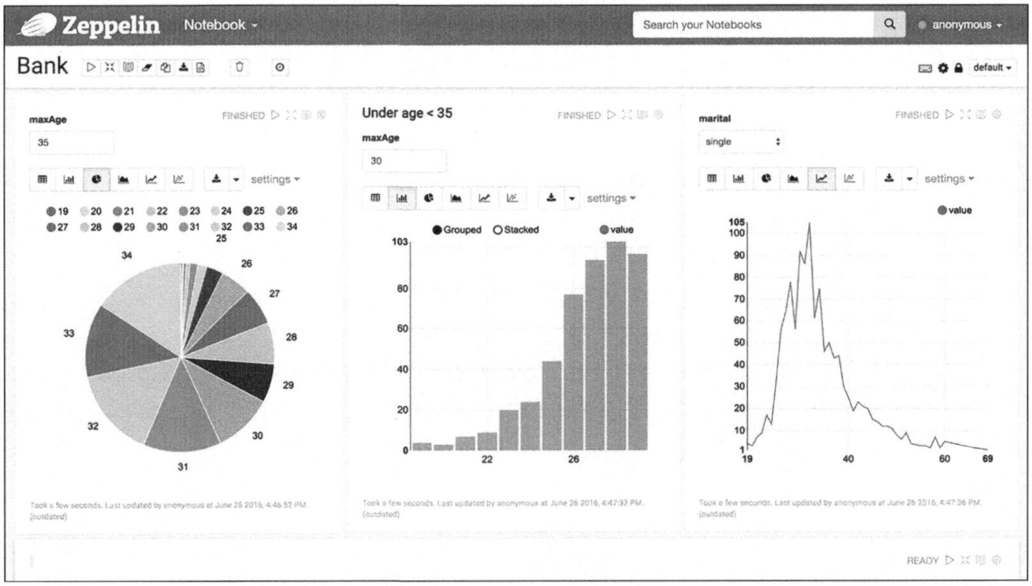

Figure 2.9: *Sample Zepplin Notebook. Source: https://zeppelin.apache.org/docs/0.6.0/*

Key Benefits of Using Notebooks for Development

Key benefits of using notebooks for development include working in their interactive, cell-based environment that allows for immediate feedback and quick experimentation. Their ability to seamlessly integrate code, visualizations, and narrative text makes them ideal for exploratory data analysis and creating reproducible research documents.

Local versus Cloud Environments

Local environments refer to running software and data analysis directly on a user's personal computer, which provides them full control and offline access. On the other hand, cloud environments utilize remote servers, offering scalable resources, collaboration features, and easy access from any location. Each has distinct advantages and limitations, which influence their suitability for different data science tasks.

Local Environments

Local environments can include dedicated local servers as well as personal computers. These servers are super-fast and easy to use, and do not require users to access an internet connection in order to work locally.

With local development, users have full control over configurations and software installations. Their performance depends on the hardware capabilities of the local machine, which can be optimized for specific tasks. However, this development choice can face scalability issues due to limited resources. As data expands and algorithms become more complex, more resources are required. Additionally, users must maintain the environment and its dependencies themselves.

Cloud Environments

Cloud environments utilize remote servers hosted by cloud service providers such as AWS, Google Cloud Platform, and Microsoft Azure to run data science applications. This option eliminates the scalability constraints of local environments. It is also ideal for collaborating with teammates in different locations using different systems, as everyone can access the same codebase from different systems if they have an internet connection. Providers offer managed services for data storage and maintenance, reducing the overhead of environment management.

However, cloud environments can be expensive, especially for large-scale projects or continuous use, and costs can quickly add up. Additionally, users might face latency issues depending on internet speed and reliability.

Hybrid Environments

Many data scientists use a hybrid approach, leveraging local environments for initial development and testing, and cloud environments for large-scale computations and deployment.

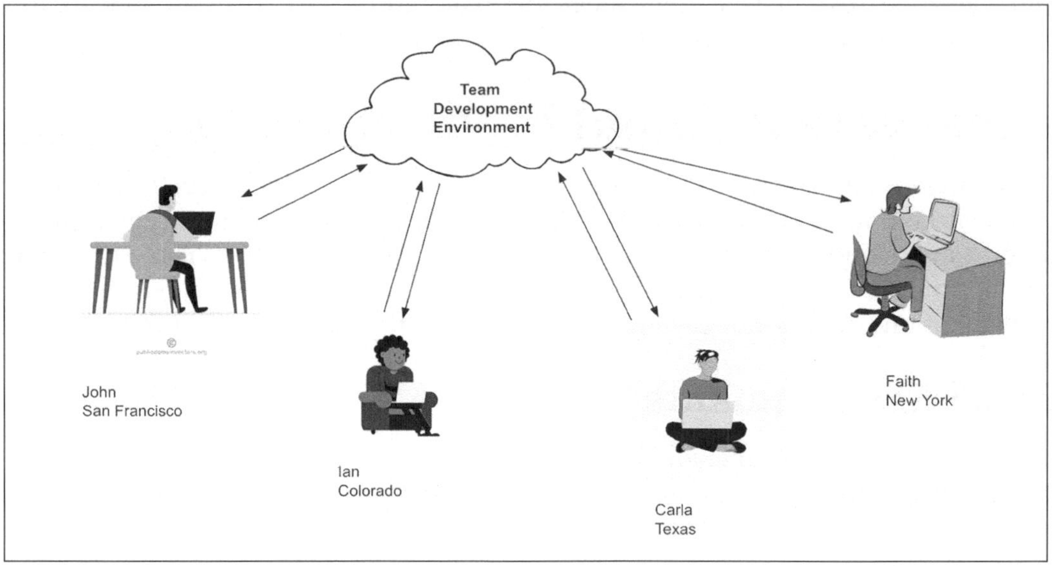

Figure 2.10: *Hybrid Approach for Development*

In the above figure, four teammates are located in different geographical locations. Each has their own local system where they can run tests on their parts of the project. Once they are ready, they can share their work in a common cloud environment. Updates made by one team member can be seen by all others, who can then download these updates to their own systems and continue developing from there.

A hybrid approach combines the advantages of both local and cloud environments while minimizing their drawbacks. This solution can be customized to fit specific use cases.

Conclusion

This chapter provided a comprehensive overview of the key programming languages, tools, and development environments in data science, while highlighting their unique features, strengths, and appropriate use cases. Whether you are just starting or looking to expand your toolkit, understanding these foundational elements will set you on the path to successful data science projects. In the next chapter, we will start setting up the environment on our local systems. So, get your laptops out, because it's time to turn theory into action and let the coding adventures begin!

CHAPTER 3
Setting Up Data Science Environment

Introduction

In today's data-driven world, the ability to harness the power of programming languages like Python and R is not just an advantage, but a necessity for anyone serious about data analysis, machine learning, or any form of data science. The first step on this journey is to set up your development environment, which is the foundation upon which all your future work will be built. This chapter is designed to guide you meticulously through the process of installing and configuring Python and R on both Windows and Mac operating systems.

Installing Python and R might seem daunting if you are new to programming, but this chapter will simplify the process. We will start with the installation of Python, guiding you through the process of downloading the latest version, setting up your development environment, and configuring necessary environment variables. For R, we will walk you through downloading and installing R itself, as well as RStudio, which is the most popular IDE for R. RStudio offers a comprehensive interface that includes a console, a syntax-highlighting editor, and tools for plotting, history, and workspace management. This setup will allow you to write, test, and run your R code efficiently, thereby making it easier to focus on your data rather than the intricacies of the toolset.

By the end of this chapter, you will have successfully installed Python and R on your system, while ensuring that your environment is optimized for performance and reliability. Whether you are using a Windows machine or a Mac, we have provided comprehensive instructions tailored to each operating system, which will result in a seamless setup experience regardless of the platform you are using.

Structure

This chapter will address the following topics:

- Installing Python on Windows and Mac

- Installing R on Windows and Mac
- Setting Up Jupyter Notebooks
- Setting Up RStudio
- Essential Packages and Libraries

Installing Python on Windows and Mac

Installing Python on both Windows and Mac is a straightforward process, but it requires attention to detail to configure the installation correctly for optimal performance.

On Windows, you can install Python by downloading its latest version from the official website. During installation, it is crucial to check the option to add Python to the system PATH, which will allow you to run Python from the command prompt without having to specify its full path. This step simplifies running scripts and managing packages.

On Mac, Python typically comes pre-installed with the operating system, but it is often an older version which you might want to update later. Be it on Windows or Mac, the installation process also includes setting up a suitable Integrated Development Environment (IDE) like PyCharm or VS Code to enhance the coding experience with features like code completion and debugging tools.

Installing Python on Windows

Here are the step-by-step instructions on installing Python on a Windows device:

1. **Downloading the Installer**

    a. Visit the official Python website at python.org. Now navigate to the Downloads section and select Windows.

    b. Click on the latest stable release to download the installer (for example, **`python-3.9.1-amd64.exe`**). Make sure to download the correct system type - 32 bit or 64 bit operating system. You can check this in your Windows settings.

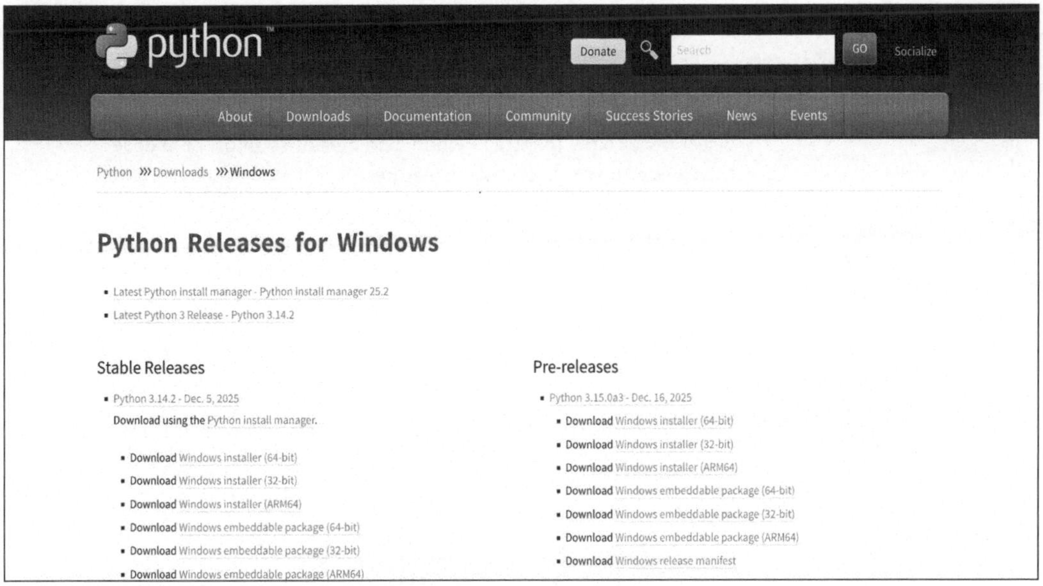

Figure 3.1: *Installing Python*

2. **Running the Installer**

   a. Open the downloaded file to start the installation process.

   b. Ensure you check the box that says "`Add Python to PATH`." This step is crucial because if Python is not added to PATH, users will not be able to run Python from the Command Prompt (`cmd`) without specifying the full path.

      If you have missed this step, you can add the installer later via Environment Variables in Windows settings.

   c. Click on "`Install Now`" and follow the prompts.

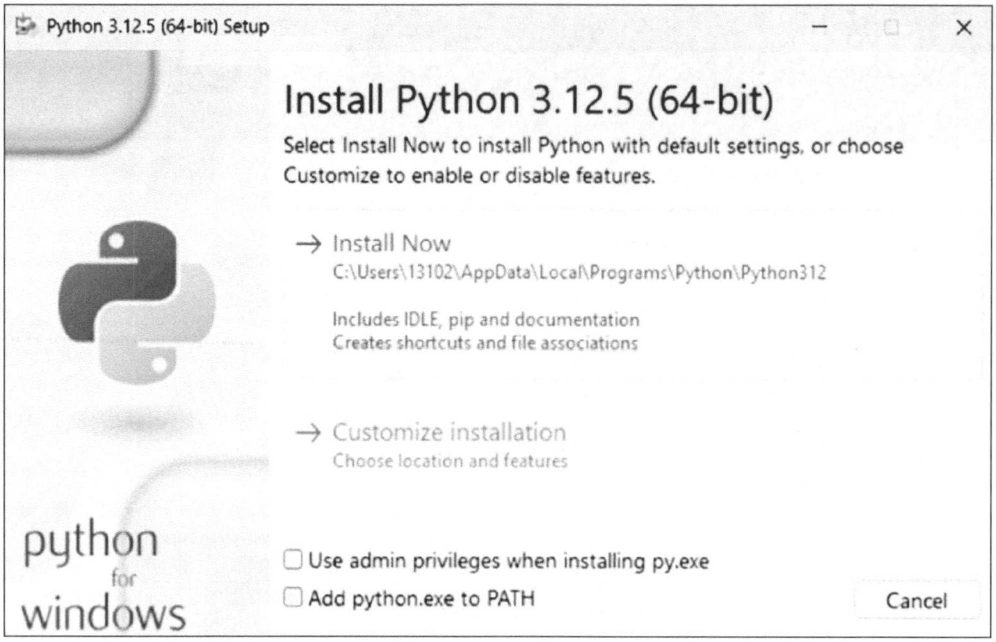

Figure 3.2: *Installing Python in Windows*

3. **Verifying the Installation**

    a. Open Command Prompt. Type **py** and press *Enter*. You will see the Python version you installed.

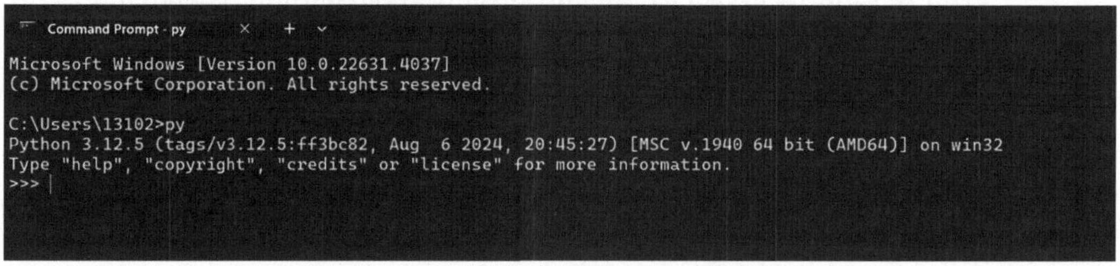

Figure 3.3: *Verification of Installation*

Installing Python on Mac

Here are step-by-step instructions on installing Python on your Mac device:

1. **Downloading the Installer**

    a. Visit python.org and navigate to the Downloads section. Select macOS and download the latest stable release.

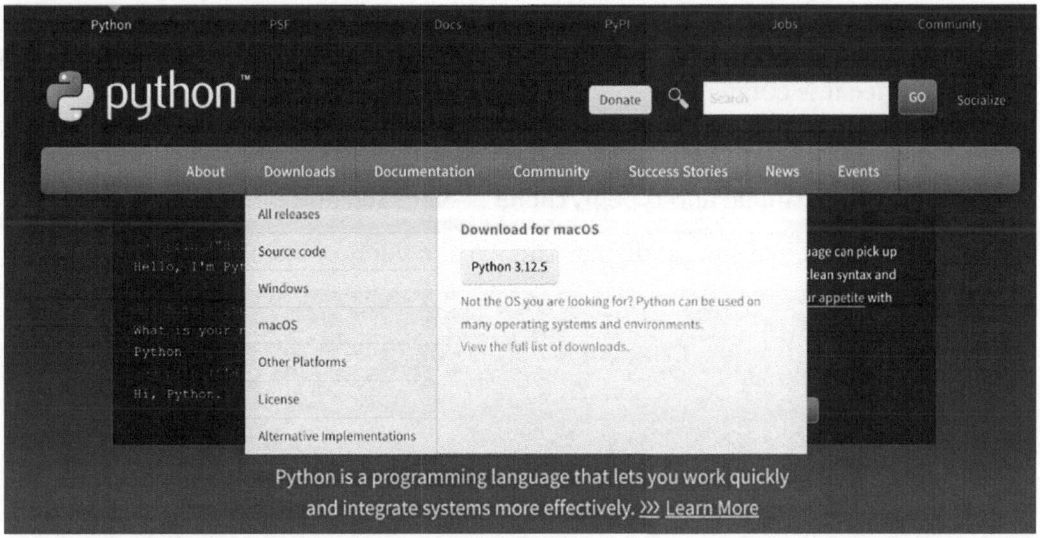

Figure 3.4: *macOS Python Download*

2. **Running the Installer**

   a. Open the downloaded **.pkg** file.

   b. Follow the on-screen instructions to complete the installation.

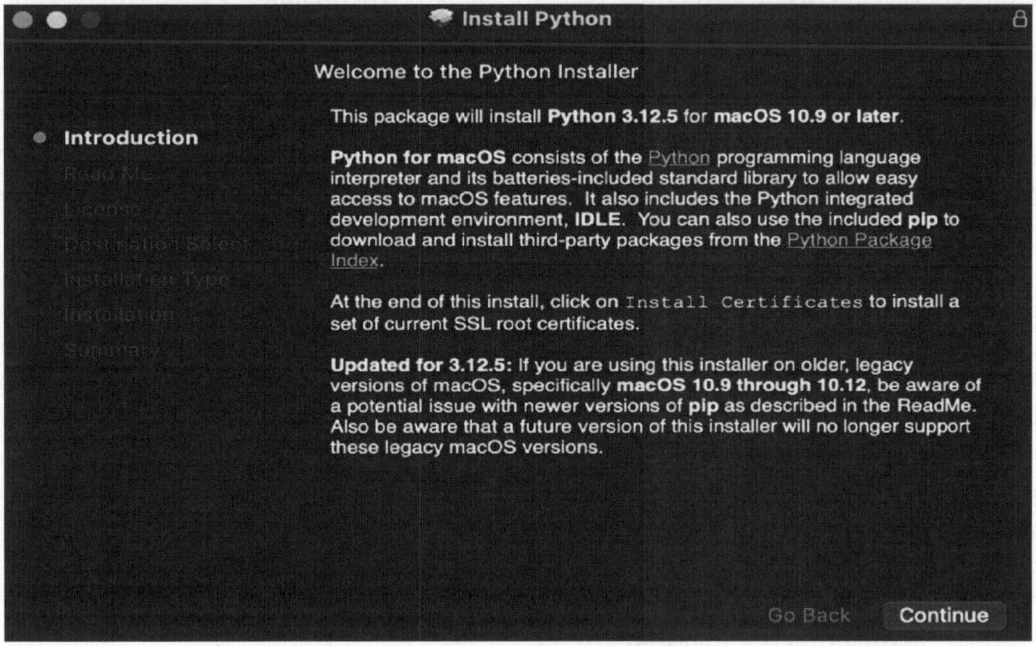

Figure 3.5: *macOS Installation*

   c. You will need to agree to the terms of the software license agreement to proceed. The step can take some time to run. You can close this window once it is complete.

3. **Verifying the Installation**
   a. Open Terminal and type **`python3 --version`** and press *Enter*.
   b. The terminal should display the Python version installed.

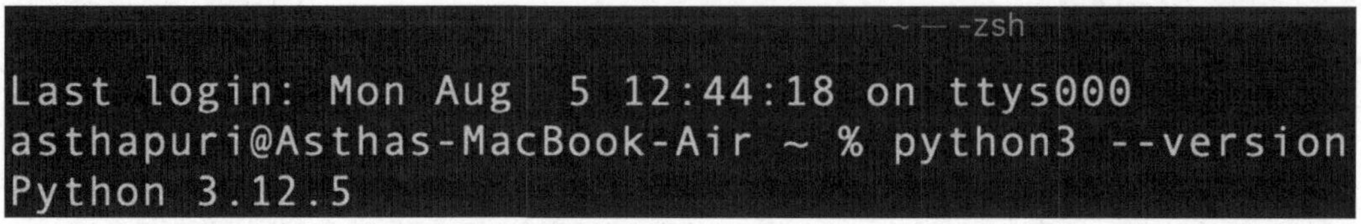

***Figure 3.6**: macOS Python Verification*

Installing R on Windows and Mac

Installing R on both Windows and Mac is a relatively simple process that acts as the foundation for powerful statistical analysis and data visualization.

On Windows, the installation begins by downloading the R installer from the Comprehensive R Archive Network (CRAN) website. The installer guides you through the setup, where you can choose the default options for most users. However, you may want to customize the installation path or select additional components depending on your needs.

On Mac, the installation process is similarly straightforward, as the R package can be downloaded from the CRAN website. After downloading, you can follow the installation prompts to ensure that R is installed correctly, and is ready to use.

Additionally, it is highly recommended to install RStudio, which is a popular Integrated Development Environment (IDE) for R. RStudio is available for both Windows and Mac. It provides an intuitive interface that includes features such as a console, script editor, and visualization tools, which significantly enhance the efficiency and ease of working with R. Once installed, both Windows and Mac users can start writing and running R scripts, loading essential packages, and diving into data analysis.

Installing R on Windows

Here are the step-by-step instructions on installing R on your Windows device:

1. **Downloading the Installer**
   a. Visit the CRAN website at **`cran.r-project.org`**.

b. Click on the "**`Download R for Windows`**" link.

c. Click on "**`base`**" and download the installer (for example, **`R-4.0.3-win.exe`**).

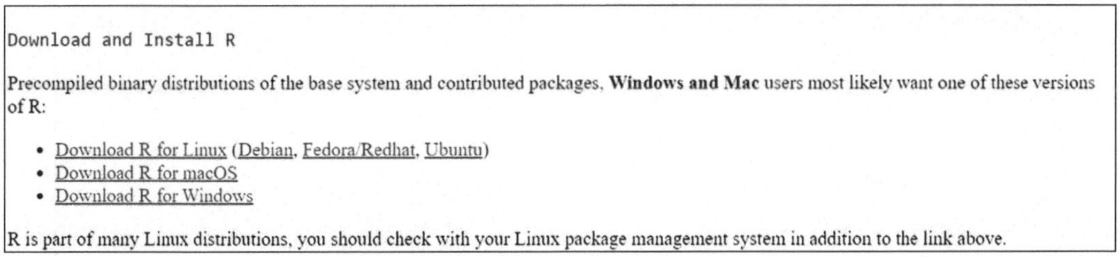

Figure 3.7: *Windows Download of R*

2. **Running the Installer**

   a. Open the downloaded file to start the installation.

   b. Follow the prompts to install R. The default settings are typically fine.

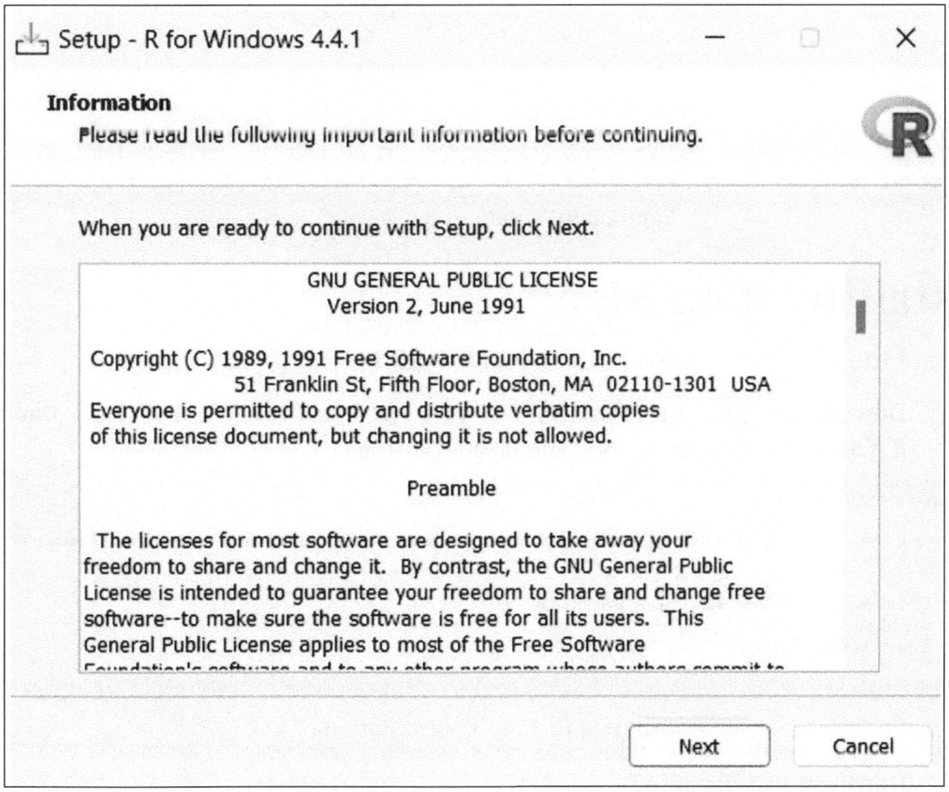

Figure 3.8: *Windows Installation of R*

3. **Verifying the Installation:** You can open R with its version name like R 4.4.1 from the start menu to see if it is installed. The R console inside the R GUI will look like how it does in the following figure during start up:

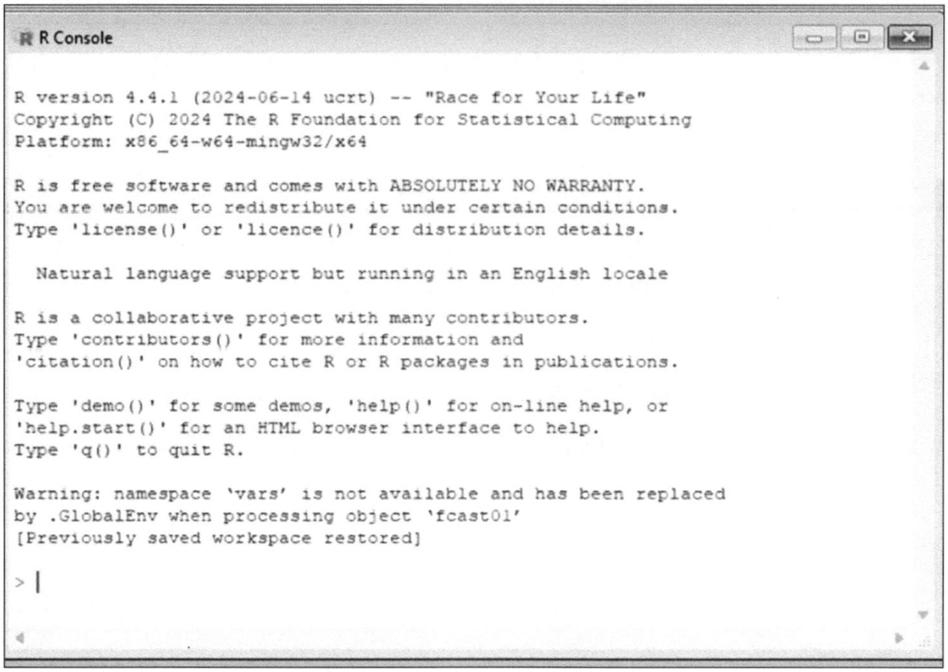

Figure 3.9: *Windows R Console View*

Installing R on Mac

Here are the step-by-step instructions on installing R on a Mac device:

1. **Downloading the Installer:** Visit `cran.r-project.org`, and click on "`Download R for macOS`" to download the latest package.

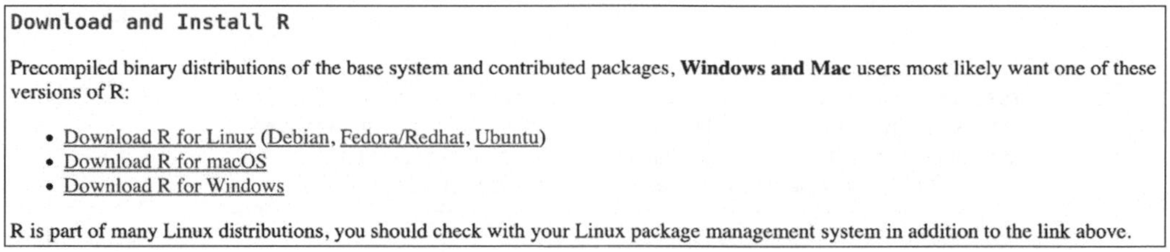

Figure 3.10: *macOS Installation of R*

2. **Running the Installer**

   a. Open the downloaded `.pkg` file.

   b. Follow the on-screen instructions to install R.

3. **Verifying the Installation**

   a. Open Terminal.

   b. Type `R --version` and press Enter to check the R version.

While R as a programming language can be run from the R console or terminal, it is not the ideal development environment for an amateur. After installing R, user should install R studio to get the IDE, which will be covered in the subsequent section.

Setting Up Jupyter Notebooks

Setting up Jupyter Notebooks is an essential step for anyone wanting to create interactive and user-friendly environments for data analysis, scientific computing, and machine learning. Jupyter Notebooks provide a powerful platform where you can write and execute code, visualize data, and document your work in a single, cohesive document. To begin, you will first need to install Python on your system. Jupyter Notebooks are an indispensable for experimentation, iterative development, and sharing your work with others.

Installing Jupyter Notebooks

Here are the step-by-step instructions to install Jupyter Notebooks on your system:

1. **Installing Jupyter Notebooks via PyCharm**

   a. It can be overwhelming at the beginning, but it is recommended that you use IDE like PyCharm or VSCode for your data science journey.

   b. Download and install PyCharm from https://www.jetbrains.com/pycharm/. Make sure to install the community edition that is available for free. To install the community edition, scroll further down on the download page.

Figure 3.11: *Downloading PyCharm (Similar for Windows and MacOS)*

c. Follow the instructions on the screen to complete the installation. Once installed, you need to select the terminal inside PyCharm and install Jupyter with the command **`pip install jupyter`**.

d. Remember to type this command in the terminal, and not in the Python console.

e. After the installation is complete, type **`jupyter notebook`** in the terminal to open the notebook view in your web browser where a local host would display the Jupyter notebook view.

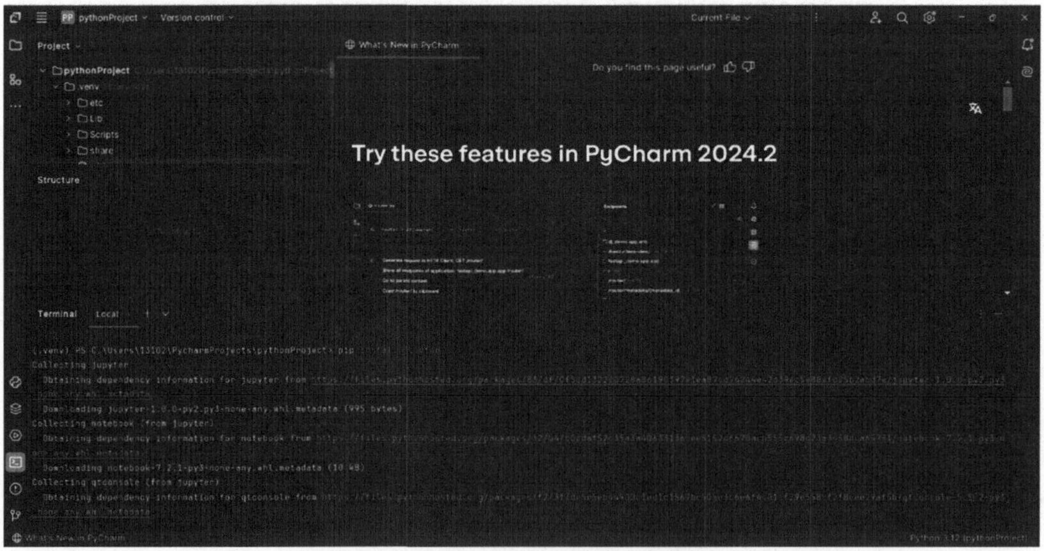

Figure 3.12: *Using Terminal inside PyCharm to Install and Launch Notebooks*

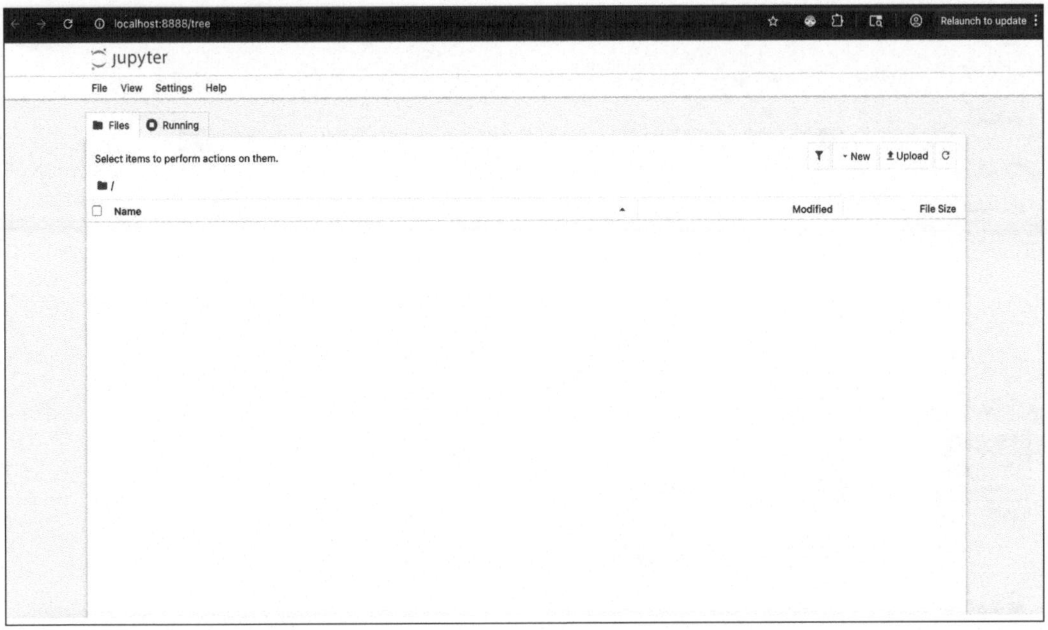

Figure 3.13: *Jupyter Notebook UI in Web Browser*

2. **Installing Anaconda Navigator**
   a. Anaconda Navigator is a Graphical User Interface (GUI) that comes with the Anaconda distribution, which is a popular platform for data science and machine learning.
   b. Navigator simplifies the management of packages, environments, and various tools used in Python and R development. It allows users to easily install, update, and launch applications like Jupyter Notebooks, Spyder, RStudio, and others, without needing to use the command line.
   c. While Anaconda navigator has everything like Jupyter Notebooks, PyCharm, and even R studio, we will still recommend installing R studio and PyCharm individually and launch notebooks through them, as Anaconda is a bulky software since it is used to launch multiple softwares.
   d. You can download and install Anaconda Navigator from https://www.anaconda.com/products/navigator.
   e. Install it locally using the standard steps. Installing Anaconda Navigator can take a few minutes to complete. Once it is done, the Navigator will show a marketplace of softwares, which you can run by simply clicking them.

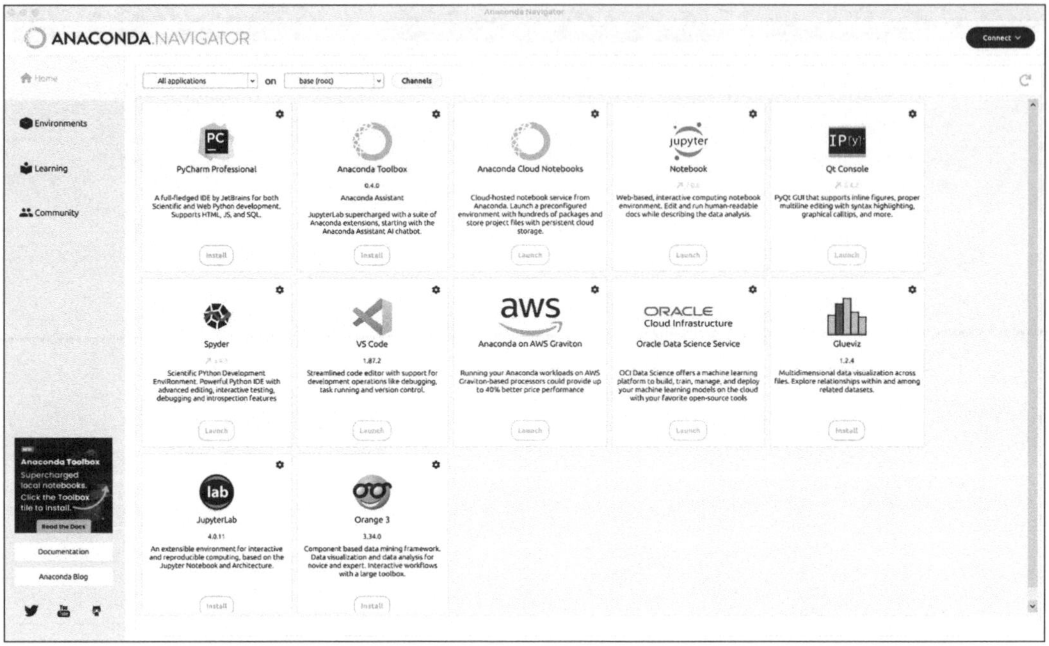

Figure 3.14: *Marketplace View inside Anaconda Navigator*

Setting Up RStudio

RStudio is a powerful and versatile Integrated Development Environment (IDE) which is specifically designed for R. As the go-to tool for R users, RStudio provides an intuitive and user-friendly interface that simplifies the process of writing and running R code, which makes it accessible for both beginners and experienced programmers.

The IDE is equipped with a variety of features that enhance productivity, like a code editor with syntax highlighting, an interactive console for executing R commands, and an integrated environment for managing scripts, data, and plots. Additionally, RStudio offers built-in tools for debugging, package management, and version control, which allows users to efficiently develop and maintain complex projects. One of its standout features is the ability to seamlessly generate and view dynamic visualizations, as well as to produce high-quality reports and documents using R Markdown. Whether you are conducting statistical analysis, building predictive models, or creating interactive visualizations, RStudio will provide a cohesive platform that integrates all aspects of your workflow, which makes it an essential tool for anyone working with R.

Installing RStudio

Here are the step-by-step instructions to install RStudio:

1. **Downloading the Installer:** Visit https://posit.co/download/rstudio-

desktop/ to download R studio. You can also download R language via the same link. Download the appropriate installer for your operating system.

Figure 3.15: *RStudio Installation Screen on the posit Website*

2. **Running the Installer:** Open the downloaded file and follow the installation instructions.

Figure 3.16: *RStudio Setup Process*

3. **Launching RStudio**
   a. Open RStudio from your applications menu.
   b. You can now start writing and executing code written in R.

Essential Packages and Libraries

There are numerous packages and libraries that can assist you in your data science journey. Your choice of package would depend on your specific tasks and preferences. Let us look at some of the most common packages and libraries used by data scientists:

Python Packages

Here are some of the most common packages used by data scientists:

- **Pandas:** Pandas is a Python package widely used for data manipulation and analysis. It provides powerful tools to handle structured data, like data frames, which allow for easy data cleaning, filtering, aggregation, and transformation. Pandas is essential for tasks like reading and writing data from various file formats (for example, CSV, Excel), performing statistical operations, and preparing data for further analysis or visualization.
  - You can read more about Pandas here: https://pypi.org/project/pandas/
  - To install it, use this pip: **`pip install pandas`**
- **NumPy:** NumPy is used for numerical computing in Python. It provides support for large, multi-dimensional arrays and matrices, besides a suite of mathematical functions to operate on these arrays. Due to its efficient handling of operations like linear algebra, random number generation, and Fourier transforms, NumPy is critical for data manipulation and numerical analysis. Whether you need to perform element-wise operations on arrays or solve complex linear algebra problems, NumPy offers the necessary tools to tackle these tasks effectively.
  - You can read more about the package here: https://pypi.org/project/numpy/
  - Install it via the **`pip`**: **`pip install numpy`**
- **Scikit-learn:** Scikit-learn is a popular Python package used for machine learning. It provides simple and efficient tools for data mining and data analysis, including algorithms for classification, regression, clustering, and dimensionality reduction. Scikit-learn also offers utilities for model selection, cross-validation, and preprocessing data, making it a go-to library for building and evaluating machine learning models in Python:

  - You can read more about the package here: https://pypi.org/project/Scikit-learn/
  - Install it via **pip**: **pip install scikit-learn**
- **Matplotlib:** Matplotlib is a widely used Python package for data visualization. It allows users to create a variety of static, animated, and interactive plots like line graphs, bar charts, histograms, and scatter plots. Matplotlib is highly customizable, which allows users to exercise detailed control over plot elements like labels, colors, and scales. These functions make it essential for visualizing data and presenting analysis results in Python.
  - You can read more about the package here: https://pypi.org/project/matplotlib/
  - Install it via the **pip**: **pip install matplotlib**

R Packages

Here are some of the most common R packages used by data scientists:

- **tidyverse:** The **tidyverse** is a collection of R packages designed for data science and provides tools for data manipulation, exploration, and visualization. Core packages include **dplyr** for data manipulation, **ggplot2** for data visualization, **tidyr** for tidying data, and **readr** for data imports. The **tidyverse** promotes a consistent and intuitive syntax, which makes it easier for users to perform complex data transformations and analyses in R.
  - Install the **tidyverse** in R console : **install.packages("tidyverse")**

  Run **library(tidyverse)** to load the core **tidyverse** in your current R session.
- **caret:** The **caret** (Classification And Regression Training) package in R is a comprehensive toolset for building and evaluating machine learning models. It simplifies the process of model training by providing functions for data preprocessing, feature selection, model tuning, and resampling. It also supports a wide range of machine learning algorithms and allows users to compare different models easily.
  - Install caret in R console via: **install.packages("caret")**

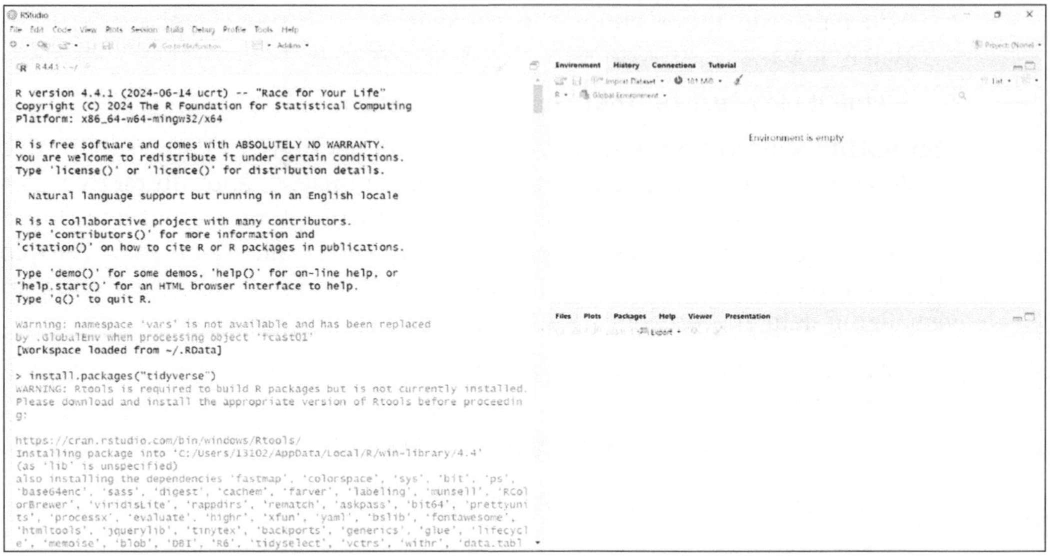

Figure 3.17: *RStudio View with Package Installation Running in Console*

Conclusion

After following the steps in this chapter, you should now have Python and R installed on your Windows or Mac system. You might also have the Jupyter Notebooks and RStudio environments set up, and essential packages installed. With your development environment ready, you are now equipped to dive deeper into data science and machine learning. This chapter marks the beginning of your foray into the world of data science. With a fully functioning Python and/or R environment at your disposal, you are now equipped to tackle the exciting challenges ahead. The tools and libraries you have installed are the building blocks for analyzing complex datasets, developing predictive models, and transforming data into actionable insights.

In the next chapter, we will put these packages to use. You will start exploring datasets with the help of these packages to do exploratory data analysis, visualize and understand your datasets to derive insights. Let us dive in!

Chapter 4

Importing and Cleaning Data in Python and R

Introduction

In the era of big data and AI (Artificial Intelligence), data has become the lifeblood of innovation and decision-making across industries. Whether you are developing a machine learning model to predict customer behavior, conducting in-depth statistical analysis, or simply trying to gain insights from a dataset, the quality and accessibility of your data are paramount. Data, however, only sometimes comes in a neat, ready-to-use format. It often originates from disparate sources like CSV files, Excel spreadsheets, JSON files, or SQL databases, where each has its own structure, quirks, and potential pitfalls. Moreover, raw data is seldom clean–it may contain missing values, inconsistent formats, outliers, and various other issues that can compromise the accuracy and reliability of your analysis or model.

Given the diversity of data sources and the challenges inherent in data preprocessing, one of the most crucial steps in any data-driven project is ensuring that the data is properly imported, thoroughly cleaned, and well-prepared for subsequent analysis or machine learning algorithms. This chapter will guide you through these essential processes while focusing on two popular programming languages widely used in data science: Python and R.

Data cleaning is an indispensable part of the data preprocessing pipeline. It involves various tasks like handling missing values, correcting bad data formats, and detecting and managing outliers. Poor data quality can lead to misleading results, inaccurate models, and flawed decision-making. Therefore, understanding effective data-cleaning strategies is as important as the analysis phase itself. In this chapter, we will delve into various data-cleaning techniques, demonstrating how to implement them in Python and R. Through practical examples and code snippets, you will learn how to transform raw, messy data into a polished dataset ready for analysis or machine learning.

By the end of this chapter, you will have a solid foundation in importing and cleaning data using Python and R. These skills are fundamental for any data scientist or analyst and will enable you to tackle a wide range of data-driven projects confidently and efficiently. Whether you are dealing with small datasets stored in CSV files or large-scale databases, the techniques covered in this chapter will equip you with the tools necessary to prepare your data for the next stages of your workflow, ensuring that your analyses and models are built on a solid, reliable foundation.

Structure

This chapter will cover the following topics:

- Importing Data in Python
- Importing Data in R
- Data Cleaning Techniques in Python
- Data Cleaning Techniques in R

Importing Data in Python

Python offers several libraries to import data from various sources. Python libraries are collections of pre-written code that help you perform common tasks without having to write everything from scratch. They act like toolkits and provide functions and modules to solve specific problems such as data manipulation, visualization, web development, and machine learning. For instance, the **`pandas`** library is great for handling and analyzing data, while **`matplotlib`** allows you to create visualizations like charts and graphs.

To use a Python library, you first import it into your script to use the available tools. This saves time and effort and enables you to focus on building your project rather than reinventing the wheel.

The most commonly used libraries for importing data are:

- **`pandas`** for CSV and Excel files
- **`sqlite3`** or **`SQLAlchemy`** for SQL databases.

Kaggle is also an amazing place to access public datasets you can practice on.

For this chapter, we will be using the dataset from: https://www.kaggle.com/datasets/rabieelkharoua/students-performance-dataset

This dataset contains comprehensive information on 2,392 high school students, detailing their demographics, study habits, parental involvement, extracurricular activities, and academic performance.

Pre-Checks in Python Before Starting

Before getting started with importing your data files, there are a few basics that need to be checked. These are listed as follows:

1. **Installation of packages in the Python environment**

   This depends on if you are using Anaconda Navigator, PyCharm, or some other environments. These packages might come pre-installed or you might need to install them before using the libraries.

   There are a few ways to install packages in PyCharm.

   i. Use the Terminal to install the requisite package(make sure to not run it in the Python console but use Windows power shell or command prompt)

   ```
   pip install pandas
   ```

   ii. Right click on the error *pandas* - show content options and **`Install packages pandas`**.

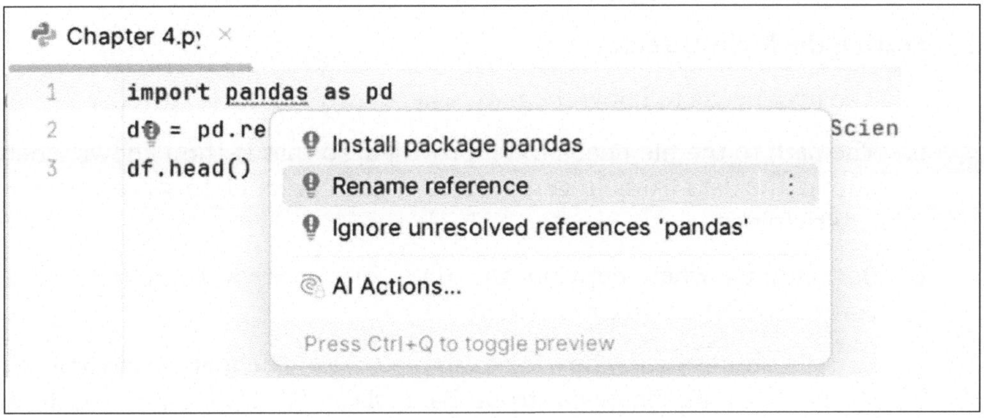

Figure 4.1: *Installing Pandas*

   iii. Another way is to click on the Python Packages and type the package name to install it.

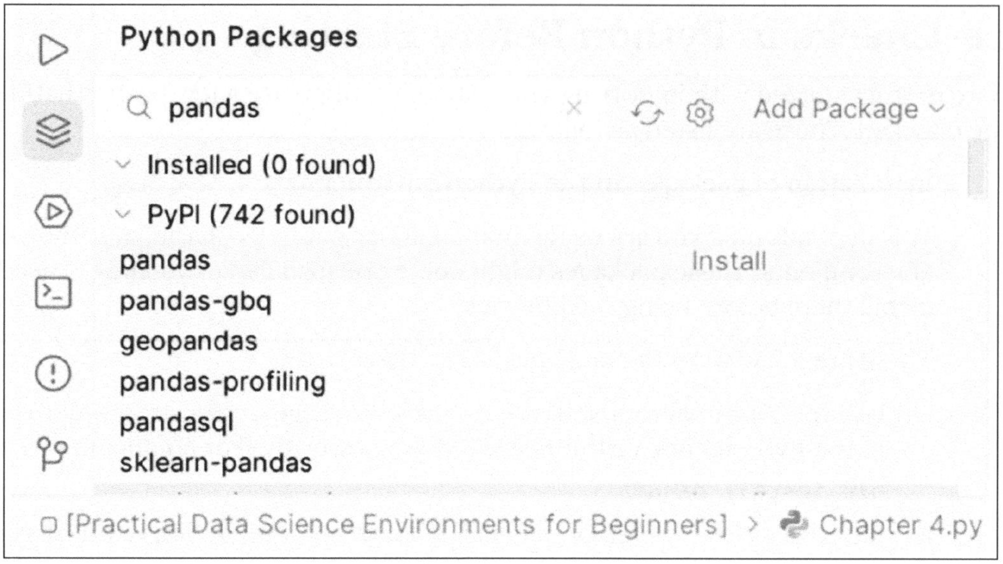

Figure 4.2: *Pandas Installation*

2. **Setting the Right Directory**

   a. The user needs to know the path where the data file is stored.

   b. The path to the file needs to be provided, so that Python knows where to import the data from. In general, it is a good practice to store your data in a **`data`** folder.

   c. Be cautious when copying the directory address from the Windows address bar in a Windows system.

      i. The address you copy for example **`C:\My Documents\Python`** would need to be changed from back-slash (\) to forward-slash while executing the following:

      ```
      pandas.read_csv('C:/My Documents/Chapter 4.py")
      ```

Importing CSV Files

Before importing your data files, there are a few basics that need to be in order and are listed as follows:

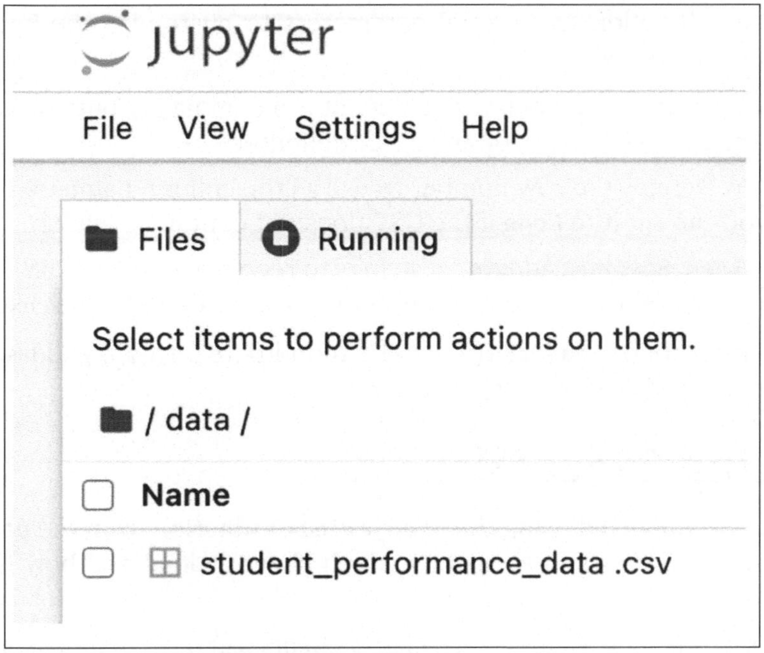

Figure 4.3: *Importing csv in Jupyter*

Create a new notebook and name it **eda.ipynb.**

The **pandas** library provides an easy way to import CSV files via the **read_csv()** function.

```
import pandas as pd

# Importing a CSV file
try:
    df = pd.read_csv('data/sample_data.csv')
Except FileNotFoundError:
    print("File not found. Check file path.")
# Display the first few rows of the dataframe
df.head()
```

The output should look something like this:

	StudentID	Age	Gender	Ethnicity	ParentalEducation	StudyTimeWeekly	Absences	Tutoring	ParentalSupport
0	1001	17	1	0	2	19.833723	7	1	2
1	1002	18	0	0	1	15.408756	0	0	1
2	1003	15	0	2	3	4.210570	26	0	2
3	1004	17	1	0	3	10.028829	14	0	3
4	1005	17	1	0	2	4.672495	17	1	3

Figure 4.4: *CSV Data Frame first 5 rows*

The **read_csv()** function has several parameters to customize the import process which are listed as follows:

- **sep**: Specifies the delimiter. The default is a comma (**,**), but you can set it to a tab (**\t**), a semicolon (**;**), or any other delimiter.
- **header**: Defines the row number to use as the column names. **0** is the default, but you can set it to **None** if the CSV does not contain a header.
- **na_values**: Specifies additional strings to recognize as NA/NaN. This is useful if your dataset uses custom representations for missing values like **NA**, **?**, or **--**.

More information about **read_csv()** can be found here: https://pandas.pydata.org/docs/reference/api/pandas.read_csv.html

Importing Excel Files

Excel files can be imported using the **read_excel()** function from the **pandas** library. This function also allows you to specify which sheet to load and how to handle NA values.

Note: *If you do not have* ***openpyxl*** *installed, you will need to do that using* ***pip install openpyxl***

For our use case, we will use the data file 'Data_SDG_India_Index_2020-21.xlsx' from https://www.kaggle.com/datasets/chandramanaha/indian-states-sdg-index-202021?select=Data_SDG_India_Index_2020-21.xlsx and place it in our 'data' folder.

The data compiles a list of 17 Sustainable Development Goals and 169 targets that several countries, including India, have pledged to comply with based on the United Nations 2030 Agenda for Sustainable Development,

This Excel file has multiple sheets which are demonstrated as follows:

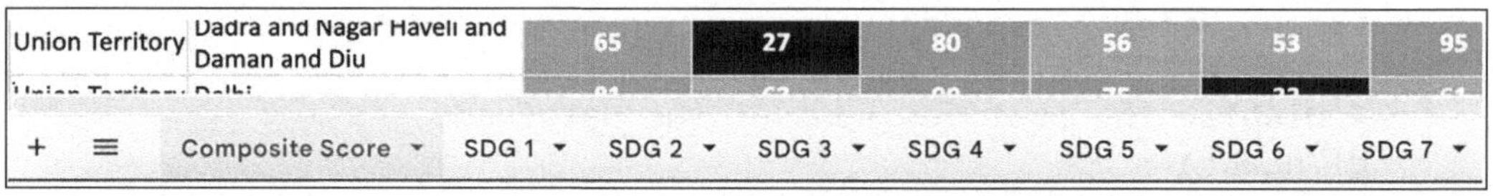

Figure 4.5: *Sample Excel File*

```
# Importing an Excel file
df = pd.read_excel('data/Data_SDG_India_Index_2020-21.xlsx')

# Display the first few rows
df.head()
```

The preceding code will only load the first sheet into the dataframe, which is the default.

Category	State/UT	SDG 1	SDG 2	SDG 3	SDG 4	SDG 5	SDG 6	SDG 7
State	Andhra Pradesh	81	52	77	50	58	92	100
State	Arunachal Pradesh	54	66	64	41	37	67	85
State	Assam	51	41	59	43	25	64	98
State	Bihar	32	31	66	29	48	91	78
State	Chhattisgarh	49	37	60	55	64	89	78

***Figure 4.6**: Excel Imported as Data Frame*

However, if you need to load another sheet, you may specify its name in the parameter **sheet_name**

```
# Importing an Excel file
df = pd.read_excel('data/Data_SDG_India_Index_2020-21.xlsx',
sheet_name='SDG 2')

# Display the first few rows
df.head()
```

Unnamed: 0	Unnamed: 1	Unnamed: 2	2.1	2.2	2.2.1	2.2.2
SNO	Category	States/UTs	Percentage of beneficiaries covered under Nati...	Percentage of children under five years who ar...	Percentage of children under five years who a...	Percentage of pregnant women aged 15-49 years ...
1	State	Andhra Pradesh	100	35.5	31.5	52.9
2	State	Arunachal Pradesh	100	16	28	33.8
3	State	Assam	94.27	29.4	32.4	44.8
4	State	Bihar	99.85	38.7	42	58.3

***Figure 4.7**: Excel Imported as Data Frame - First 5 Rows of Tab SDG 2 in the Excel*

Notice how the first three columns are called 'Unnamed' as their names were not specified in the Excel file.

Similar to **sheet_name, read_excel()** has more parameters like **na_values**, and **header** to control the import. To read more about parameters, users can visit: https://pandas.pydata.org/docs/reference/api/pandas.read_excel.html

Importing SQL Data

To import data from SQL databases, you can use the **sqlite3** library or the more flexible **SQLAlchemy** package. **pandas** provide a **read_sql()** function that can read SQL query results directly into a DataFrame.

To test this, you can look for any publicly available sample database in **.db** format and download them offline to practice.

Example with SQLite:

```
import sqlite3

# Connecting to the database
conn = sqlite3.connect('data/sample_database.db')

# Reading data from SQL
df = pd.read_sql_query("SELECT * FROM sample_table", conn)

# Closing the connection
conn.close()

# Displaying the data
print(df.head())
```

Example with SQLAlchemy:

```
from sqlalchemy import create_engine

# Creating the engine
engine = create_engine('sqlite:///data/sample_database.db')

# Reading data from SQL
df = pd.read_sql("SELECT * FROM sample_table", con=engine)

# Displaying the data
df.head()
```

Importing Data in R

R, similar to Python, provides various libraries, which are also called packages, to handle data import from different sources like CSV, Excel, and SQL databases.

The prechecks we established in Python, such as installing a package in R and setting the working directory also apply while working in RStudio.

To get started open a new file called R script, where you can write the code that will be saved as an executable script.

You can set the working directory where your CSV file is present by selecting **Session** > **Set Working Directory** > **Choose Directory**.

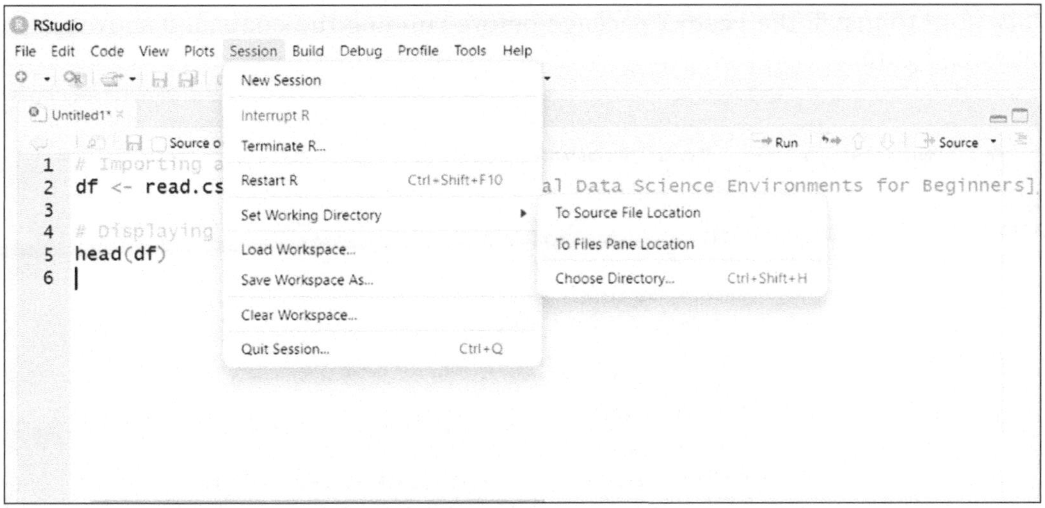

***Figure 4.8**: Setting a Working Directory in R Script*

Importing CSV Files

The **read.csv()** function in R is the most commonly used method to import CSV files, which is also demonstrated in the following example:

Example:

```
# Importing a CSV file
df <- read.csv('data/sample_data.csv')

# Displaying the first few rows
head(df)
```

You can customize the import process using parameters like **sep** for specifying the delimiter, **header** to indicate if the file contains a header, and **na.strings** to define what should be interpreted as NA.

Here is an example with these parameters:

```
df <- read.csv('data/sample_data.csv', sep=';', header=TRUE,
na.strings=c("NA", "--"))

# Displaying the first few rows
head(df)
```

Importing Excel Files

The **readxl** package is widely used for Excel files. It allows reading both **.xls** and **.xlsx** formats.

Make sure to install the **readxl** package before running the command shown in the following figure:

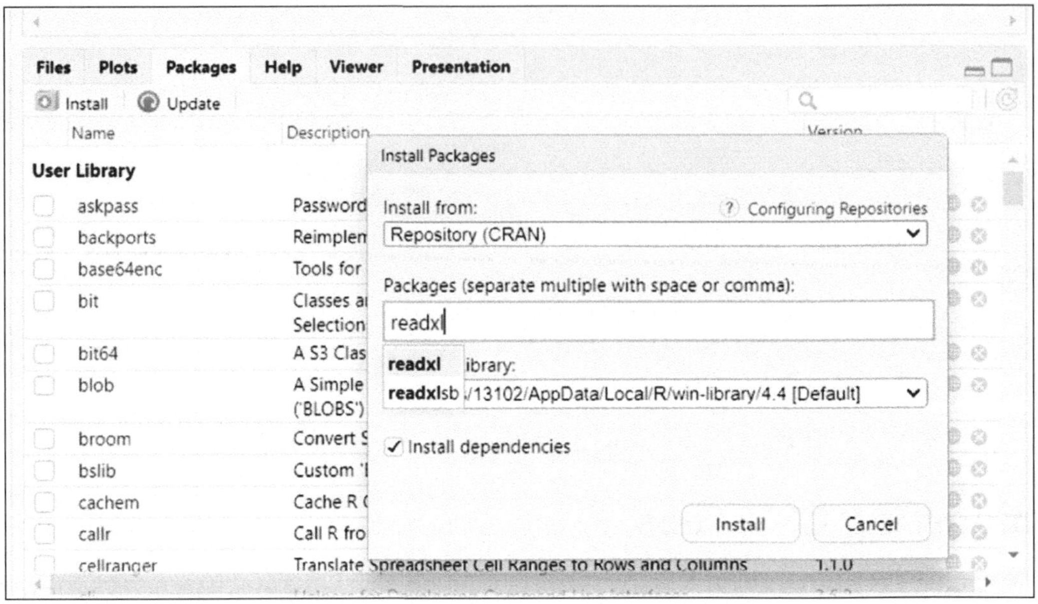

***Figure 4.9**: Installing the readxl Package in R*

Before running the following code block, set the working directory or add the complete path of the Excel sheet along with the correct location and tab name.

Example:

```
library(readxl)

# Importing an Excel file
df <- read_excel('data/sample_data.xlsx', sheet = 'Sheet1')

# Displaying the first few rows
head(df)
```

Importing SQL Data

To import SQL data, R provides the **DBI** package, which acts as a database interface, and **RSQLite** for SQLite databases. You can also use **dplyr** with **dbplyr** to handle database connections.

Example with SQLite:

```
library(DBI)
library(RSQLite)
```

```
# Connecting to the database
con <- dbConnect(SQLite(), 'data/sample_database.db')

# Reading data from SQL
df <- dbGetQuery(con, "SELECT * FROM sample_table")

# Closing the connection
dbDisconnect(con)

# Displaying the data
head(df)
```

Data Cleaning Techniques in Python

Once the data is imported, the next step is to clean it by handling missing values, dealing with bad data formats, removing outliers, and more.

Handling Missing Values

Missing values are common in datasets as they emerge from a source with data pipeline errors or when the data is simplified after it is joined with another database. This error is detrimental for analysis as it can distort statistics and also result in biased estimates.

Python's **pandas** library offers several methods to handle them, such as dropping rows/columns, filling them with specific values, or more sophisticated techniques like interpolation.

First, let us check if any column in the **'Student performance data'** DataFrame has null/missing values. If there are no import errors or alternations in the data, the following code will return as False:

```
df.isnull().values.any()
```

Now let us replace one of the values in the DataFrame with NULL to see if this works. This will also give you an idea to reference an individual scalar cell or data point using **Pandas**.

Run the following command:

```
df.iat[0,0]
#It would return the Value of the cell at 0,0 which is 1001
```

Note that Python indexes start from 0, therefore, the 1st cell of the 1st row and column will be called using [0,0]. Let us intentionally replace this cell with NULL using **numpy** library with the following snippet:

```
import numpy as np
df.iat[0,0] = np.nan
# Then re-run the above command again to check if there is indeed
a NULL value in the Data Frame
df.isnull().values.any()
```

The following code returns the column names containing missing values:

```
null_columns = df.columns[df.isnull().any()]
print(null_columns)
```

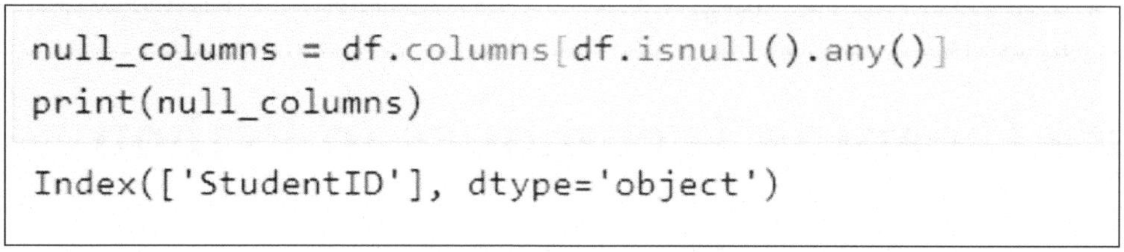

***Figure 4.10**: StudentID Column Containing Null Values*

This tells us that the columns StudentID contain missing values. There are many ways to handle null values. One of them is removing all the rows with null values. However, we might lose key information in the process because other columns of that row might it.

Another way is to fill the missing values with a specific value. Here, we do not lose information, but assume that the assigned value is pretty close to being accurate. We can later fill it with a constant, statistical average, or the same as the next or previous value. This step is shown in the following example:

```
# Drop rows with missing values
df.dropna(inplace=True)

# Fill missing values with a specific value
df.fillna(0, inplace=True)

# Fill missing values using forward fill
df.fillna(method='ffill', inplace=True)
```

Since the missing value in this instance is a **`'StudentID'`**, we cannot use any numerical manipulation to replace it. We might have to remove the row containing the missing value, as shown in the example here:

```
#count the number of rows in the data frame
df.shape[0]
# You should get 2392
# remove the row that has the missing value
df.dropna(inplace = True)
df.shape[0]
```

```
# You should get 2391
#You can also run the isnull() command again to see if it is
False now
df.isnull().values.any()
```

It is important to evaluate the use case before applying a particular treatment for the missing value. The action is important as it can critically affect your analysis and model training in the future.

Handling Bad Data Formats and Characters

Data can often appear in bad formats or with unexpected characters. These features can significantly undermine the reliability and accuracy of your data science project.

When integrating multiple datasets, bad formats can prevent successful merging or joining of data. For instance, if one dataset uses a different date format or includes unexpected characters, it may not align correctly with other datasets. A situation where a column is meant to store dates but contains a string that cannot be converted to a date format severely disrupts time-series analysis. Hence, reviewing formats and checking basic summary statistics before analyzing the data are important.

Let us use the student data set we used in the analysis above and manipulate the data intentionally, while adding bad data formats and characters.

When we obtain data from multiple sources, it should be converted before analyzing the data and running models. Now, observe the following code:

```
from datetime import datetime
df['Today_Date'] = datetime.today().strftime('%Y-%m-%d')
df.head()
print(df['Today_Date'].dtype)
```

This code uses the **`datetime`** module from Python's standard library. **`datetime.today()`** fetches the current date and time (the instance of code execution). The **`.strftime()`** method is used to format the date and time as a string. **`'%Y-%m-%d'`** is the format string that specifies how you want the date to appear.

The column **`Today_Date`** which looks like **`datatime`** format, is a string that comes as a data type object.

```
print(df['Today_Date'].dtype)

object
```

***Figure 4.11**: Output of the Column Today Date's Format*

To convert it to a date-time format, we can run the **to_datetime** function in Pandas to convert it to Python date time format. The second statement ensures that if a value in the column cannot be converted to a datetime format, the function will replace it with **NaT** (which stands for **Not a Time**, equivalent to **NaN** for datetime), instead of throwing an error.

```
df['Today_Date'] = pd.to_datetime(df['Today_Date'], errors='
coerce')
print(df['Today_Date'].dtype)
```

Similar data type conversions can be performed using **pd.to_numeric()** for numeric conversion and **.astype()** for general type conversions.

Another common situation is when some values in a column contain special characters that have to be removed or replaced. Let us see an example, where we create a new column called school city. However there is an & (ampersand) symbol instead of a space. To fix this we will run **.str.replace** as shown in the following code:

```
df['School_City'] = 'New&York'
df['School_City'] = df['School_City'].str.replace('&', ' ',
regex=True)
```

The **.str** accessor is used to perform vectorized string operations on a pandas Series (that is, the entire column).The **.replace()** method is used to replace specific characters or patterns in strings.

Handling Outliers

Handling outliers is crucial in machine learning and data analysis as they can significantly skew results and result in inaccurate models. Outliers may distort summary statistics like the mean and standard deviation, while affecting the overall data distribution. In regression models, they can promote bias in the coefficients, which leads to incorrect predictions. For algorithms like k-nearest neighbors or clustering, outliers can create misleading groupings. Additionally, outliers may represent data entry errors or rare, but valid phenomena; therefore, detecting and handling them generates more reliable and interpretable outcomes.

Let us check the distribution of GPA in our dataset via the following code:

```
plt.Figureure(Figuresize=(8, 5))
sns.histplot(df['GPA'], bins=5, kde=True)
plt.title('Distribution of GPA')
plt.xlabel('GPA')
plt.ylabel('Frequency')
plt.show()
```

Here is what the output might look like:

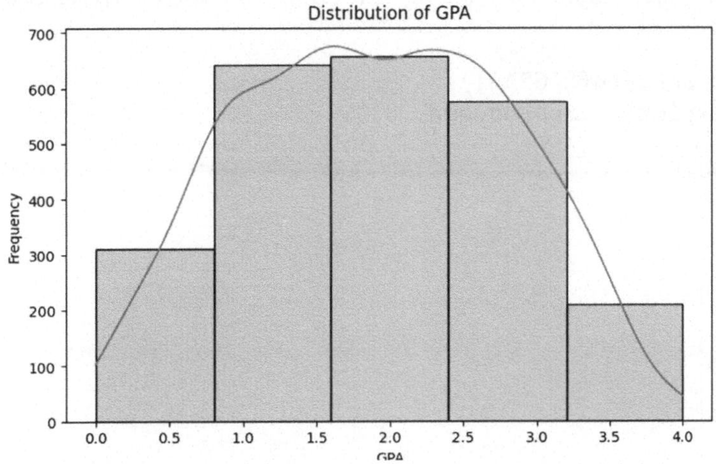

Figure 4.12: *Normal Distribution of Column GPA*

Here, the data is normally distributed without outliers. If we had any outliers, the graph would have skewed either to the left or to the right.

You can also check for outliers using boxplots. For example, try running this code on the student performance dataset:

```
plt.Figureure(Figuresize=(8, 5))
# Create a box plot
plt.boxplot(df['GPA'])
# Show the plot
plt.title('Box Plot with Percentiles')
plt.show()
```

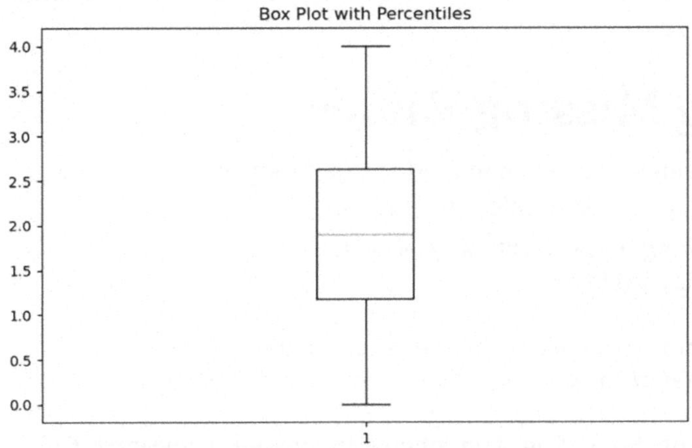

Figure 4.13: *Box Plot of Column GPA*

Here, the entire data lies within the plot. This shows that there are not any outliers. For the sake of experimentation, let us add an outlier to the GPAs and then plot the same graph:

```
gpa=np.array(df['GPA'])
plt.boxplot(np.append(gpa, 8))
```

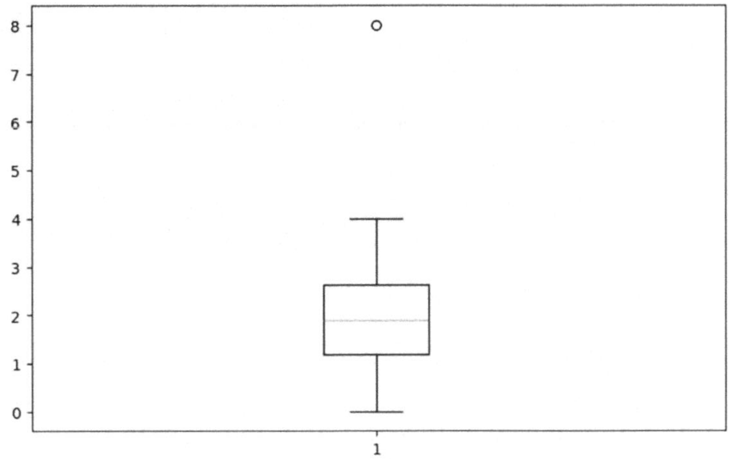

***Figure 4.14**: Box Plot of Column GPA with Outliers*

This outlier is shown on the boxplot as a dot on the topmost part of the graph. In situations like these, we might want to handle the outlier. However, from our original dataset perspective, we are good.

Data Cleaning Techniques in R

R provides a rich set of tools for data cleaning, that are most commonly used through the **dplyr** and **tidyr** packages.

Handling Missing Values

In R, missing values can be managed using functions like **na.omit()**, **is.na()**, and **replace()** as shown in the following example:

```
# Removing rows with any missing values
df <- na.omit(df)

# Replacing NA with a specific value
df[is.na(df)] <- 0

# Filling NA using the previous value (forward fill)
library(zoo)
df <- na.locf(df)
```

Let us try the same example we had tried in Python:

```
# To check if the data frame has any NULL values
print(any(is.na(df)))
# Getting the value of 1st row and column
print(df[1, 1])

# Replace the value at the first row and first column with NA

df[1, 1] <- NA
# Check if there are any NA values in the dataframe

print(any(is.na(df)))
```

To see the columns with the NULL value, run the following code:

```
# Identify columns with NA values
null_columns <- names(df)[apply(df, 2, function(x) any(is.
na(x)))]

# Print the column names with NA values
print(null_columns)
```

`apply(df, 2, function(x) any(is.na(x)))` checks each column (2 refers to columns) for NA values.

Handling Bad Data Formats and Characters

R's functions like **`as.Date()`** and **`gsub()`** are commonly used to handle data formats and clean characters.

We will manipulate the data here just like we did in Python to add a new column that looks like a date but is a "**`character`**" format:

```
# Load the required library
library(lubridate)

# Add a new column with the current date
df$Today_Date <- format(Sys.Date(), "%Y-%m-%d")

# Display the first few rows of the dataframe
head(df)

typeof(df$Today_Date)

# To convert the column back to date format

df$Today_Date <- as.Date(df$Today_Date, format = "%Y-%m-%d")
```

Here is how to fix a bad character in the data frame:

```
# Assign the string 'New&York' to the School_City column
df$School_City <- 'New&York'
# Replace '&' with a space in the School_City column
df$School_City <- gsub('&', ' ', df$School_City)

# Display the updated dataframe
print(df)
```

Handling Outliers

Outliers can be handled using the statistical functions in R or by defining thresholds based on an Interquartile Range (IQR).

Example:

```
# Load the required library
library(ggplot2)

# Create the histogram with density (KDE) plot
ggplot(df, aes(x = GPA)) +
geom_histogram(bins = 5, fill = "skyblue", color = "black", alpha
= 0.7) +
# Histogram
geom_density(aes(y = ..count..), color = "red", size = 1) +
ggtitle("Distribution of GPA") +
# Title
xlab("GPA") +
# X-axis label
ylab("Frequency") +
# Y-axis label
theme_minimal()
# Minimal theme
```

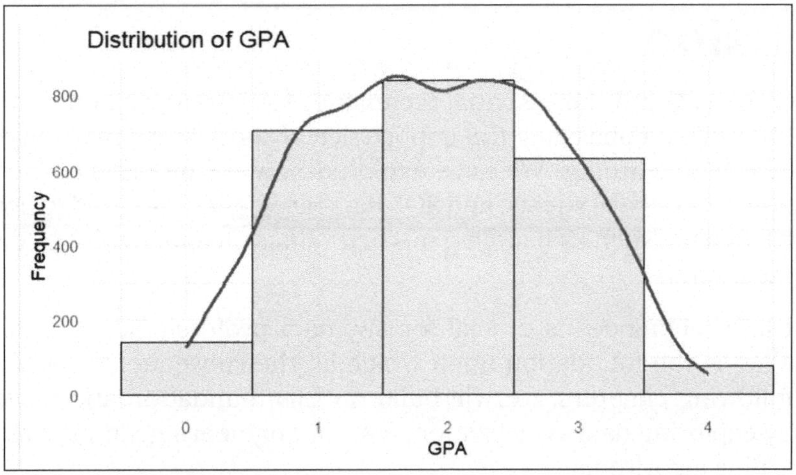

Figure 4.15: *Normal Distribution of Column GPA in R*

```
# Convert the GPA column to a numeric vector
gpa <- as.numeric(df$GPA)

# Append the value 8 to the GPA vector
gpa <- c(gpa, 8)

# Create a boxplot
boxplot(gpa, main = "Boxplot of GPA", ylab = "GPA")
```

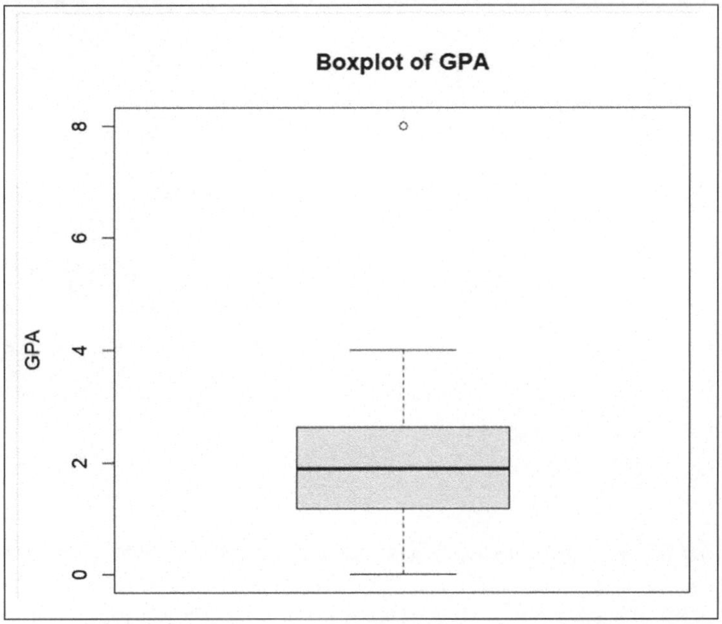

Figure 4.16: *Box Plot of Column GPA with an Outlier in R*

Conclusion

This chapter has covered the essential techniques for importing and cleaning data in Python and R, while emphasizing the importance of these steps in preparing data for analysis or machine learning. We have explored how to import data from common sources like CSV files, Excel sheets, and SQL databases, and discussed various methods for cleaning this data, such as handling missing values, dealing with bad data formats, and managing outliers.

Mastering these techniques is crucial for any data professional, as clean and well-structured data is the foundation upon which all the subsequent analysis will stand on. In the following chapters, we will build on this foundation and move on to the next steps by exploring data visualization, feature engineering, and the application of machine learning algorithms.

CHAPTER 5
Data Wrangling and Manipulation in Python and R

Introduction

Data wrangling and manipulation are essential stages in the data analysis process, where raw data is transformed into a structured format suitable for analysis. This chapter offers an in-depth guide that explains advanced wrangling techniques using Python and R, which are two of the most widely used tools by data scientists.

Structure

This chapter will address the following topics:

- Importing and Cleaning Data
- Inspecting Data - Grouping, Aggregations
- Filtering and Subsetting
- Merging and Joining

Here, we will use an interesting dataset about the most-streamed songs in 2024. The data can be downloaded from Kaggle via the following link:

https://www.kaggle.com/datasets/nelgiriyewithana/most-streamed-spotify-songs-2024/data

Importing and Cleaning Data

In many analyses, default **pd.read_csv** can be used without adding additional parameters to the method. This dataset shows the nuances of working with different data and the inherent challenges. In order to not overwhelm you with nuances even before we begin importing, we advise adding the command **encoding='unicode_escape'**. This command will instruct Pandas to interpret the file via the Unicode escape encoding, which will convert special characters into their Unicode escape sequences (for example, \uXXXX). While **unicode_escape** is a special decoding mode, you may also use **UTF-8** (Unicode Transformation Format – 8-bit), which is the default and the most common type of encoding used for text files today. It represents all Unicode characters with variable-length bytes (1–4 bytes per character) and supports every written language.

You can run the default **pd.read_csv** to check the error, infer it, and find a through a web search.

```
import pandas as pd

df = pd.read_csv('C:/My Documents/Practical Data Science
Environments for Beginners/Data/Most_Streamed_Spotify_Songs_2024.
csv', encoding='unicode_escape')

df.info()
```

Once the DataFrame is imported, you can run the **info()** method. **info()** provides a concise summary of a DataFrame, while providing you important information about its structure and the data it contains. It is useful for getting a quick overview of large datasets. You can get information about the index, entries, non-null values, data types, and even memory usage (which will be helpful as you work with larger production datasets). This will give you a fair idea of the columns that need to be converted into different data types and can also show you the nulls present in various columns.

```
RangeIndex: 4600 entries, 0 to 4599
Data columns (total 29 columns):
 #   Column                      Non-Null Count  Dtype
---  ------                      --------------  -----
 0   Track                       4600 non-null   object
 1   Album Name                  4600 non-null   object
 2   Artist                      4595 non-null   object
 3   Release Date                4600 non-null   object
 4   ISRC                        4600 non-null   object
 5   All Time Rank               4600 non-null   object
 6   Track Score                 4600 non-null   float64
 7   Spotify Streams             4487 non-null   object
 8   Spotify Playlist Count      4530 non-null   object
 9   Spotify Playlist Reach      4528 non-null   object
 10  Spotify Popularity          3796 non-null   float64
 11  YouTube Views               4292 non-null   object
 12  YouTube Likes               4285 non-null   object
 13  TikTok Posts                3427 non-null   object
 14  TikTok Likes                3620 non-null   object
 15  TikTok Views                3619 non-null   object
 16  YouTube Playlist Reach      3591 non-null   object
 17  Apple Music Playlist Count  4039 non-null   float64
 18  AirPlay Spins               4102 non-null   object
 19  SiriusXM Spins              2477 non-null   object
 20  Deezer Playlist Count       3679 non-null   float64
 21  Deezer Playlist Reach       3672 non-null   object
 22  Amazon Playlist Count       3545 non-null   float64
 23  Pandora Streams             3494 non-null   object
 24  Pandora Track Stations      3332 non-null   object
 25  Soundcloud Streams          1267 non-null   object
 26  Shazam Counts               4023 non-null   object
 27  TIDAL Popularity            0 non-null      float64
 28  Explicit Track              4600 non-null   int64
dtypes: float64(6), int64(1), object(22)
```

Figure 5.1: *Result of the Command df.info()*

For example, column SiriusXM Spins has the value of 2477 and we can see that the range index goes from 0 to 4599, which indicates that there are 4600 rows. Also, the column Track has a 4600 count, which shows 4600 tracks.

Before we begin analyzing to answer any questions, the first step is will be to conduct a basic examination of the data. It is always a better idea to examine the data set visually as a table. We can use the **head()** method to view the Data Frame. By default, the **head()** method condenses some of the columns. Since our DataFrame has 29 columns, we can run the following command to visually see all columns. This is useful when the number of columns are still comprehensive, but in the case where the DataFrame has 100s of columns, it might not be intuitive to display all the columns.

```
pd.options.display.max_columns = None
df.head()
```

As we learned in the last chapter, we need to treat the data for outliers, missing values, and any format mismatches. Apart from these basic checks, we also need to check for duplicate values. This is an intuitive and iterative process where we detect obvious issues in the data. This step also prompts more intensive thought about data. Hence, sharp business acumen and in-depth domain knowledge will be helpful here.

For instance, consider the case of duplicates in data. You should ask if is this a case of data error or just a track having the same name but a different artist (think how the song 'Photograph' can be the one by Nickelback or the one by Ed Sheeran)? There can also be instances that the same track is a part of different albums by the same artist. Setting such intuitions before analysis would prevent any erroneous results at later stages. Here, we will not go into the nuances of duplicates, but will look at such rows that contain complete duplicates.

To get the exact duplicated rows in a Pandas DataFrame, you can use the **duplicated()** method, but instead of counting them, you can filter the DataFrame to show the rows that are marked as duplicates. To remove duplicate rows from the DataFrame **df**, we can use the method **drop_duplicates()**. This method is used to drop rows duplicated in the DataFrame. The argument **keep="first"** tells Pandas to retain the first occurrence of each duplicated row, and remove any subsequent duplicates.

```
# To see the total number of rows that are duplicated
df.duplicated().sum()

# DataFrame has 2 duplicate rows, visually see them using the
below statement
df[df.duplicated(keep=False)]

# To remove duplicates
df.drop_duplicates(keep="first", inplace = True)

#Running a validation to check if the duplicate values are
removed
df.duplicated().sum()
```

Running the analysis in R will look like this:

```
df <- read.csv('C:/My Documents/Practical Data Science Environments
for Beginners/Data/Most_Streamed_Spotify_Songs_2024.csv')

# Displaying the first few rows
head(df)

#Equivalent of.info() method that gives you column names and data
types
str(df)
```

```
# To see the total number of rows that are duplicated
sum(duplicated(df))

# Remove duplicate rows, keeping the first occurrence
df <- df[!duplicated(df), ]
```

`!duplicated(df)` returns a logical vector that is **`TRUE`** for unique rows and **`FALSE`** for duplicates, except for the first occurrence.

`df[!duplicated(df), ]` subsets the DataFrame to keep only the rows that are not duplicated (first occurrences are kept). The result is then assigned back to df to make the change "in place," similar to the inplace=True argument in Pandas.

Missing Value Analysis

Based on the output of the **`info()`** method, we can see that columns have missing values. We can sum the NULL values in each column to see the actual number of NULL values.

```
df.isna().sum()
```

```
Track                           0
Album Name                      0
Artist                          5
Release Date                    0
ISRC                            0
All Time Rank                   0
Track Score                     0
Spotify Streams               113
Spotify Playlist Count         70
Spotify Playlist Reach         72
Spotify Popularity            804
YouTube Views                 308
YouTube Likes                 315
TikTok Posts                 1173
TikTok Likes                  980
TikTok Views                  981
YouTube Playlist Reach       1009
Apple Music Playlist Count    561
AirPlay Spins                 498
SiriusXM Spins               2123
Deezer Playlist Count         921
Deezer Playlist Reach         928
Amazon Playlist Count        1055
Pandora Streams              1106
Pandora Track Stations       1268
Soundcloud Streams           3332
Shazam Counts                 577
TIDAL Popularity             4598
Explicit Track                  0
```

Figure 5.2: *Columns Showing Missing Values*

The column TIDAL Popularity is entirely NULL, while other columns like SiriusXM Spins and Soundcloud Streams have high levels of NULL values. Let us start by removing only the TIDAL Popularity column. We will use the **drop()** method in Pandas in the following example:

```
df.drop('TIDAL Popularity', axis = 1, inplace = True)
```

In the **drop()** method you start by adding the column name; **axis=1** specifies that you are dropping a column (for rows, you would use **axis=0**) and **inplace=True** (optional) modifies the DataFrame in place without returning a new one.

There are other methods like the **'del'** statement and **pop()** method to remove the columns. **pop()** is useful when you want to store the deleted column as a series.

Let us remove other columns '**Soundcloud Streams**', '**SiriusXM Spins**', and 'Pandora Track Stations' which have higher values of NULLs. From an analysis perspective, we can gather similar information from other streaming services with more data. To remove multiple columns at once, you can pass the list of column names shown in the following example:

```
df.drop(['Soundcloud Streams', 'SiriusXM Spins', 'Pandora Track
Stations','Pandora Streams'], axis = 1, inplace = True)

# To check if the columns are removed.
df.info()
```

An alternative to dropping columns or rows with missing values is to impute them using meaningful defaults. For numerical columns, missing values can be replaced with measures of central tendency like the mean or median, while preserving the overall data distribution. For categorical variables, you can substitute missing entries with the most frequent (mode) category to maintain consistency in classification features.

This approach helps retain more data for analysis and reduces potential information loss, especially in smaller datasets where every record is valuable.

```
# Add median value as the missing value
df['Column_Name'].fillna(df['Column_Name'].median(), inplace=True)

# Add Mode as the missing value
df['Column_Name'].fillna(df['Column_Name'].mode()[0], in-
place=True)
```

Running the analysis in R will look like:

```
colSums(is.na(df))
# Remove the 'TIDAL Popularity' column from the dataframe
df <- df[ , !(names(df) %in% 'TIDAL Popularity')]
# Remove multiple columns from the dataframe
df <- df[ , !(names(df) %in% c('Soundcloud Streams', 'SiriusXM
Spins', 'Pandora Track Stations', 'Pandora Streams'))]
```

```
# Check the structure of the dataframe to confirm columns are
removed
str(df)
```

Data Type Conversion

The **info()** method also shows the data type of each column. We can see some obvious mismatches, like the column '**Release Date**' is an object and so are some of the other columns like '**YouTube Views**', '**YouTube Likes**', '**TikTok Posts**', '**TikTok Likes**', '**TikTok Views**', 'YouTube Playlist Reach', which appear numerical but are object data type.

```
# Using errors='coerce' ensures that invalid values become NaT
instead of throwing an error.
df['Release Date'] = pd.to_datetime(df['Release Date'], format
='%Y-%m-%d', errors='coerce')
```

To convert multiple columns from object to numeric, we will run the following snippet:

```
columns_list = ['All Time Rank', 'YouTube Views', 'YouTube
Likes', 'TikTok Posts', 'TikTok Likes', 'TikTok Views', 'YouTube
Playlist Reach']

# Convert specified columns to numeric, assigning them back to
DataFrame
df[col_names] = df[col_names].apply(pd.to_numeric, errors='
coerce')

# Now the columns in the original DataFrame df are numeric
df.info()
```

We have created a list of columns (see **columns_list** above). The snippet **apply(pd.to_numeric, errors='coerce')** applies the **pd.to_numeric** function to each column and converts all of them into numeric types.

The **errors='coerce'** argument ensures that any non-numeric values (such as strings or invalid values) are converted to **NaN**. The **df[col_names]=...** reassigns the converted columns back to the original DataFrame df, while replacing the old columns with the new numeric ones.

Running the analysis in R will look like:

```
# Convert the 'Release Date' column to the Date type
df$`Release Date` <- as.Date(df$`Release Date`, format="%Y-%m-%d")

# List of columns to convert to numeric
columns_list <- c('All Time Rank', 'YouTube Views', 'YouTube
Likes', 'TikTok Posts', 'TikTok Likes', 'TikTok Views', 'YouTube
Playlist Reach')
```

```
# Convert specified columns to numeric, coercing any invalid
values to NA
df[columns_list] <- lapply(df[columns_list], function(x)
as.numeric(as.character(x)))

# Check the structure of the dataframe
str(df)
```

as.Date(df$'Release Date', format="%Y-%m-%d") converts the **Release Date** column to **Date** format in R. You can adjust the date format based on the actual format of the date in your data.

lapply(df[columns_list], function(x) as.numeric(as.character(x))) converts the selected columns to numeric. The **as.character()** is used to handle cases where columns might be factors, and **as.numeric()** converts them while coercing any invalid values to **NA**.

Inspecting Data: Grouping, Aggregations

Grouping and performing various aggregations on data is one of the most common operations a data professional can perform. The **groupby** function in both Python (**pandas**) and R (**dplyr**) is used to group data based on one or more columns or variables, allowing for operations to be performed on each group independently. Once grouped, you can apply aggregation or transformation functions (for example, **mean()**, **sum()**, **min()**, **max()**, or custom functions) to each group.

Let us find the number of unique songs each Artist has in our data. So in this case, the group is the Artist and the aggregation function we are performing is finding unique values. To do this, we will group column 'Artist' and count the column 'ISRC' (ISRC is the International Standard Recording Code is a 12-digit code that uniquely identifies a specific recording of a song or music video). Let us sort it based on the artist having the most unique songs in the data.

```
df.groupby('Artist')['ISRC'].nunique().sort_values
(ascending=False)
```

You can also format the output of the above command through the following code snippet:

```
result = df.groupby('Artist')['ISRC'].nunique().sort_values
(ascending=False)

 # Convert to DataFrame with default index
result_df = result.reset_index()

# Rename columns
```

```
result_df.columns = ['Artist', 'Unique ISRC Count']

# Styling pandas using 'Styler'
styled_df = result_df.style.hide_index().background_gradient
(cmap='Blues')
styled_df
```

`.hide_index()`: Hides the index and **`.background_gradient(cmap='Blues')`** applies a gradient background with the color map **`'Blues'`**. You can use other color maps, if needed.

Artist	Unique ISRC Count
Taylor Swift	63
Drake	63
Bad Bunny	60
KAROL G	32
The Weeknd	31
Travis Scott	30
Billie Eilish	27
Ariana Grande	26
Future	23

***Figure 5.3**: Taylor Swift and Drake Have the Maximum ISRC Count in this Dataset*

Running the analysis in R will look like:

In R, you can achieve the same task using functions from the **`dplyr`** and **`gt`** packages. Here is how you can replicate the functionality of grouping by "**`Artist`**," counting unique "**`ISRC`**" values, sorting them, and then creating a styled table.

`dplyr` is one of the most widely used R packages for data manipulation, part of the **`tidyverse`** ecosystem. It provides a suite of functions that make it easier to transform and manipulate data using a clear, consistent syntax. **`gt`** is used to create professional-looking tables from the data you have manipulated, often after summarizing or transforming it with **`dplyr`**.

In the Python code above, we displayed the unique ISRC count as gradient colors. We will implement the same logic using **library(scales)** in the following example:

```
# Load required packages
library(dplyr)
library(gt)

# Group by 'Artist', count unique 'ISRC', and sort in descending
order
result_df <- df %>%
  group_by(Artist) %>%
  summarise(`Unique ISRC Count` = n_distinct(ISRC)) %>%
  arrange(desc(`Unique ISRC Count`))

# Display result_df as a styled table using 'gt'
result_df <- result_df %>%
  mutate_all(~iconv(., from = "latin1", to = "UTF-8"))

# Ensure the column 'Unique ISRC Count' is numeric
result_df$`Unique ISRC Count` <- as.numeric(result_df$`Unique
ISRC Count`)

# Define a gradient fill for the 'Unique ISRC Count' column using
'Blues'
result_df %>%
  gt() %>%
  data_color(
       columns = vars(`Unique ISRC Count`),
       colors = scales::col_numeric(
       palette = c("white", "blue"),
       domain = NULL
       )
  )
```

Artist	Unique ISRC Count
Drake	63
Taylor Swift	63
Bad Bunny	60
KAROL G	32
The Weeknd	31
Travis Scott	30
Billie Eilish	27
Ariana Grande	26
Future	23
Peso Pluma	22
Post Malone	22

Figure 5.4: *Taylor Swift and Drake Have the Maximum ISRC Count Here*

Instead of the artist, you might want to check the album that has the most songs. Additionally, you would also want the artist's name to show up beside the album name. This is the condition where you can group by multiple columns:

```
result = df.groupby(['Artist','Album Name'])['ISRC'].nunique().
sort_values(ascending=False)
result_df = result.reset_index()
result_df.columns = ['Artist','Album Name', 'Unique ISRC Count']
# Use
styled_df = result_df.style.hide(axis='index').background_
gradient(cmap='Blues')
styled_df
```

Artist	Album Name	Unique ISRC Count
Bad Bunny	Un Verano Sin Ti	20
Taylor Swift	THE TORTURED POETS DEPARTMENT	18
Bad Bunny	nadie sabe lo que va a pasar maï¿½ï¿	16
Travis Scott	UTOPIA	15

Figure 5.5: *Bad Bunny's Album Has the Maximum ISRC Count*

Now let us add another aggregation to the same grouping level. For each album and artist, we already know the unique count of songs. Now we want to add the average

'**Track Score**' for each song in that album. Then let us sort the DataFrame by **'ISRC'** as demonstrated in the code here:

```
result = df.groupby(['Album Name', 'Artist']).agg(
    unique_ISRC=('ISRC', 'nunique'),
    avg_track_score=('Track Score', 'mean')
)
result_sorted = result.sort_values(by='unique_ISRC', ascending
=False)
result_df = result_sorted.reset_index()
result_df.columns = ['Album Name','Artist', 'Unique ISRC Count','
Average Track Score']
styled_df = result_df.style.hide(axis='index').background_
gradient(cmap='Blues')
styled_df
```

After grouping, the **data.agg()** allows you to apply multiple aggregation functions to different columns in the grouped data.

It considers a dictionary-like syntax, where the keys are the new column names and the values are tuples specifying the column on which the function will be applied, as well as the function itself.

Album Name	Artist	Unique ISRC Count	Avergae Track Score
Un Verano Sin Ti	Bad Bunny	20	59.035000
THE TORTURED POETS DEPARTMENT	Taylor Swift	18	55.183333
nadie sabe lo que va a pasar maï¿½ï¿	Bad Bunny	16	40.187500
For All The Dogs	Drake	15	44.153333
UTOPIA	Travis Scott	15	52.793333

Figure 5.6: *Adding the Average Track Score*

Running the analysis in R will look like:

```
# Group by 'Artist' and 'Album Name', and count unique 'ISRC'
values
result_df <- df %>%
group_by(Artist, Album.Name) %>%
summarise(`Unique ISRC Count` = n_distinct(ISRC)) %>%
arrange(desc(`Unique ISRC Count`))

# Group by 'Album Name' and 'Artist', and calculate unique ISRC
count and average track score
```

```
result_df <- df %>%
  group_by(`Album.Name`, Artist) %>%
  summarise(
       `Unique ISRC Count` = n_distinct(ISRC),
       `Average Track Score` = mean(`Track.Score`, na.rm = TRUE)
# Calculate average track score
  ) %>%
  arrange(desc(`Unique ISRC Count`))  # Sort by 'Unique ISRC
Count' in descending order
```

Filtering and Subsetting

Let us say your 10-year-old niece wants a playlist of the top songs in 2024 for a road trip. You want to remove all the explicit tracks from this list so that she does not pick a bad word. Let us create a subset of this data as a new DataFrame that has all the non-explicit tracks. Now, let us check how many songs we have for each type in the Data Frame. To do this, we will group the column Explicit Track and count the unique values of the column ISRC:

```
result = df.groupby('Explicit Track')['ISRC'].nunique()
result.columns = ['Explicit Track', 'Unique ISRC Count']
result
```

Based on this, we have 1,651 explicit tracks in the data set. Let us keep those rows with the column '**Explicit Track**' as 0 and save it as a new DataFrame called '**clean_tracks**'.

```
clean_tracks = df[df['Explicit Track'] == 0]
clean_tracks = clean_tracks.reset_index()
clean_tracks
```

There are 2,947 tracks in this new **clean_tracks** DataFrame. You now realize that the list is too big and would want to keep the songs with an 'All Time Rank' under 100. In cases like these, terms like filtering and subsetting are used interchangeably for all practical reasons. Usually, filtering focuses on selecting rows that meet a condition. Meanwhile, subsetting selects specific columns or specific rows based on indices or labels.

Let us create a subset of our **clean_top_tracks** which only has columns '**ISRC**', '**Track**', and '**Album Name**':

```
import pandas as pd

# Convert 'All Time Rank' column to numeric, forcing errors='
coerce' to handle any non-numeric values
df['All Time Rank'] = pd.to_numeric(df['All Time Rank'],
errors='coerce')
```

```
# Now, apply filtering
clean_top_tracks = df[(df['Explicit Track'] == 0) & (df['All Time
Rank'] <= 100)]
clean_top_tracks = clean_top_tracks[['ISRC','Track','Album
Name']]
clean_top_tracks = clean_top_tracks.reset_index()
clean_top_tracks
```

`clean_top_tracks` is a new DataFrame with only three columns and has non-explicit tracks and songs in the top 100. In this example, we used the main df to show how to filter rows on more than one condition. This also shows how to keep only selective columns in the DataFrame.

```
clean_top_tracks['Track'].nunique()
```

Let us also keep all the non-explicit tracks of Billie Eilish and Taylor Swift in a separate playlist for the road trip:

```
your_fav_tracks = df[(df['Explicit Track'] == 0) & (df['Artist'].
isin(['Billie Eilish', 'Taylor Swift']))]
your_fav_tracks = your_fav_tracks[['ISRC','Track','Album Name']]
your_fav_tracks = your_fav_tracks.reset_index()
your_fav_tracks
```

In the above code, **`df['Artist'].isin(['Billie Eilish', 'Taylor Swift'])`** creates a boolean mask that selects rows where the **`'Artist'`** column contains either **`'Billie Eilish'`** or **`'Taylor Swift'`**. **`&`** combines the two conditions via the logical AND operator. Both conditions must be **`True`** for a row to be selected.

	index	ISRC	Track	Album Name
0	12	USUM72401991	LUNCH	HIT ME HARD AND SOFT
1	16	USUG12401028	Fortnight (feat. Post Malone)	THE TORTURED POETS DEPARTMENT
2	18	USUM72401996	BLUE	HIT ME HARD AND SOFT
3	40	USUM72401994	BIRDS OF A FEATHER	HIT ME HARD AND SOFT
4	68	USUM72307484	What Was I Made For? [From The Motion Picture "Barbie"]	What Was I Made For? (From The Motion Picture "Barbie")
...	...	...	...	...
70	4023	USUM71900766	all the good girls go to hell	WHEN WE ALL FALL ASLEEP, WHERE DO WE GO?
71	4148	USUG12402543	How Did It End?	THE TORTURED POETS DEPARTMENT: THE ANTHOLOGY
72	4487	USUG12100622	You Belong With Me (Taylorï¿½ï¿½ï¿½s Ve	Fearless (Taylor's Version)
73	4492	USUG12306688	Say Don't Go (Taylor's Version) (From The Vault)	1989 (Taylor's Version)
74	4556	USUM72013019	my future	my future

75 rows × 4 columns

***Figure 5.7**: Tracks Filtered by Artist*

Running the analysis in R will look like:

```
# Load necessary library
library(dplyr)

result_df <- df %>%
  group_by(`Explicit.Track`) %>%
  summarise(`Unique ISRC Count` = n_distinct(ISRC))  # Count
unique ISRC values


# df is your dataframe and 'Explicit Track' is a numeric column

clean_tracks <- df %>%
  filter(`Explicit.Track` == 0) %>%
  mutate(row_num = row_number())  # Reset index manually in R
(optional)

# View the result
head(clean_tracks)

# Filter for clean top tracks and select specific columns
clean_top_tracks <- df %>%
  filter(`Explicit.Track` == 0, `All.Time.Rank` <= 100) %>%
  select(ISRC, Track, `Album.Name`) %>%
  mutate(row_num = row_number())  # Reset index manually (optional)

# View the result
head(clean_top_tracks)

# Filter for tracks by specific artists and explicit track == 0
your_fav_tracks <- df %>%
  filter(`Explicit.Track` == 0, Artist %in% c('Billie Eilish',
'Taylor Swift')) %>%
  select(ISRC, Track, `Album.Name`) %>%
  mutate(row_num = row_number())  # Reset index manually (optional)

# View the result
head(your_fav_tracks)
```

Merging and Joining

In the context of manipulating data with Pandas, merging and joining are used to combine two DataFrames. These methods are used in slightly different contexts and are different with respect to application. Merging is conceptually similar to SQL joins that combine DataFrames based on one or more columns or indexes. Pandas support multiple types of joins: inner, outer, left, and right.

Types of Merges

- **Inner join (default)**: Keeps only the rows with keys that are present in both DataFrames
- **Left join**: Keeps all rows from the left DataFrame and fills in **NaN** for missing matches from the right DataFrame
- **Right join**: Keeps all rows from the right DataFrame and fills in **NaN** for missing matches from the left DataFrame
- **Outer join**: Keeps all rows from both DataFrames and fills in **NaN** where there are no matches

The syntax for merging follows this template:

```
pd.merge(left_df, right_df, on='key_column', how='join_type')
```

Let us try to see this as an example: the DataFrame **your_fav_tracks** does not have the artist's name, but our main df - DataFrame has. In this case, we can do an inner join between the two DataFrames on the column '**ISRC**', as shown in the following example:

```
merged_df = pd.merge(your_fav_tracks, df, on='ISRC', how='inner')
merged_df
```

	index	ISRC	Track_x	Album Name_x	Track_y	Album Name_y	Artist	Release Date	All Time Rank	Track Score
0	12	USUM72401991	LUNCH	HIT ME HARD AND SOFT	LUNCH	HIT ME HARD AND SOFT	Billie Eilish	2024-05-17	13.0	316.3
1	16	USUG12401028	Fortnight (feat. Post Malone)	THE TORTURED POETS DEPARTMENT	Fortnight (feat. Post Malone)	THE TORTURED POETS DEPARTMENT	Taylor Swift	2024-04-18	17.0	297.6
2	18	USUM72401996	BLUE	HIT ME HARD AND SOFT	BLUE	HIT ME HARD AND SOFT	Billie Eilish	2024-05-17	19.0	292.6
3	40	USUM72401994	BIRDS OF A FEATHER	HIT ME HARD AND SOFT	BIRDS OF A FEATHER	HIT ME HARD AND SOFT	Billie Eilish	2024-05-17	41.0	212.8

Figure 5.8: *A Merged DataFrame*

From the join, we can see something peculiar in the new **merged_df**. While we got the 'Artist' column we wanted, we also got duplicate columns that were present in both the **DataFrame (column_x, column_y)**.

To deal with this, we can:

1. Manually drop the duplicate columns and then rename the columns to their original names.

```
merged_df = merged_df.drop(columns=['Album Name_y','Track_y'])
merged_df = merged_df.rename(columns={'Album Name_x': 'Album
Name','Track_y' : 'Track'})
merged_df
```

2. Selectively merge, which means keeping only those columns that we want in the final DataFrame.

```
merged_df = pd.merge(your_fav_tracks, df[['ISRC', 'Artist']],
on='ISRC', how='inner')
merged_df.reset_index()
merged_df
```

Even if we manually drop and then rename the columns, we might still end up retaining only selective columns. Hence in this case, it is simpler to merge the DataFrames selectively.

When merging or joining DataFrames, there are several important considerations and best practices to ensure the process goes smoothly and the resultant data is accurate. Here are some of the essential points to consider during an analysis:

1. Choose the right join type based on the type of analysis. Avoid unintended cases where you create a Cartesian product, which happens when every row in the left DataFrame is combined with every row in the right DataFrame. This can lead to a massive increase in the size of the resultant DataFrame
2. Ensure the column names are consistent, in case the names of the keys are different, you can use **`left_on`** and **`right_on`** parameters to specify the column names.
3. Check for duplicate keys. It is critical to ensure that the column you are merging on does not contain duplicate values (unless it is intended for a many-to-many merge)
4. Handing Missing data before merging could present erroneous analysis. You can fill the missing values with **`.fillna()`** or drop the rows using **`.dropna()`** command.
5. Factor in the following performance considerations while joining:
    a. While these fields are small DataFrames, industrial tables are likely to be large datasets.
    b. Indexing the columns significantly speeds up the merging process. You can also subset columns to make sure you merge only the essential columns

6. Ensure that the columns you are merging have the same data type in both DataFrames. Cases where one DataFrame is int and the other is str would fail the merge.

Running the analysis in R will look like:

In R, you can achieve the same functionality of merging two dataframes on a specific column via the **merge()** function or the **dplyr::inner_join()** function for an inner join.

```
library(dplyr)

# Perform an inner join using dplyr
merged_df <- inner_join(your_fav_tracks, df, by = "ISRC")

# View the result
head(merged_df)

# merged_df is your dataframe from the previous inner join

merged_df <- merged_df %>%
# Drop columns 'Album Name_y' and 'Track_y'
  select(-`Album Name_y`, -`Track_y`) %>%

# Rename 'Album Name_x' to 'Album Name' and 'Track_x' to 'Track'
  rename(`Album Name` = `Album Name_x`, Track = `Track_x`)

# View the result
head(merged_df)
# Assuming your_fav_tracks and df are your dataframes
# Select 'ISRC' and 'Artist' columns from df and perform an inner
join with your_fav_tracks
merged_df <- inner_join(your_fav_tracks, df %>% select(ISRC,
Artist), by = "ISRC")

# Reset the index by adding row numbers as a new column (optional
in R)
merged_df <- merged_df %>%
  mutate(index = row_number())  # Add an index column if needed

# View the result
head(merged_df)
```

Best Practices in Data Wrangling

There are several ways in which you can manipulate and analyze data. This chapter sets a template you can follow to analyze the data. As you encounter more examples and develop intuitions, we will be able to find different methodologies for data analysis.

When performing data wrangling, it is important to follow best practices to ensure efficiency and reproducibility. Document your work by maintaining detailed records of every data cleaning step such as transformations, imputation methods, and dropped columns, all of which helps to track changes and improve transparency. Write modular code by breaking down the wrangling process into smaller, reusable functions or scripts, making it easier to debug, maintain, and apply to new datasets. Finally, treat wrangling as an iterative process by revisiting and refining the steps as new insights emerge, and ensure that the data is consistently prepared for analysis.

Conclusion

In this chapter, we explored the essential techniques of data wrangling using Python and R and learned how to clean, transform, and prepare raw data for analysis. We covered key processes such as handling missing values, restructuring datasets, and applying various transformations to ensure that the data is in the right format for further exploration. By mastering these techniques, we can improve data quality and reliability and lay a strong foundation for meaningful analysis.

In the next chapter, we will shift our focus to data visualization, exploring how graphical representations can uncover patterns, trends, and insights within a dataset. We will discuss different types of visualizations, their applications, and how tools in Python and R can be used to create compelling and informative visuals. Understanding data visualization is crucial for effectively communicating findings and making data-driven decisions, which will be our primary focus in the upcoming chapter.

CHAPTER 6
Data Visualization in Python and R

Introduction

Data visualization is an essential aspect of data science, as it bridges raw data and actionable insights. The ability to present complex data in a clear and effective manner is critical for storytelling, decision-making, and identifying trends. In an era of big data and real-time analytics, effective visualization helps stakeholders quickly interpret results and act with confidence. Visual representations are widely used across domains such as business intelligence, healthcare, finance, marketing, and scientific research to communicate insights to both technical and non-technical audiences. Well-designed visualizations not only enhance understanding but also reveal patterns and anomalies that may be difficult to detect through raw data alone. In this section, we will explore the significance of data visualization, fundamental concepts of charts and plots, and a comparison of visualization capabilities in Python and R.

Structure

This chapter addresses the following topics:

- Introduction to Data Visualization
- Visualization Libraries Overview and Basic Plots
- Advanced and Interactive Visualizations
- Best Practices for Data Visualization

For this chapter, we will continue using the dataset we experimented with in the last chapter. The dataset is about the most streamed songs in 2024. The data can be downloaded from Kaggle via the following link:

https://www.kaggle.com/datasets/nelgiriyewithana/most-streamed-spotify-songs-2024/data

Introduction to Data Visualization

The impact and adoption of data-driven insights often depend on how effectively they are communicated to stakeholders.

Even groundbreaking analysis can fail to drive change if it is not presented in an accessible, compelling way. Strong visualization turns abstract numbers into concrete understanding by creating an emotional resonance through storytelling that connects data to real business outcomes and human experiences. When stakeholders can understand and relate with the implications of the data, they are more likely to take action.

Different audiences have different approaches to visualization. Technical teams may want detailed statistical visualizations, while executives often need high-level dashboards focused on KPIs and strategic implications. The same insights often need multiple visualization approaches to reach different stakeholders effectively. Interactive exploration capabilities allow stakeholders to investigate the data themselves and answer their own questions. This builds trust in the analysis and helps us glean novel insights through collaborative discovery.

Organizations benefit from establishing data visualization standards and best practices to ensure consistency, reduce confusion, and make insights more readily actionable. When everyone speaks the same visual language, communication barriers drop and insights flow more smoothly across teams and departments. Combining qualitative context with quantitative data through techniques such as annotations, highlights, and supporting narrative is crucial, as raw charts alone rarely tell the full story that is required to make informed decisions.

Another key aspect of data visualization is building data literacy over time by helping stakeholders interpret sophisticated visualizations. As their fluency in visualization grows, so does their ability to derive value from complex analyses. This investment in data literacy pays dividends as organizations become more adept at turning data into decisions.

Data visualization plays a crucial role in various stages of the data science workflow. These implications are mentioned as follows:

- **Exploratory Data Analysis (EDA):** Visuals help users and clients understand patterns, distributions, and anomalies in the data during the exploratory phase. For example, histograms reveal the distribution of numerical data, while scatter plots show relationships between variables.
- **Communication of Insights:** Data scientists often work with non-technical stakeholders like business managers or clients, who need to understand insights without diving into raw data or statistical jargon. Visuals simplify complex ideas and them into easily digestible insights.

- **Pattern Recognition and Trend Identification:** Visuals are particularly useful in spotting patterns, correlations, and trends that may not be immediately apparent from viewing the data alone. For instance, time series plots can uncover seasonal trends, while heatmaps can highlight correlations between variables.
- **Decision Making:** Data-driven decision-making relies on clear presentations of key metrics. Visualizations provide a means for decision-makers to quickly grasp the state of the business, allowing them to make informed decisions based on the data at hand.

Before diving into visualization tools in Python and R, it is essential to understand the key concepts behind common plot types:

- **Line Plots:** Line plots are typically used for time series data, where one variable (often time) is plotted on the x-axis and another variable on the y-axis. Line plots display trends over time and are often used in financial and business reporting.
- **Bar Charts:** Bar charts display categorical data with rectangular bars representing the magnitude of the data points. Bar charts can be used for comparing quantities across different categories like sales per region or website traffic per device.
- **Histograms:** Histograms visualize the distribution of numerical data by grouping values into bins. They are ideal for showing the underlying distribution of a dataset, including variables such as age or income distribution.
- **Scatter Plots:** Scatter plots represent relationships between two numerical variables. Each point on the plot corresponds to an observation in the dataset. Scatter plots are commonly used to analyze any correlation or clustering in data.
- **Box Plots:** Box plots provide a summary of the distribution of data by showing the median, quartiles, and potential outliers. They are particularly useful in identifying skewness and detecting the presence of outliers in the data.
- **Heatmaps:** Heatmaps use color to represent the intensity of values in a matrix-like structure. They are often used to represent correlations between variables or visualize complex relationships.

Visualization Libraries Overview and Basic Plots

A visualization library is a collection of pre-built tools and functions that help programmers create charts, graphs, and other visual representations without having to write all the code from scratch. These libraries simplify the process of turning raw numbers into meaningful images, which eventually makes data easier to understand and analyze.

Data Visualization in Python

Python offers a plethora of libraries for data visualization, each with its unique features and capabilities. In this section, we will focus on two widely used libraries: Matplotlib and Seaborn. Before we begin, make sure that you have installed Python on your system, along with all the necessary libraries. You can install the required libraries using the following pip:

```
pip install pandas matplotlib seaborn
```

First, we will load the dataset using the Pandas library:

```
import pandas as pd

# Load the dataset
df = pd.read_csv('most_streamed_spotify_songs_2024.csv')

# Display the first few rows of the dataframe
print(df.head())
```

Now, to visualize the top 10 most-streamed songs, we can create a horizontal bar plot:

```
convert_to_float = ['All Time Rank','Spotify Streams', 'Spotify
Playlist Count', 'Spotify Playlist Reach', 'YouTube Views',
                    'YouTube Likes', 'TikTok Posts', 'Tik-
Tok Likes', 'TikTok Views', 'YouTube Playlist Reach', 'AirPlay
Spins',
                    'SiriusXM Spins', 'Deezer Playlist Reach',
'Pandora Streams', 'Pandora Track Stations', 'Soundcloud
Streams', 'Shazam Counts']

df[convert_to_float] = df[convert_to_float].replace({',': ''},
regex=True).astype(float)

import matplotlib.pyplot as plt
import seaborn as sns

# Select the top 10 most streamed songs
top_10_songs = df.nlargest(10, 'Spotify Streams')

# Create the plot
plt.figure(figsize=(10, 6))
sns.barplot(x='Spotify Streams', y='Track', data=top_10_songs,
palette='viridis')
plt.title('Top 10 Most Streamed Spotify Songs in 2024')
```

```
plt.xlabel('Number of Streams')
plt.ylabel('Track Name')
```

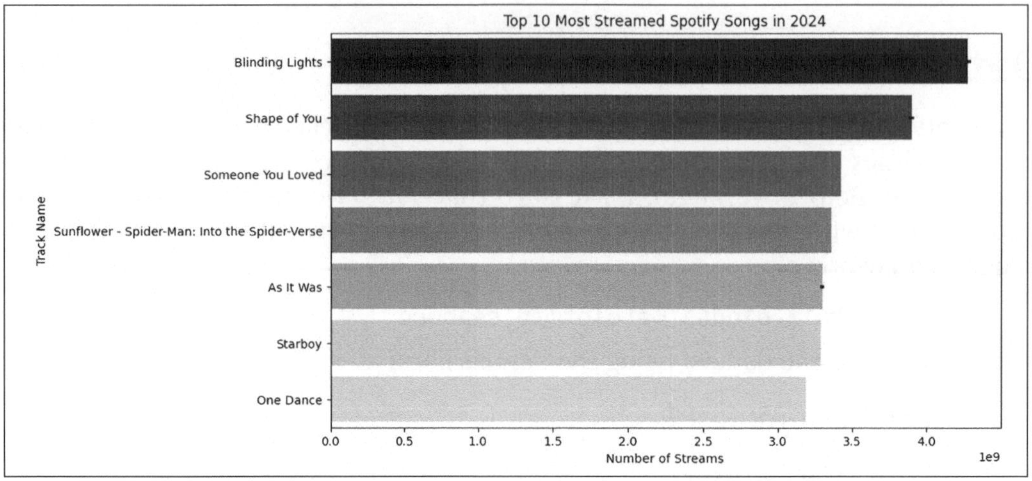

Figure 6.1: *Songs Organized by Number of Streams*

This bar plot provides a clear comparison of the top 10 songs based on the number of streams.

To examine the relationship between the release year and the number of streams, we can create a scatter plot like the following one:

```
# Convert 'Release Date' to datetime format and extract the year
df['Release Date'] = pd.to_datetime(df['Release Date'])
df['Release Year'] = df['Release Date'].dt.year

# Create the scatter plot
plt.figure(figsize=(10, 6))
sns.scatterplot(x='Release Year', y='Spotify Streams', data=df,
hue='Release Year', palette='coolwarm', alpha=0.6)
plt.title('Streams by Release Year')
plt.xlabel('Release Year')
plt.ylabel('Number of Streams')
plt.show()
```

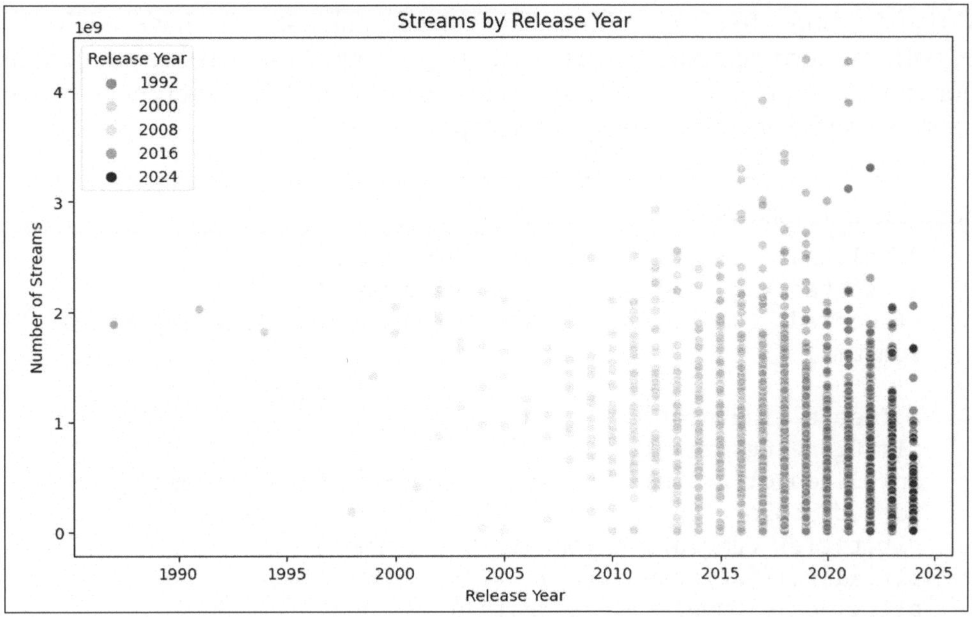

Figure 6.2: *Streams Organized by Release Year*

The scatter plot allows us to observe the trends in streaming numbers since the respective years each song was released in. We see data across different release years, spanning from around 1990 to 2024. Here are the key insights one can gather from the plot:

The y-axis shows the "*Number of Streams*" (in billions, given the 1e9 scale), while the x-axis shows the "*Release Year*" of the content. The data points are color-coded by the year the content was released, ranging from 1992 (blue) to 2024 (dark red).

There are several notable patterns which are mentioned as follows:

- **Increasing Variance**: As we move from left to right (older to newer releases), the number of streams increase progressively. Recent releases show widespread variability in streaming numbers, which has created a distinctive fan or cone shape.
- **Higher Peaks**: More recent releases (2015 onwards) have achieved significantly higher streaming numbers, with some songs reaching over 4 billion streams.
- **Density:** There are far more data points that can be observed in recent years compared to the 1990s and early 2000s, which suggests that either more content is being released or the data has been collected more efficiently during this time.
- **Base Level:** While recent releases show high variability, there is a consistent pattern of many releases achieving relatively low streaming numbers (near zero), regardless of the year they were released in.

This visualization effectively shows how streaming patterns have evolved over time, with modern releases having both the potential for massive success and a higher risk of minimal streams. These patterns indicate the emergence of a more competitive and diverse streaming landscape.

To visualize the trend of cumulative streams over time, we can draw line plot demonstrated as follows:

```
# Calculate cumulative streams over time
df_sorted = df.sort_values('Release Date')
df_sorted['Cumulative Streams'] = df_sorted['Spotify Streams'].
cumsum()

# Create line plot
plt.figure(figsize=(10, 6))
sns.lineplot(x='Release Date', y='Cumulative Streams', data=df_
sorted, color='green')
plt.title('Cumulative Streams Over Time')
plt.xlabel('Release Date')
plt.ylabel('Cumulative Streams')
plt.show()
```

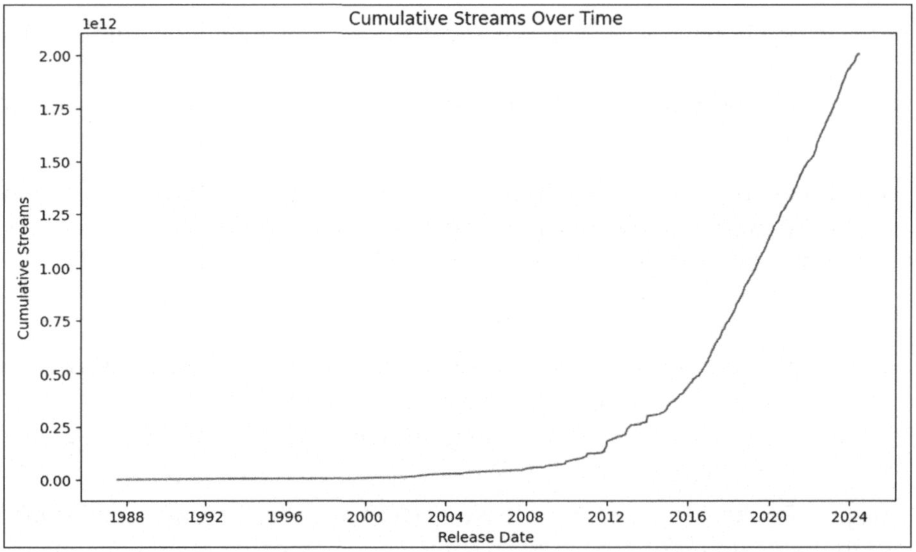

Figure 6.3: *A Line Graph Showing Explosive Growth in Cumulative Streams by Year*

This graph shows the cumulative total number of streams over time from 1988 to 2024, while narrating a compelling story about the explosive growth of streaming:

The y-axis shows cumulative streams at the scale of 1e12 (trillions), while the x-axis shows the timeline spanning 35 years. The green line represents the total accumulated streams over time.

The growth pattern clearly shows the following distinct phases:

- **1988-2008:** A relatively flat period with minimal growth, showing streaming was not yet a mainstream trend. This represents the pre-streaming era, where one could have seen the dominance of physical media and downloads.
- **2008-2016:** A gradual increase begins, which implies the early adoption of streaming services. The curve starts to bend upwards, but growth is still observed to be moderate.
- **2016-2024:** Exponential growth kicks in, with the line becoming increasingly steep. This suggests a massive acceleration in streaming adoption and usage. By 2024, the cumulative streams have approached 2 trillion.

The most striking feature one might observe from the graph is the dramatic acceleration in recent years, when the curve takes on a near-vertical trajectory around 2020-2024. This indicates an unprecedented surge in streaming activity. The pattern can be attributed to factors like increased streaming platform adoption, more available content, improved internet infrastructure, and possibly changes in consumption patterns during global events.

To explore the distribution of streams, we can draw a histogram as follows:

```
plt.figure(figsize=(10, 6))
sns.histplot(df['Spotify Streams'], kde=True, color='blue',
bins=30)
plt.title('Distribution of Streams')
plt.xlabel('Number of Streams')
plt.ylabel('Frequency')
plt.show()
```

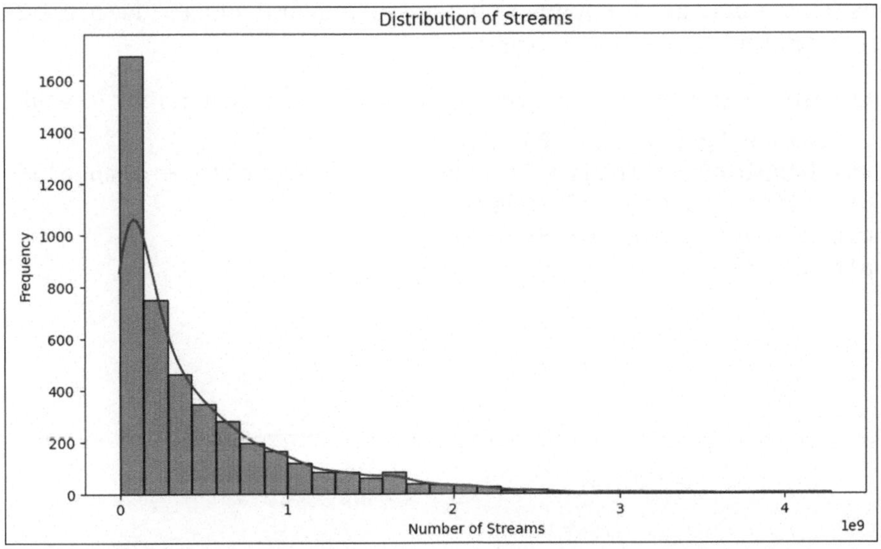

Figure 6.4: *A Histogram Showing the Distribution of Streams*

This histogram shows the distribution of streams across content and reveals a classic "*long tail*" distribution pattern which is commonly observed in digital media consumption. Here is what it tells us:

The vast majority of content (shown by the highest bars on the left) has received relatively few streams, with the number ranging between 0 and 500 million. This is represented by the extremely tall bars in the first few instances.

As we move along the x-axis (which shows the number of streams up to 4 billion) towards the right, we see that the frequency (y-axis) drops dramatically. Very few pieces of content achieve stream counts in the billions, as shown by the very low bars on the right side of the distribution.

The blue curve overlaid on the histogram appears to be a probability density function, which shows the theoretical distribution of the data. The shape strongly suggests that this follows a power law or a similar highly skewed distribution.

This pattern tells us several important things about streaming behavior:

- There is a huge disparity between the most and least streamed content.
- Only a tiny fraction of content becomes massively popular.
- The streaming market appears to follow the "80-20 *rule*" or possibly an even more extreme version of the Pareto principle, where a small percentage of content accounts for the majority of total streams.
- This type of distribution suggests a "*winner-takes-most*" dynamic in the streaming market.

This kind of distribution has important implications for content creators and platforms. This is because it suggests that achieving viral success is rare, but when it happens, the potential reach is enormous.

To examine the spread of streams, we can draw a boxplot which may look like:

```
plt.figure(figsize=(10, 6))
sns.boxplot(x='Spotify Streams', data=df, color='orange')
plt.title('Boxplot of Streams')
plt.xlabel('Number of Streams')
plt.show()
```

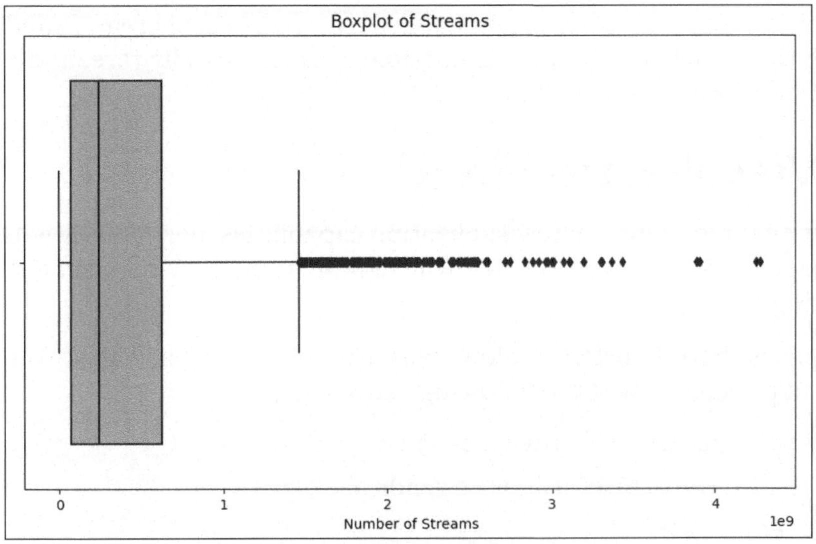

***Figure 6.5:* A** *Boxplot Indicating the Number of Streams*

This boxplot provides a clear visualization of the highly skewed distribution of streaming numbers and reveals several key insights. The box (which represents the interquartile range containing the middle 50% of the data) is compressed near the bottom of the scale, which suggests that most content has received relatively few streams. The vertical line inside the box (the median) is positioned very low, indicating that a typical piece of content has a low number of streams.

What is particularly striking is the large number of outliers, which are shown as individual dots extending far to the right. These represent the "hits" or viral content that achieved exceptionally high numbers of streams (up to 4 billion). The presence of these outliers and their distance from the box demonstrates just how rare and extreme it is to achieve viral success.

The whiskers extend from the box to show the range of the data and exclude outliers. The very long right whisker compared to the size of the box indicates extreme right-skewed data, which reinforces what we saw in the previous distribution graph.

This visualization effectively shows that:

- The vast majority of content receives a relatively small number of streams.
- There is an enormous gap between typical performance and viral hits.
- The streaming landscape has extreme outliers that perform far above the norm.
- Achieving success in streaming follows a highly uneven distribution.
- The "superstar" effect is very strong in this market, with a few pieces of content achieving astronomical success compared to the median.

This type of distribution has important implications for content creators and platforms, suggesting that while viral success is possible, it is statistically rare, and most of the content will perform closer to the median.

Data Visualization in R

R is renowned for its robust data visualization capabilities, particularly with packages such as ggplot2. In this section, we will demonstrate how to visualize the same dataset using R.

Ensure that you have R installed, along with the necessary packages. You can install the required packages using the following commands:

```
install.packages('tidyverse')
```

First, we will load the dataset using the **readr** package:

```
library(readr)

# Load the dataset
df <- read_csv('most_streamed_spotify_songs_2024.csv')

# Display the first few rows of the dataframe
head(df)
```

To visualize the top 10 most-streamed songs, we can create a horizontal bar plot using ggplot2 in the following way:

```
library(ggplot2)
library(dplyr)

# Select the top 10 most streamed songs
top_10_songs <- df %>%
  arrange(desc(`Spotify Streams`)) %>%
  slice(1:10)

# Create the plot
ggplot(top_10_songs, aes(x = `Spotify Streams`, y = reor-
der(`Track`, `Spotify Streams`))) +
  geom_bar(stat = 'identity', fill = 'steelblue') +
  labs(title = 'Top 10 Most Streamed Spotify Songs in 2024',
       x = 'Number of Streams',
       y = 'Track Name') +
  theme_minimal()
```

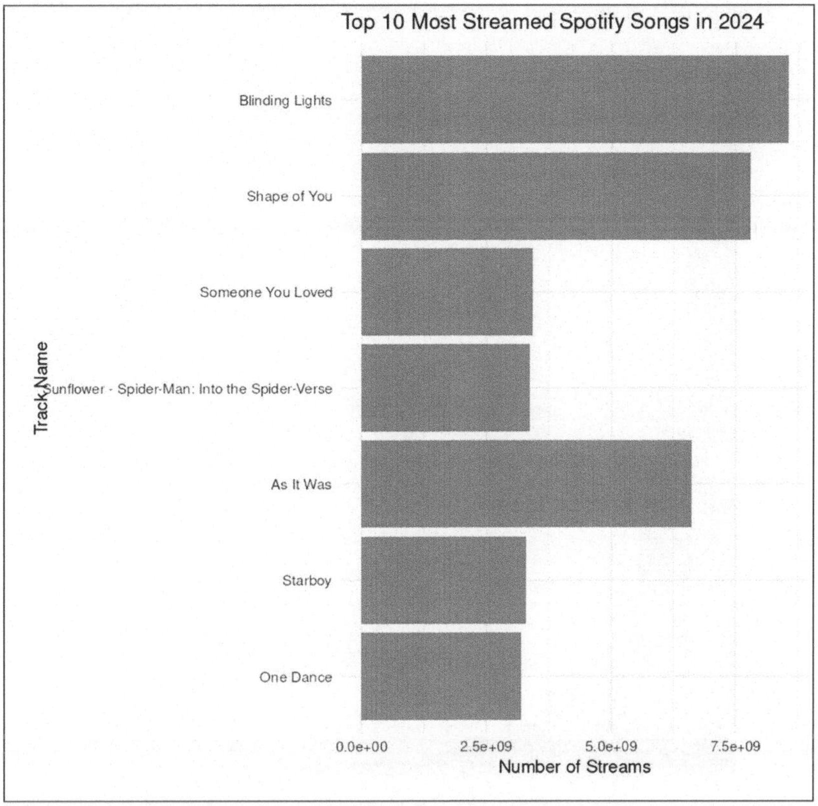

Figure 6.6: *Songs Organized by Number of Streams*

This bar plot provides a clear comparison of the top 10 songs based on the number of streams.

A histogram can be used to see the distribution of streams by frequency. In **geom_histogram()**, **bins** specifies how many intervals the data is divided into, controlling the histogram's granularity. **fill** sets the interior color of the bars, while **alpha** adjusts the transparency level (ranging from 0 = fully transparent to 1 = fully opaque), which allows overlapping elements to retain their visibility.

```
# Create histogram
ggplot(df, aes(x = `Spotify Streams`)) +
  geom_histogram(fill = 'blue', bins = 30, alpha = 0.7) +
  labs(title = 'Distribution of Streams',
       x = 'Number of Streams',
       y = 'Frequency') +
  theme_minimal()
```

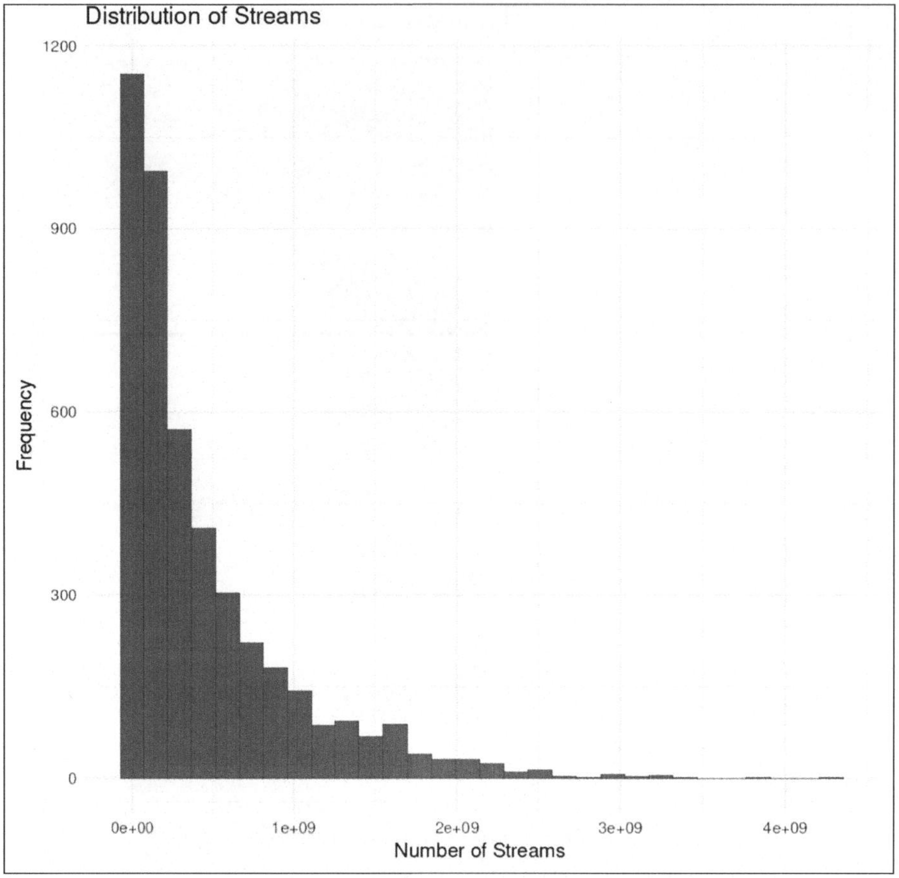

Figure 6.7: *A Histogram Showing the Distribution of Streams*

A boxplot can be built in R just like Python, to see the distribution of streams and get a clear view of normal and outlier points.

```
# Create boxplot
ggplot(df, aes(x = "", y = `Spotify Streams`)) +
  geom_boxplot(fill = 'orange') +
  labs(title = 'Boxplot of Streams',
       x = '',
       y = 'Number of Streams') +
  theme_minimal()
```

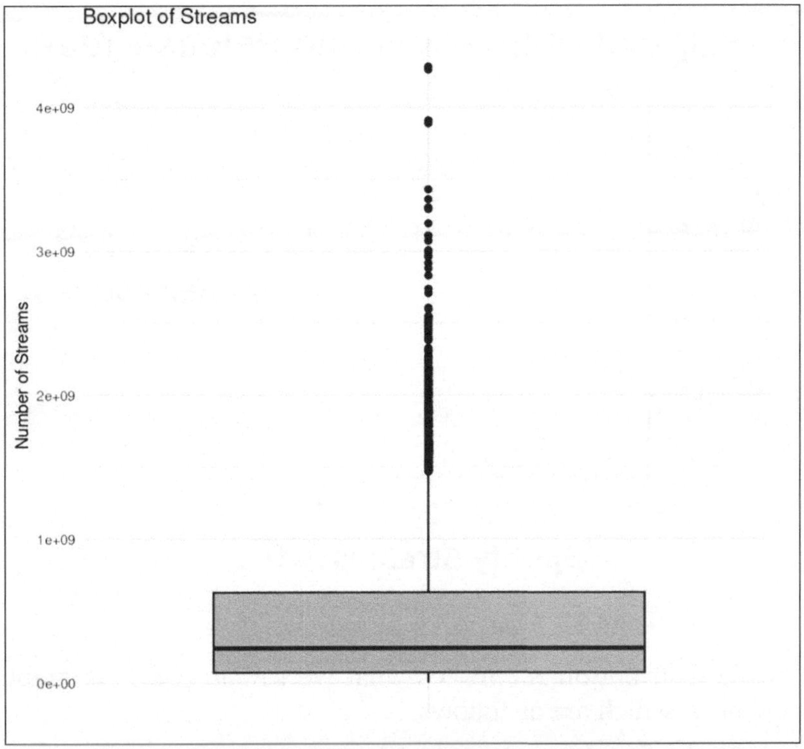

Figure 6.8: *A Boxplot Indicating Streams*

Advanced and Interactive Visualization

To elevate your data visualization capabilities, we will explore advanced and interactive visualization techniques. These enable deeper engagement and flexibility in exploring datasets like Spotify's Most Streamed Songs of 2024.

Pair Plot (Python)

A pair plot displays the relationships between all the numerical columns in the dataset. We can create one for the specific distribution in the following way:

```
# Pair plot to visualize relationships
sns.pairplot(df[['Spotify Streams', 'Release Year']], hue='
Release Year', palette='viridis')
plt.suptitle('Pair Plot of Streams and Release Year', y=1.02)
plt.show()
```

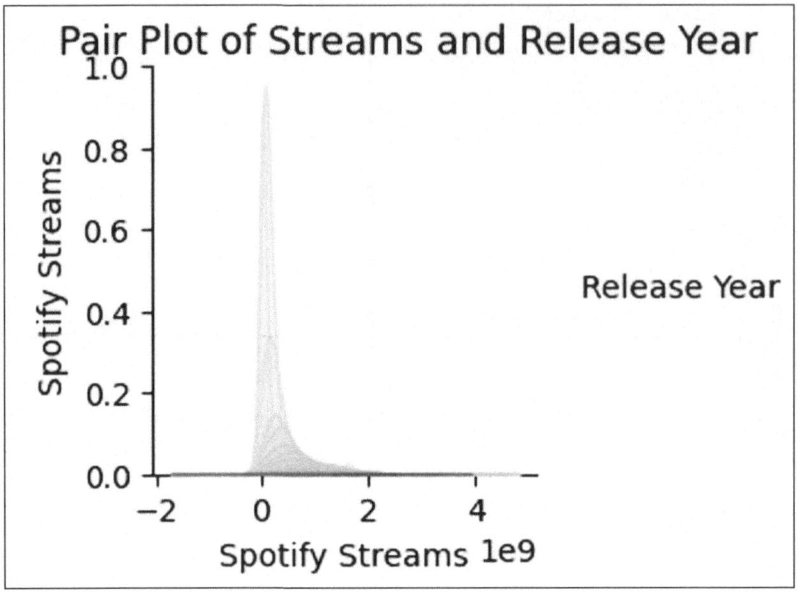

Figure 6.9: *A Pairplot of Streams by Release Year*

The shape of the distribution reinforces what we saw in previous graphs but with some more nuances, which are as follows:

1. The highest density (shown by the tallest yellow peak) is concentrated near zero streams, which confirms that most content received relatively few streams.
2. The distribution has a very sharp peak and long right tail (extending to 4 billion streams), showing the extreme skew in streaming success.
3. The color gradient from blue to yellow represents different release years, with newer releases (likely shown in yellower/greener colors) demonstrating higher density in lower stream counts.
4. The shape suggests that while extremely high stream counts (over 2 billion) are possible, they are exceedingly rare, which is shown by a very thin extension of the distribution towards the right.

This visualization effectively combines the insights from both the histogram and boxplot we saw earlier and adds the dimension of release year through color. It elegantly shows how streaming success follows a power distribution, where the vast majority of content is clustered near zero streams and an increasingly rare set of outliers have achieved higher stream counts.

The sharp peak at zero with rapid fall off particularly emphasizes just how concentrated the distribution is at the lower end of the streaming spectrum, reinforcing the '`winner-takes-all`' nature of the streaming market.

3D Scatter Plot (Python)

A 3D scatter plot adds an additional dimension for richer insights. It can be created in the following way:

```
from mpl_toolkits.mplot3d import Axes3D
import matplotlib.pyplot as plt
# 3D scatter plot
fig = plt.figure(figsize=(10, 8))
ax = fig.add_subplot(111, projection='3d')
ax.scatter(df['Release Year'], df['Spotify Streams'], df['Spotify Streams']**0.5, c=df['Spotify Streams'], cmap='viridis', s=50)
ax.set_xlabel('Release Year')
ax.set_ylabel('Streams')
ax.set_zlabel('Square Root of Streams')
plt.title('3D Scatter Plot of Streams')
plt.show()
```

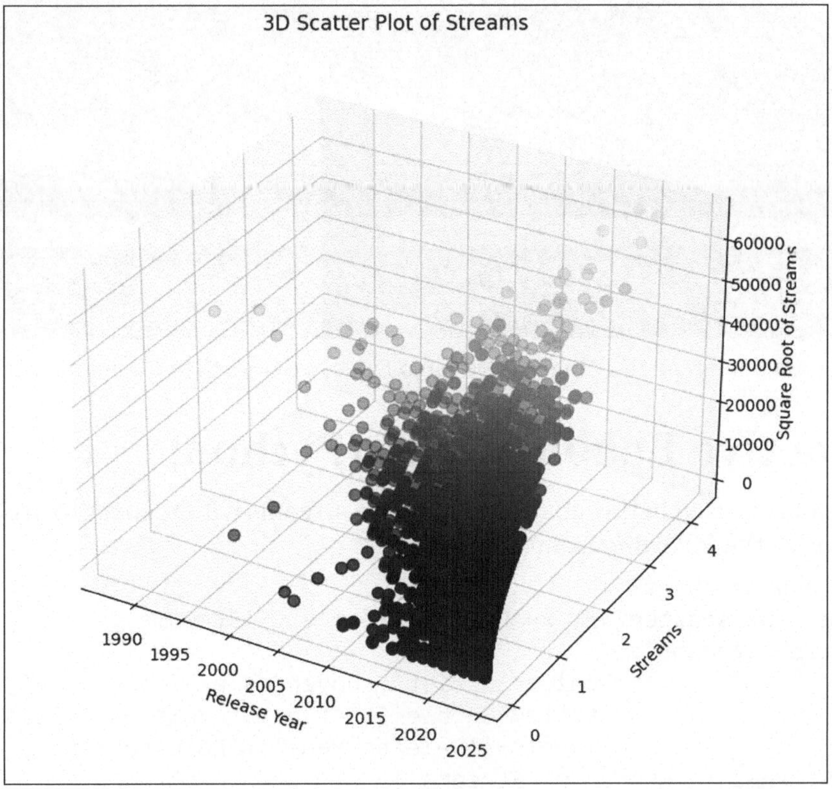

Figure 6.10: **A** *3D Visualization of the Number of Streams in Different Release Years*

Interactive Line Plot (Python)

An interactive line plot can be created to explore cumulative streams over time. You may do so through the following steps:

```
import plotly.express as px

# Interactive line plot
fig = px.line(df_sorted, x='Release Date', y='Cumulative Streams',
              title='Cumulative Streams Over Time',
              labels={'Release Date': 'Release Date', 'Cumulative
Streams': 'Cumulative Streams'},
              template='plotly_dark')
fig.show()
```

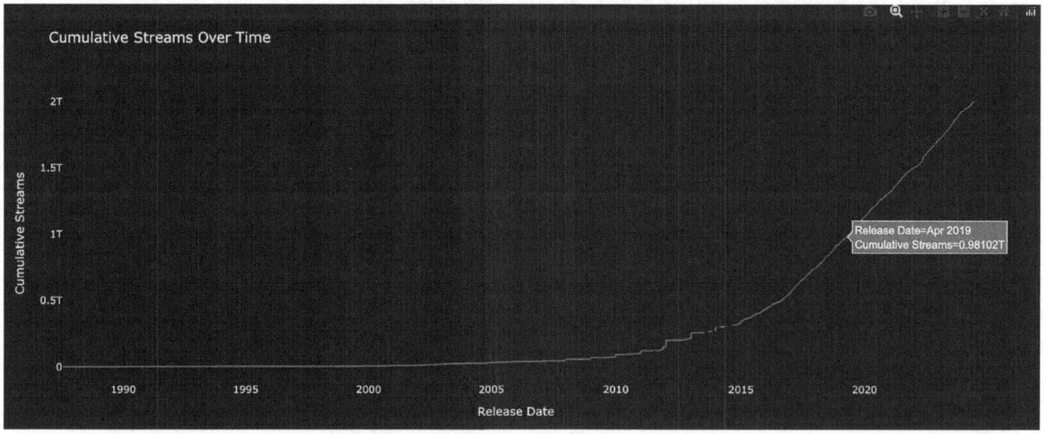

***Figure 6.11**: An Interactive Line Plot Showing Explosive Growth in Cumulative Streams*

Interactive Bubble Chart (Python)

A bubble chart is used in this chapter to explore streams with respect to artist impact. Have a look at the following example:

```
# Bubble chart
fig = px.scatter(df, x='Release Year', y='Streams',
size='Streams',
                 color='Artist', hover_name='Track Name',
                 title='Bubble Chart of Streams by Release Year',
                 labels={'Release Year': 'Release Year',
'Streams': 'Number of Streams'},
                 template='plotly')
fig.show()
```

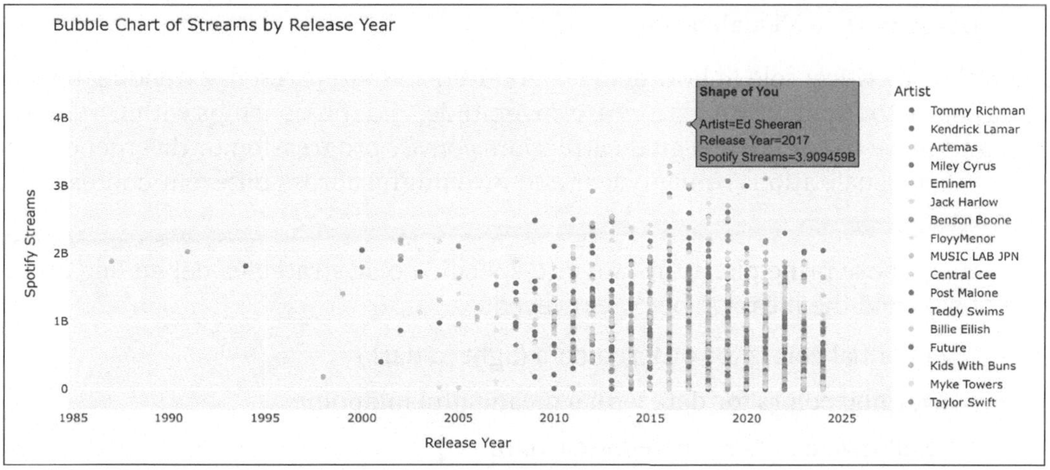

Figure 6.12: *Interactive Bubble Chart Indicating Streams by Release Year and Artist Impact*

Best Practices for Data Visualization

Understanding your audience requires you to be familiar with the context and their needs. For instance, if you are dealing with executives, focus on high-level insights and business implications. You should ideally use clear metrics and minimal technical detail to keep things simple. If you are dealing with analysts, remember to include more detailed statistical information and methodological notes. For public presentations, emphasize storytelling and focus on providing relatable examples. You must also factor in any cultural differences and the varying levels of data literacy among different clients.

Choosing the right type of chart is more nuanced than just simple categorization. While bar charts work well for categories, consider grouped bars for subcategories, stacked bars for composition, or horizontal bars for long labels. Line charts can be enhanced with confidence intervals or overlaid with event markers. Scatter plots might benefit from size variations (bubble charts) or color coding to highlight additional dimensions.

Simplifying data visualization is about making intentional design choices. Remember to remove redundant information, decorative elements, and unnecessary gridlines. Consider using small multiples instead of cramming everything into one chart. Think about using minimum elements to convey your message effectively. Additionally, you may use negative (white) spaces strategically to guide attention to different components.

Color Usage in Data Visualization:

Color plays a critical role in how data is perceived and interpreted, extending beyond visual appeal to communicate structure, magnitude, and relationships within a dataset. Thoughtful use of color helps guide attention, convey progression or divergence, and ensure that visualizations remain clear and meaningful across different contexts and audiences.

In practice, these principles translate into specific color strategies depending on the type of data and the message being conveyed:

- Sequential colors for ordered data (light to dark)
- Diverging colors for data with a meaningful midpoint
- Qualitative colors for categorical data
- Contextual color associations for more impact. For example: in healthcare red is associated with risk and in finance it is associated as loss
- Test visualizations in grayscale to ensure they can work without color

Effective Labeling Strategies:

Clear and well-designed labels help viewers quickly understand what a visualization represents without unnecessary effort or misinterpretation. Thoughtful labeling reduces cognitive load, provides essential context, and ensures that insights are communicated accurately and efficiently.

Some of the points to keep in mind while creating labels are:

- Direct labeling often works better than legends.
- Position labels to minimize overlapping.
- Use consistent formatting for numbers.
- Consider using subtitles to provide context.
- Include units of measurement clearly.

Effective data visualization also depends on maintaining proportionality for authenticity. Start axes at zero for bar charts, but consider exceptions for line charts that show small, but significant changes. Use consistent scales when comparing multiple charts. Consider logarithmic scales for data spanning multiple orders of magnitude. However, do not forget to indicate the choices you make.

Best Practices for Highlighting Insights:

Highlighting insights effectively ensures that viewers quickly recognize the most important patterns, trends, and anomalies in a visualization. By guiding attention intentionally, data visualizations can support clearer storytelling and more informed decision-making without overwhelming the audience.

- Use color sparingly to draw attention.
- Add reference lines for important thresholds.
- Include contextual annotations.
- Consider before/after comparisons.
- Highlight outliers when they matter to the story.

Best Practices for Accessibility:

Accessible data visualizations ensure that insights can be understood and used by a diverse range of audiences, including individuals with visual, motor, or cognitive impairments. Designing with accessibility in mind improves clarity, usability, and inclusivity without compromising analytical value.

- Ensure sufficient text contrast.
- Use patterns or shapes in addition to color.
- Make interactive elements keyboard-accessible.
- Provide alternative text descriptions.
- Test with screen readers.

Final Checks:

Systematic validation is essential to ensure that visualizations are accurate, trustworthy, and ready for decision-making. Performing final checks helps prevent errors, misinterpretation, and the unintended communication of misleading insights.

- Check that the figures are accurate.
- Verify all the calculations.
- Test different data scenarios.
- Get the visualizations and calculations peer reviewed.
- Document assumptions and limitations for further reference.

Including Interactive Features:

Interactive elements can enhance data visualizations by allowing users to explore information dynamically while preserving overall context. When designed thoughtfully, interactivity helps users uncover deeper insights, ask follow-up questions, and engage more meaningfully with the data.

These principles should work together cohesively. A visualization might be technically accurate, but might fail if it does not engage its audience sufficiently. Conversely, an engaging visualization that misrepresents data is equally problematic. Therefore, balancing these elements while staying focused on the core message can help you create and curate impactful visualizations.

Conclusion

In this chapter, we explored a range of techniques for visualizing data and examined how different types of visual representations can be used to communicate patterns, trends, and insights effectively. We discussed how choosing the right visualization can enhance data interpretation, as it makes complex information more accessible and meaningful. By leveraging various visualization methods, we can transform raw data into compelling stories that facilitate better decision-making and analysis.

As we move forward, the next chapter will introduce fundamental data science algorithms, their core principles, functionalities, as well as their real-world applications. We will explore how these algorithms process and analyze data to uncover hidden patterns, make predictions, and drive informed decision-making. From supervised learning models like regression and classification, to unsupervised techniques such as clustering and dimensionality reduction, we will examine their role in solving complex problems across various domains. By understanding how these algorithms work, we will be able to better harness the power of data science and extract meaningful insights, while driving innovation.

CHAPTER 7
Introduction to Data Science Algorithms

Introduction

An algorithm is more than just a sequence of instructions–it is the backbone of modern computational problem-solving. At its core, an algorithm is a step-by-step procedure or formula for addressing a specific challenge, which transforms a complex problem into a set of manageable tasks. In the realm of data science, algorithms act as powerful tools that sift through vast amounts of data and enable systems to recognize patterns, draw conclusions, and even forecast future trends. They transform raw data into actionable insights, driving decision-making across industries ranging from healthcare to finance to marketing. Whether it is classifying images, recommending products, or predicting stock market trends, these algorithms are meticulously crafted to handle a diverse range of data types, from numbers to text to multimedia. They provide the foundation for automation, which allows machines to mimic human decision-making, learn from experience and make intelligent choices without explicit programming.

Structure

This chapter will address the following topics:

- Fundamentals of Algorithms in Data Science
- Types of Data Science Algorithms
- Algorithm Selection and Performance Evaluation
- Real-World Applications of Data Science Algorithms

Fundamentals of Algorithms in Data Science

An algorithm is a set of well-defined, step-by-step instructions or rules designed to solve a specific problem or perform a task. It is essentially a recipe for achieving a desired outcome. The process outlined in an algorithm is meant to be clear, logical, and repeatable, which ensures that the same result can be achieved every time the guidelines are followed.

In the context of computing and data science, algorithms are used to process data, perform calculations, or make decisions. For example, when you use a search engine, the algorithm determines the results that are the most relevant to your query. In Machine Learning (hence abbreviated as ML), algorithms analyze large data sets to identify patterns and make predictions.

An algorithm can vary in complexity—from simple tasks, like sorting numbers, to more advanced ones, like image recognition or natural language processing. The key feature of an algorithm is that it operates in a structured, predictable manner, while solving problems accurately and efficiently.

Characteristics of Effective Algorithms

Effective data science algorithms should possess the following characteristics:

- **Accuracy** refers to how well an algorithm produces results reflecting the true nature of the problem being solved. A good algorithm should be able to deliver correct or nearly correct predictions, classifications, or insights, especially when they are compared to a known ground truth or expected outcome.

  For example, in a spam email classification algorithm, the accuracy would be measured by how many spam and non-spam emails is the algorithm able to identify correctly. If the algorithm incorrectly marks legitimate emails as spam (false positives) or misses spam emails (false negatives), the accuracy will consequently decrease. Therefore, a high-accuracy algorithm would have minimal errors in classifying emails.

- **Efficiency** refers to an algorithm's ability to solve a problem in minimal time and with the least computational resources (like memory and processing power). Efficient algorithms are especially important when working with large datasets or in environments with limited resources (for example, real-time applications or mobile devices).

  For example, in a recommendation system for an online retailer, the algorithm needs to quickly suggest products to users while considering their preferences and past behaviors. If the algorithm takes too long to generate recommendations, the users may get frustrated. An efficient algorithm would return recommendations almost instantaneously, even if the platform has millions of products and users. Techniques like Matrix Factorization or Collaborative Filtering are commonly used to make such recommendation algorithms both fast and resource-efficient.

- **Scalability** means an algorithm's ability to maintain its performance as the size of the dataset grows. A scalable algorithm can handle large volumes of data without a significant decrease in performance or speed. As businesses grow and data increases exponentially, scalable algorithms become crucial for continued success.

  For example, consider an ML algorithm used for customer segmentation in a retail company. If the algorithm works well with 1,000 customers, it should still be effective enough to handle the data of a million customers. An algorithm that can "*scale*" handles increasing data size effectively, often by utilizing parallel processing or distributed systems. MapReduce and Apache Spark are commonly used frameworks that help scale data-processing algorithms by distributing tasks across many machines.

- **Robustness** refers to an algorithm's ability to maintain its performance and reliability when it confronts varying conditions, including noisy, incomplete, or biased data. A robust algorithm will perform well despite the data deviating from ideal conditions or when there are slight anomalies or outliers.

  For example, imagine an ML model trained to predict house prices. If the model is robust, it will provide reasonable predictions despite missing values in some features (like the number of bedrooms) or if the dataset includes some extreme outliers (for example, a mansion priced unusually low). For instance, if a dataset includes a few properties with drastically different prices, a robust algorithm will adjust its predictions accordingly to avoid being skewed by those outliers, rather than making guesses randomly.

- **Interpretability** refers to how easily the results of an algorithm can be understood by humans, especially when they are used for critical decision-making. In certain fields (for example, healthcare, finance, law), it is important not only to make predictions but also to explain how and why those predictions were made. An algorithm with high interpretability helps decision-makers trust and act upon the results.

  For example, in a healthcare setting, imagine an algorithm is used to predict whether a patient is at risk for a heart attack. If the algorithm produces a risk score, interpretability allows doctors to understand which factors (such as cholesterol levels, blood pressure, or smoking history) have contributed most to the risk prediction. If the model is a "*black box*" (like a deep neural network), the decision may be trusted less. On the other hand, simpler models like decision trees are often more interpretable because they show which features (for example, cholesterol level > 200) may lead to a higher likelihood of cardiac arrest.

Categories of Algorithms

Data science algorithms are broadly classified into the following categories:

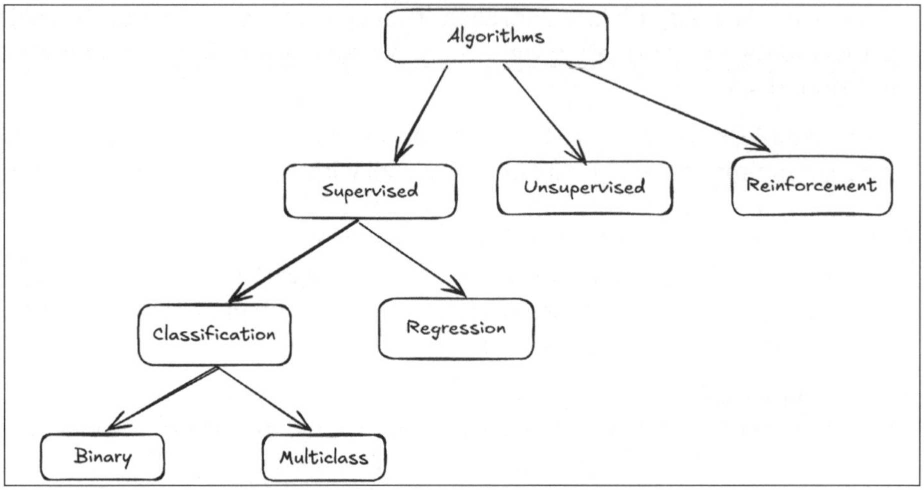

***Figure 7.1**: Categories of Algorithms*

Supervised Algorithms

Supervised Learning Algorithms are a type of ML where the algorithm is trained on a labeled dataset, which means that the input data comes with corresponding output labels or target values. The goal is for the algorithm to learn a mapping from inputs to outputs and make predictions on new, unseen data based on the patterns it learned during training.

In supervised learning, **labeled data** refers to the data that is paired with a known outcome or target value. The algorithm learns by observing the relationships between the **input features** (variables used to describe the data) and the **output labels** (the corresponding known result). These labels act as a teacher that guides the learning process.

- **Input Features**: These are the variables or attributes that describe the data. For example, in a dataset of housing prices, the input features can include the number of bedrooms, square footage, location, and age of the house.
- **Output Labels**: These are the known outcomes or values that we want to predict. In the housing dataset example, the output label might be the price of the house.

The key idea here is that the data points are already labeled with the correct outcome, which allows the model to understand how inputs relate to the outputs. The algorithm uses these labeled examples to learn a mapping function, which it can then use to make predictions on new, unseen data.

Example: Consider a dataset that contains the number of hours a student studies and whether they pass or fail a course. The input features would be the number of study hours, and the output label would be either "*Pass*" or "*Fail.*" The model learns to detect the pattern between study hours and the likelihood of passing the course. Later, it can predict whether a new student will pass or fail based on the number of hours they studied for.

Study Hours	**Result (Label)**
1	Fail
2	Fail
3	Pass
4	Pass

Table 7.1: *Dataset Mapping Hours Studies to Result*

The central goal of supervised learning is to **predict** the output label based on input features. Once a model is trained on the labeled data, it can make predictions on new, unseen data by applying the learned relationship between the input and output.

The **model** uses the patterns it learned during training to generalize and predict outcomes for new instances where the labels are unknown.

The accuracy of the model is determined by how well its predictions match the actual outcomes, which are usually evaluated on a separate set of labeled data called the **test data**.

Example: Let us take the earlier example of predicting, where we have to determine whether a student will pass based on their study hours. After training the model, you might want to predict whether a new student with 6 hours of study time will pass or fail. Based on the relationships the model learned from the previous data, it would predict "*Pass.*"

In this case, the **input features** are the student's study hours, and the **output** is the predicted result, which could be a categorical outcome (Pass/Fail) or a continuous value (for example, a probability score, if you are using logistic regression).

Types of Supervised Learning

Supervised learning tasks can be broadly categorized into two types based on the nature of the prediction task: **Classification** and **Regression**.

Classification: Predicting a Categorical Label

Classification refers to the task of predicting a **categorical** label, where the output variable is a category or class. The goal is to assign each input data point to one of the predefined classes. Classification problems often involve binary outcomes (for example, yes/no, true/false) or multiclass problems (for example, classifying an animal as a dog, cat, or bird).

- **Binary Classification**: The output label has two possible classes. Common examples include:
  - **Spam Detection**: Predicting whether an email is '*Spam*' or '*Not Spam*'
  - **Medical Diagnosis**: Predicting whether a patient has a disease ('Positive') or does not ('*Negative*')
- **Multiclass Classification**: The output label has more than two possible classes. Examples include:
  - **Image Classification**: Predicting whether an image contains a dog, a cat, or a bird
  - **Sentiment Analysis**: Predicting whether a piece of text has positive, negative, or neutral sentiment

Example of Classification: Consider the task of predicting whether a customer will buy a product based on their age and income. The model may classify customers into two categories: "*Will Buy*" or "*Won't Buy*." The output labels are categorical, meaning the model predicts which class a customer belongs to.

Age	**Income**	**Will Buy (Label)**
25	$30,000	Won't Buy
45	$60,000	Will Buy
30	$50,000	Will Buy
50	$80,000	Won't Buy

Table 7.2: *Dataset with Age and Income as Factors to Predict the Label "Will Buy"*

Regression: Predicting a Continuous Value

Regression refers to predicting a **continuous** value as the output label rather than a category. The goal is to find a function that can map the input features to a real-valued number.

Examples of Regression:

- **House Price Prediction**: Predicting the price of a house based on features such as size, location, and number of bedrooms

- **Stock Price Prediction**: Predicting the future price of a stock based on historical data

Suppose we want to predict the **price of a house** based on features like the number of bedrooms, square footage, and location. The output label is continuous (a price in dollars). Therefore, this is a regression problem.

Square Footage	Bedrooms	Price (Label)
1000	2	$150,000
1500	3	$200,000
2000	4	$250,000
1200	3	$180,000

Table 7.3: *Dataset with Square Footage and Bedrooms as Factors to Predict the Label "Price"*

The model learns the relationship between the input features (square footage, number of bedrooms) and the price of the house. Once trained, the model can predict the price of a new house based on its features.

Unsupervised Learning Algorithms

These are a type of ML where the model is trained on data that **does not have labeled outputs**. Unlike supervised learning, where each input is paired with a known label or target value, in unsupervised learning, the algorithm tries to find hidden patterns or structures in the data on its own. Its main goal is to explore the data and uncover relationships or groupings without being explicitly told what to look for.

In unsupervised learning, the data provided to the algorithm does **not** include any labels (that is, there is no target variable). The algorithm has to discover patterns, groupings, or structures within the data without any direct supervision or correct answers provided.

- **Input Data**: The input consists of raw data points, such as customer attributes (age, income, location) or a set of items (for example, products in a store).
- **No Output Labels**: Unlike supervised learning, there are no target values for the algorithm to predict. The model's task is to uncover hidden patterns in the data.

The algorithm is free to explore the data, identify natural groupings or relationships, and sometimes even reduce the complexity of the data.

For example, consider a dataset with customer purchase data, but without any labels. The data might include customer features such as age, spending habits, and frequency of visits. Without predefined labels (like "*High spender*" or "*Low spender*"), the algorithm might group customers into clusters based on their behavior.

In unsupervised learning, the main goal is to **discover underlying patterns, groupings, or structures** in the data. The model does not predict outcomes, but instead attempts to organize the data in a meaningful way.

A classic example is **customer segmentation** in marketing. Without any predefined categories, an unsupervised learning algorithm might identify different types of customers based on their buying behavior, such as:

- High-value, frequent buyers
- Occasional shoppers
- Price-sensitive buyers

The algorithm finds these groupings based on patterns in the data, without knowing about the labels beforehand.

Reinforcement Learning Algorithms

These are a type of ML where an agent learns how to make decisions by interacting with an environment. Unlike supervised learning, where the model learns from labeled data, or unsupervised learning, where the model identifies patterns without supervision, reinforcement learning involves an agent that learns by **trial and error**. The agent takes actions in an environment and receives feedback in the form of rewards or penalties, which helps the agent adjust its behavior to maximize cumulative rewards over time.

In reinforcement learning, the learning process revolves around the following key components:

- **Agent**: The learner or decision-maker that interacts with the environment
- **Environment**: The external system with which the agent interacts; it could be anything from a video game world to a robot's physical surroundings
- **Actions**: The set of possible moves or decisions the agent can take at any given time
- **Rewards**: The feedback the agent receives after taking an action; rewards can be positive (indicating a good decision) or negative (indicating a poor decision). The agent's goal is to maximize the cumulative reward over time.

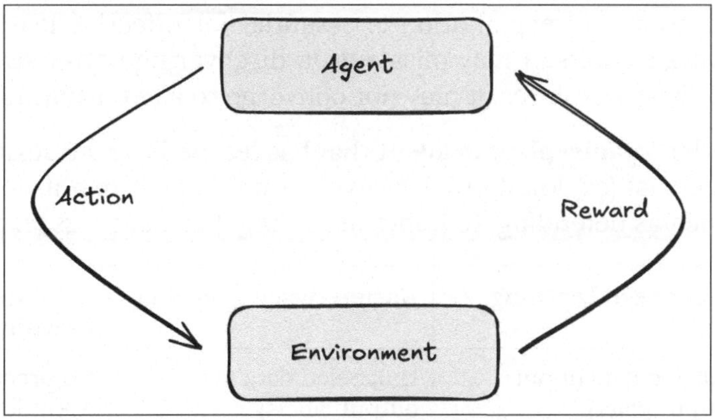

***Figure 7.2**: Agent and Environment Interaction*

For instance, consider a **robot** navigating a maze:

- The **agent** is the robot.
- The **environment** is the maze.
- The **actions** are the moves the robot can make (for example, move forward, turn left, or turn right).
- The **reward** could be +1 for reaching the goal (exit) or -1 for hitting a wall.

In an RLA, the agent learns by taking actions in the environment and observing the outcomes. The agent makes decisions based on its current knowledge and aims to **maximize long-term rewards**. The agent is not explicitly told what to do; instead, it must explore different strategies and learn from feedback. The agent faces a balance between exploring new actions to discover better strategies (exploration) and leveraging known actions that give high rewards (exploitation). Instead of focusing on immediate rewards, RLAs aim to maximize the **cumulative (long-term) reward**. This encourages the agent to think ahead and make decisions that lead to better outcomes in the future, not just short-term gains.

Example: In a **self-driving car**, the car (agent) takes actions like speeding up, slowing down, or turning. Initially, the car may make mistakes, but over time, it learns that stopping at a red light (action) yields a positive reward (safety) while running a red light results in a penalty (accident, ticket).

A major challenge in reinforcement learning is balancing **exploration** (trying new actions to discover their effects) and **exploitation** (using known actions that yield the highest reward).

- **Exploration**: Trying out actions that may not have been previously tested, which might lead to discovering new, better strategies.
- **Exploitation**: Repeating actions that are known to result in high rewards, using the knowledge gained so far.

Balancing exploration and exploitation is essential for effective learning in an RLA. If the agent always exploits, it may miss out on discovering better strategies. On the other hand, if it always explores, it may not converge to a good solution.

Example: Consider a **game-playing agent** that has learned that attacking an opponent is generally beneficial (exploitation). However, sometimes it might need to explore a new strategy, such as defending, to improve its long-term success (exploration).

Feature	Supervised Learning	Unsupervised Learning	Reinforcement Learning
Data Type	Labeled data (input-output pairs)	Unlabeled data (no output labels)	No predefined data; agent learns from interactions with the environment
Goal	Learn to predict the output from input features	Discover hidden patterns or groupings in the data	Learn to make decisions by maximizing cumulative rewards over time
Task	Classification or Regression	Clustering, Dimensionality Reduction, Anomaly Detection	Decision-making, Game-playing, Robot control, Strategy learning
Learning Process	The model learns from the labeled training data and generalizes to unseen data	The model identifies patterns, groupings, or structures in the data without labels	The agent learns through trial and error by interacting with the environment, receiving rewards or penalties
Training Data	Data with both input features and corresponding labels (for example, inputs and outputs)	Data with only input features (no labels)	No labels; agent interacts with the environment to learn what actions lead to rewards
Output	Known output label (classification or continuous value in regression)	Hidden patterns or groups (clusters, reduced features)	Sequence of actions (policy) that maximizes long-term rewards
Types of Problems	Classification (for example, spam detection) and Regression (for example, house price prediction)	Clustering (for example, customer segmentation) and Dimensionality Reduction (for example, image compression)	Game-playing (for example, chess, Go), Robotics (for example, robot navigation), Self-driving cars

Table 7.4: *Comparison of ML Algorithms*

Types of Data Science Algorithms

So far, we have studied the categories of data science algorithms. In this section, we will go over each of them in more detail. We will also look at the various types of algorithms within each category.

Supervised Learning Algorithms

SLAs learn from labeled datasets, meaning the model is trained on input-output pairs. There are various types of supervised learning algorithms which are mentioned as follows:

- Linear Regression
- Logistic Regression
- Decision Trees
- Random Forest
- Support Vector Machines
- Neural Networks

Let us look at these in further detail:

Linear Regression

Linear regression is used to model the relationship between a dependent variable and one or more independent variables by fitting a linear equation to the observed data. At its core, linear regression attempts to draw a straight line that best represents the connection between variables, which allows us to predict outcomes and understand underlying patterns.

Imagine that you want to understand how a person's study time relates to their exam score. Linear regression helps you answer questions like: "*If a student studies for X hours, what exam score can we expect?*" The method creates a mathematical model that captures this relationship.

The basic linear regression equation will look like this:

$$y = mx + b$$

Where:

- y is the dependent variable (what we are trying to predict)
- x is the independent variable (the predictor)
- m is the slope (how much y changes for each unit change in x)

- b is the y-intercept (the value of y when x is zero)

Simple Linear Regression is a type of supervised learning algorithm that models the relationship between **one independent variable (x)** and **one dependent variable (y)** using a straight-line equation. It is called "*simple*" because it involves only **one predictor variable.**

The goal of simple linear regression is to find the best-fitting straight line that **minimizes the difference between actual and predicted values.**

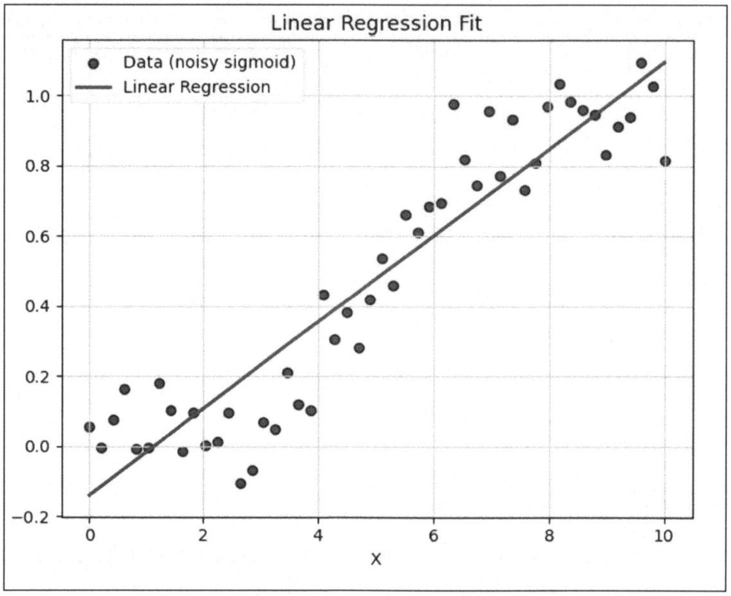

***Figure* 7.3:** *Simple Linear Regression*

Logistic Regression

Logistic regression is a fundamental statistical method used for predicting binary outcomes. Unlike linear regression which predicts continuous values, logistic regression is designed to estimate the probability that an instance belongs to a particular class. It is a powerful technique that bridges statistical analysis and machine learning, which is particularly useful for classification problems.

Imagine that you want to predict whether an email is spam or not spam, or whether a tumor is malignant or benign. These are binary classification problems where the outcome is one of two possible classes. Logistic regression provides a probabilistic approach to making these predictions.

At the heart of logistic regression is the sigmoid (or logistic) function. This special mathematical function takes any real-valued number and maps it to a value between 0 and 1, which can be interpreted as a probability.

The sigmoid function is defined as: `f(x) = 1 / (1 + e^(-x))`

Here are the key properties of the sigmoid function:

- Always outputs a value between 0 and 1
- Creates an S-shaped curve
- Allows us to convert linear combinations of features into probabilities

The model combines linear regression with the sigmoid function:

$$P(y=1) = 1 / (1 + e^{-(\beta_0 + \beta_1 x_1 + \beta_2 x_2 + ... + \beta_n x_n)})$$

Where:

- P(y=1) is the probability of the positive class
- β_0 is the intercept
- $\beta_1, \beta_2, ..., \beta_n$ are coefficients for each feature
- $x_1, x_2, ..., x_n$ are the input features

The model creates a decision boundary at 0.5 probability. Predictions above 0.5 are classified as the positive class, while those below are classified as the negative class.

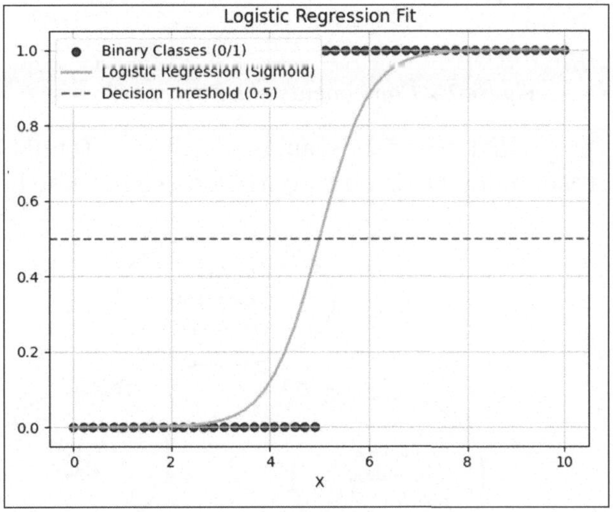

Figure 7.4: *Logistic Regression*

Decision Trees

Decision trees are a powerful ML algorithm that mimic the way humans make decisions. Imagine a flowchart that breaks down complex choices into a series of simple yes-or-no questions. Just like navigating through a choose-your-own-adventure book, a decision tree guides you from the root to a final decision by asking strategic questions about your data.

A decision tree consists of three main components:

- **Root Node**: The starting point of the tree, representing the entire dataset
- **Internal Nodes**: Decision points where the data is split based on specific features
- **Leaf Nodes**: Final nodes that represent the predicted outcome or classification

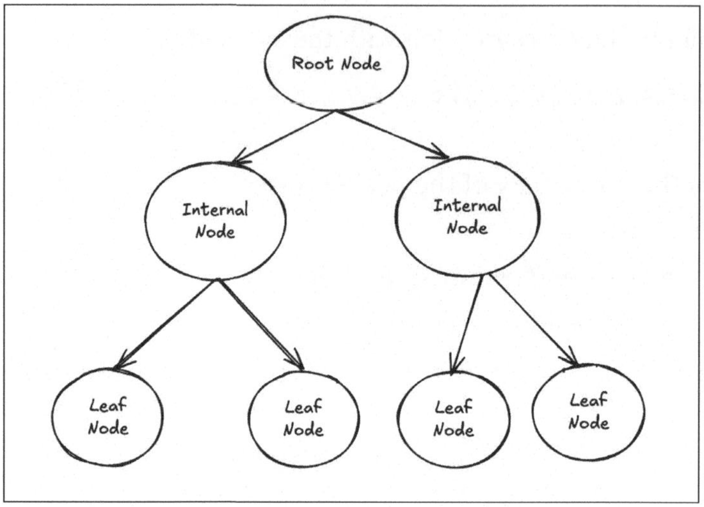

Figure 7.5: *Components of a Decision Tree*

Imagine you want to predict whether someone will play tennis based on weather conditions. The corresponding decision tree will look something like this:

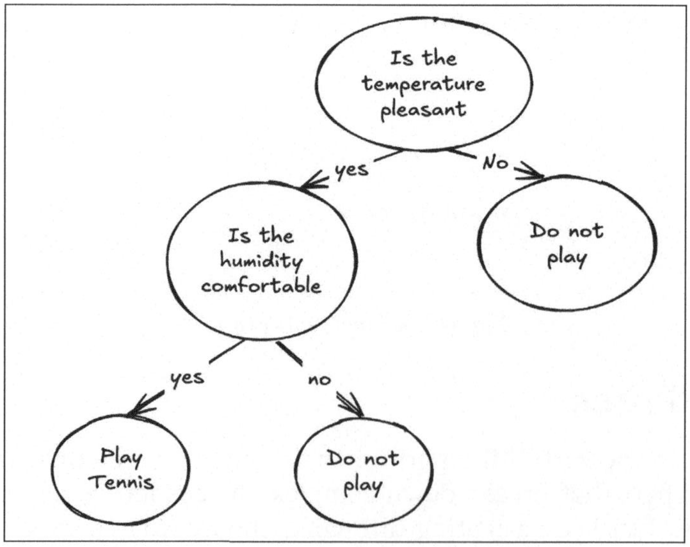

Figure 7.6: *Decision Tree Used for Prediction*

In this simple tree, the algorithm breaks down the decision into more questions that become progressively specific at each turn.

Random Forest

This algorithm works by combining the results of multiple decision trees to create a more accurate and stable model. The first step involves **bootstrap sampling**, where the algorithm creates multiple subsets of the training data by randomly sampling with replacement. This means that some data points may appear more than once in a single subset, while others may not appear at all. This introduces variation and helps reduce overfitting by ensuring that the model does not become too dependent on any specific part of the data. Next, for each sample, a decision tree is built. However, instead of considering all available features at each split, the algorithm selects a random subset of features. This further introduces randomness and prevents trees from becoming too similar to each other, which reduces correlation among them and improves the overall performance of the model. Finally, the predictions from all the individual trees are combined to make a final prediction. For classification tasks, the final prediction is determined by majority voting–whichever class gets the most votes is assumed as the final prediction. For regression tasks, the final prediction is the average of all the tree outputs. This ensemble approach helps the model generalize better and reduces the risk of overfitting.

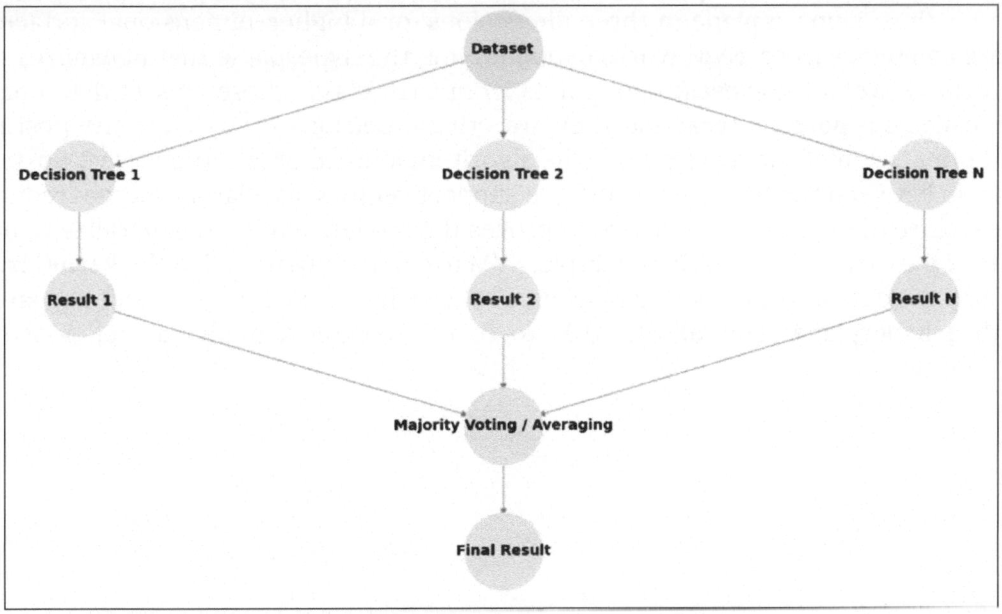

Figure 7.7: *Random Forest*

One of the main advantages of Random Forest is its high accuracy and robustness. Since it averages the predictions of multiple decision trees, the model is less sensitive to noise and outliers, and is thus highly stable and reliable. Unlike a single decision tree which tends to overfit the data, Random Forest reduces overfitting through bagging and feature randomness. It also handles high-dimensional data effectively because it considers only a subset of features at each split, which speeds up computation and improves generalization. Another benefit is the measure of **feature importance**–the algorithm ranks features based on how useful they are for prediction, which can be valuable to understand the underlying structure of the data. This makes it easier to perform feature selection and reduce the complexity of the model.

Despite its strengths, Random Forest has some limitations. It can be computationally expensive because it involves training multiple decision trees, which increases the processing time and memory requirements, especially with large datasets. The larger the forest is, the longer it will take to make predictions. As a result, it will also consume more memory. Another unique feature of Random Forest is that it is less interpretable than individual decision trees due to its complexity.

Support Vector Machines (SVM)

These are powerful supervised learning algorithms that are used for both **classification** and **regression** tasks, though they are most commonly used for classification. The main idea behind SVMs is to find a **hyperplane** that best separates data points into different classes. A hyperplane is essentially a decision boundary–it can be a line in two dimensions, a plane in three dimensions, or a higher-dimensional surface in more complex spaces. SVM works by identifying the hyperplane that maximizes the **margin** between the closest data points from each class. These closest data points are called **support vectors**, and they are critical because they define the position and orientation of the hyperplane. The algorithm aims to create the largest possible margin between the hyperplane and the support vectors, as a larger margin reduces the chance of misclassification and improves the model's ability to generalize to new data. If the data is not linearly separable, SVM uses a technique called the **kernel trick** to map the data into a higher-dimensional space where it becomes easier to separate with a hyperplane. This allows SVM to handle complex, nonlinear relationships effectively.

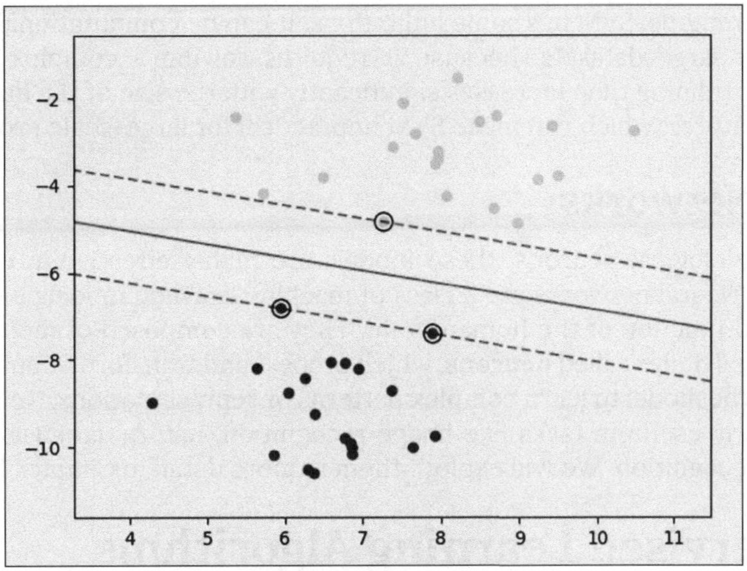

Figure 7.8: SVM. Source: *sklearn doc*

SVM is effective because it can maximize the margin between classes, which improves the model's ability to generalize to unseen data. Unlike other models that aim to minimize classification error directly, SVM tries to create the widest possible separation between the classes, which reduces the risk of overfitting. Using **support vectors** ensures that the model is influenced only by the most informative data points, which makes it less sensitive to noise and outliers. The **kernel trick** is another key factor behind the success of SVM. When data cannot be separated by a straight line (or hyperplane) in its original space, the kernel function projects it into a higher-dimensional space where it becomes linearly separable. Common kernels include **linear**, **polynomial**, and **radial basis function (RBF)** kernels, which allow the model to adapt to different patterns in data. By combining margin maximization with flexible kernel functions, SVM is able to capture both linear and nonlinear relationships effectively.

One of the key advantages of SVM is its ability to handle both linear and nonlinear data using the kernel trick. This makes it highly versatile and capable of adapting to different types of data structures. SVM is particularly effective in high-dimensional spaces where other models might struggle, as it focuses on the most important data points (support vectors) rather than the entire dataset. SVM tends to perform well even when the number of dimensions (features) is greater than the number of samples, which ends up making it suitable for tasks like text classification and image recognition. Another advantage is that SVM is relatively resistant to overfitting, especially when the margin is well-optimized. Additionally, SVM can provide a clear geometric interpretation of the decision boundary, which can help us understand how a model makes decisions.

Despite its strengths, SVM has some limitations. It can be computationally expensive, especially for large datasets, because it requires solving a complex optimization problem. The training time increases significantly with the size of the dataset and the number of features, which can make SVM impractical for large-scale problems.

Neural Networks

Inspired by biological neurons, these models are highly effective in deep learning applications. Neural networks are a class of machine learning models inspired by the structure and function of the human brain. They are composed of multiple layers of interconnected nodes called **neurons**, which process and transform input data in a way that enables the model to learn complex patterns or representations. Neural networks are particularly useful in tasks like image recognition, natural language processing, and speech recognition. We will explore them in more detail in *Chapter* 11.

Unsupervised Learning Algorithms

These algorithms analyze unlabeled data to discover patterns and structures.

Clustering

Clustering is an unsupervised learning technique that groups data points based on similarity, so that items within the same cluster are more alike than those in different clusters. It is commonly used to explore data, identify natural groupings, and uncover hidden structures without prior labels.

- **K-Means**: Partitions data into clusters based on similarity. This is a centroid-based algorithm that partitions data into a predefined number of clusters, denoted as K. The algorithm begins by selecting K initial centroids either randomly or via strategies like k-means++. Thereafter, each data point is assigned to the cluster whose centroid is closest based on a distance metric, which is often the Euclidean distance. After the points are assigned, the centroids are recalculated as the mean of the data points in each cluster, and the process repeats until the centroids stabilize. K-Means is computationally efficient and works well for large datasets with well-separated, spherical clusters. K-means minimizes within-cluster variance, which is also known as the inertia or sum of squared distances. However, it is sensitive to the initial selection of centroids and may struggle with clusters of varying sizes or shapes. Moreover, since the number of clusters, K, needs to be specified beforehand, it can be a limitation in scenarios where the ideal number of clusters is unknown.

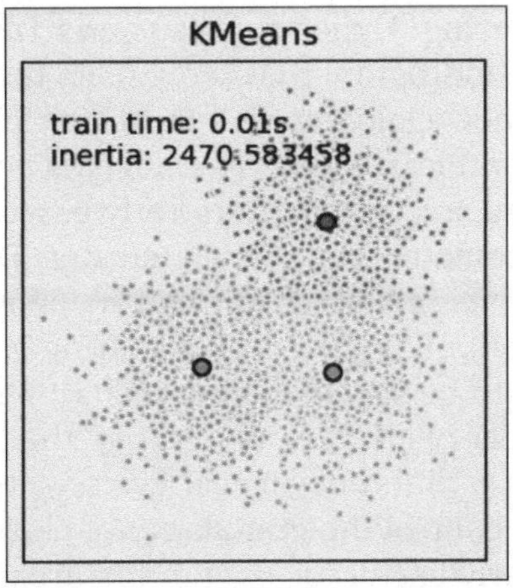

***Figure 7.9**: K-means. Source: sklearn doc*

- **DBSCAN** (Density-Based Spatial Clustering of Applications with Noise): This is a density-based clustering algorithm that groups data points based on the density of their neighborhoods, rather than assuming spherical clusters. The algorithm defines clusters as regions of high point density, which are separated by areas of lower density. A core point has a sufficient number of neighboring points within a given radius which is known as epsilon (ε); the points that lie within the radius of a core point but do not have enough neighbors are labeled as border points. Points that do not meet the criteria for being core or border points are considered noise or outliers. One of the major advantages of DBSCAN is that it does not require specifying the number of clusters in advance and can detect arbitrarily shaped clusters. It also handles noise well by identifying outliers. However, it is highly sensitive to the choice of the ε and minPts parameters, and may not perform well on datasets with varying density.

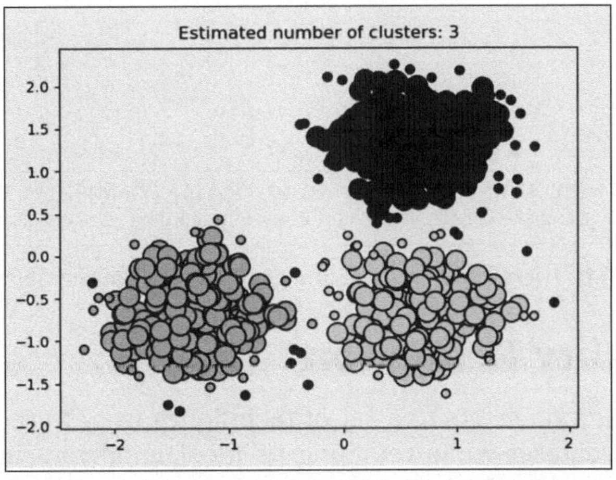

***Figure 7.10**: Clusters from* DBSCAN **Source: sklearn doc**

- **Hierarchical Clustering**: Unlike K-Means and DBSCAN, it builds a tree-like structure called a dendrogram that represents the hierarchy of clusters. This method can be either agglomerative (bottom-up) or divisive (top-down). In agglomerative hierarchical clustering, each data point starts as its own cluster, and pairs of clusters are merged iteratively based on a distance metric until all the points are combined in a single cluster. Divisive clustering works by starting with all points in one cluster and recursively splitting it into smaller clusters. A key benefit of hierarchical clustering is that it does not require the number of clusters to be specified beforehand. The dendrogram allows users to choose the number of clusters by "*cutting*" the tree at a desired level. If you cut the dendrogram at different vertical levels, you get clusters of various sizes, which allow you to control the granularity of clustering (coarse vs. fine). This method is particularly useful for data in hierarchical relationships. However, hierarchical clustering can be computationally expensive for large datasets, and its results can be sensitive to noise. It is because the progressive merging or splitting of clusters can be affected by outliers. Additionally, the distance metric and the linkage method used to define the distances between clusters can greatly influence the results.

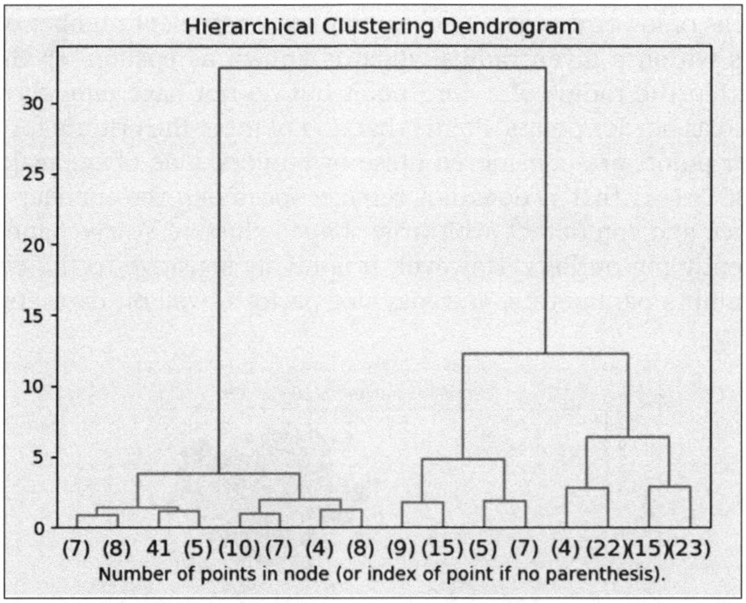

Figure 7.11: *Hierarchical Clustering Dendogram. Source: sklearn doc*

Dimensionality Reduction

Dimensionality reduction refers to a set of techniques used to reduce the number of input features in a dataset while retaining its most important information. It helps address challenges such as high computational cost, noise, and overfitting in high-dimensional data. By simplifying data representations, these methods improve model efficiency, interpretability, and visualization.

- **Principal Component Analysis (PCA):** It is used for dimensionality reduction while preserving as much of the data's variance as possible. PCA transforms the original data into a new coordinate system where the axes, also known as **principal components**, represent the directions in which the data varies the most. The first principal component captures the largest variance; the second captures the next largest variance, and so on. Each subsequent component is orthogonal to the previous ones. By selecting the first few principal components, PCA can significantly reduce the dimensionality of the data, which is especially helpful while dealing with high-dimensional datasets. This reduction simplifies the data for analysis and eliminates noise and redundancy. A major advantage of PCA is that it retains the most important features of the data while reducing complexity, which makes it particularly useful for tasks like data compression, exploratory data analysis, and noise reduction. However, while PCA is effective for linear relationships, it may not perform well when the data contains non-linear relationships. Additionally, PCA requires the data to be centered (that is, have a mean of zero) and can be influenced by the scaling of features. Therefore, careful preprocessing is often necessary.
- **t-Distributed Stochastic Neighbor Embedding (t-SNE):** This is a non-linear dimensionality reduction technique that is particularly useful for visualizing high-dimensional data in two or three dimensions. Unlike PCA, which focuses on maximizing variance in the data, t-SNE preserves the local structure of the data. It works by modeling pairwise similarities between data points; in the original high-dimensional space, similar data points are placed closely, while dissimilar points are kept farther apart in the lower-dimensional representation. t-SNE minimizes the divergence between probability distributions that represent pairwise similarities in both the original and lower-dimensional spaces. This allows t-SNE to capture complex, non-linear relationships within the data. One of the key strengths of t-SNE is its ability to reveal the underlying structures of data that may not be apparent in higher dimensions. It is widely used for data exploration, particularly in fields like ML, where it uncovers hidden patterns in high-dimensional feature spaces. However, t-SNE comes with some limitations. The algorithm can be computationally expensive, especially for large datasets, and requires tuning hyperparameters like the perplexity. These factors affect how the data is clustered. Furthermore, while t-SNE excels at local structure preservation, it can distort the global structure, which makes it challenging to interpret distances between distant points accurately. It also does not provide a direct way to project new data points once the model has been fitted, unlike PCA.

Reinforcement Learning Algorithms

Reinforcement learning focuses on sequential decision-making, where an agent improves its behavior through trial and error based on feedback from the environment. It is particularly useful in problems where explicit labeled data is unavailable and actions influence future outcomes, such as robotics, game playing, recommendation systems, and resource optimization. By balancing exploration and exploitation, these algorithms aim to maximize long-term rewards rather than immediate gains.

- **Markov Decision Processes (MDP)**: This is a mathematical framework used to model decision-making in environments where outcomes are partially random and under the control of an agent. An MDP consists of several components such as states, actions, rewards, transition probabilities, and a discount factor. The states represent all possible configurations or situations of the system, while actions are the choices the agent can make to transition from one state to another. In each state, the agent chooses an action, which results in a transition to a new state. It also receives a reward, which quantifies the benefit (or cost) of taking that action. The goal of the agent is to learn a **policy**, which specifies which action to take in each state in order to maximize the expected cumulative reward over time.

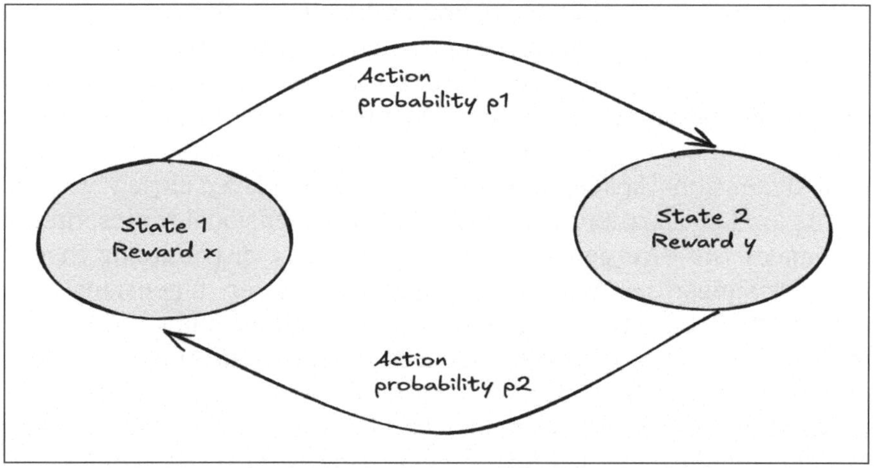

Figure 7.12: *Markov Decision Process between Two States*

The transition between states is governed by **transition probabilities**, which describe the likelihood of moving from one state to another given a particular action. Additionally, a **discount factor** is often applied to future rewards to account for the fact that immediate rewards are typically preferred over future rewards. The Markov property implies that the future state depends only on the current state and action, not on the history of past states or actions. This makes MDP a powerful tool for modeling sequential decision-making problems in applications such as robotics, game playing, and resource allocation.

- **Q-Learning**: This is a model-free, value-based reinforcement learning algorithm used to learn the optimal policy in an MDP. The key idea behind Q-Learning is to estimate the **Q-values**, which represent the expected cumulative reward of taking a specific action in a given state and then following the current policy (ideally the optimal policy) thereafter. Q-Learning involves learning a **Q-table** where each entry corresponds to a specific state-action pair, which is denoted as Q(s, a). Initially, Q-values are typically set to zero or some arbitrary value, and the algorithm updates them as the agent interacts with the environment. The agent explores the environment by taking actions and receiving rewards, using a process called **temporal difference (TD) learning** to iteratively update the Q-values. Through repeated interactions with the environment, Q-Learning gradually converges towards the optimal Q-values, and the agent can derive the optimal policy by selecting the action with the highest Q-value in each state.

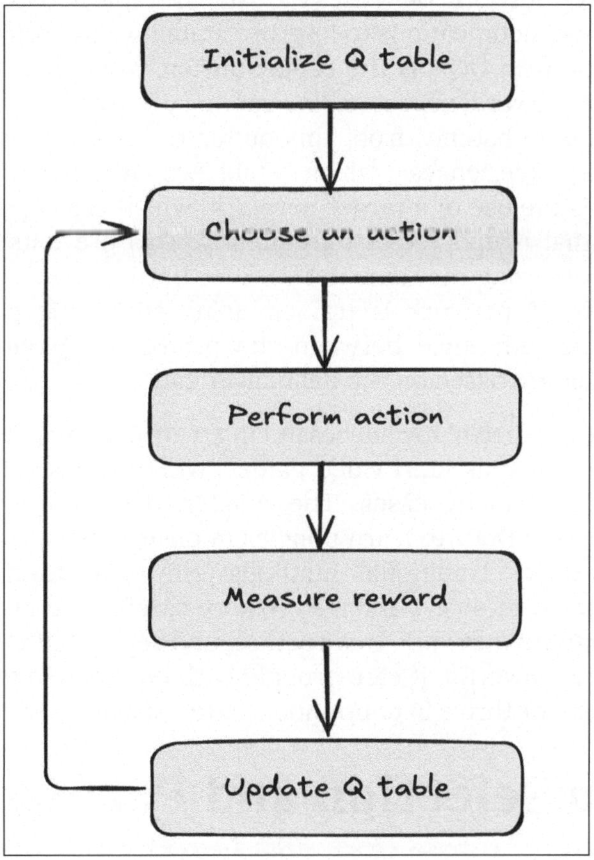

Figure 7.13: Q-Learning

Q-Learning is powerful because it is model-free. In other words, it does not require knowledge of the environment's transition probabilities or reward function. This makes it applicable to a wide range of decision-making problems. However, Q-Learning can struggle with large state and action spaces because it relies on maintaining a Q-table, which becomes infeasible when the space is vast.

- **Deep Q Networks (DQN)**: These are an extension of Q-Learning designed to address the challenges of large state and action spaces. While Q-Learning stores Q-values in a table, DQN leverages a **neural network** to approximate the Q-values, further allowing it to scale to environments with very large or continuous state spaces, such as video games or real-world robotics. The core idea behind DQN is to replace the Q-table with a **Q-network**, which is a neural network that takes a state as input and outputs Q-values for all possible actions. This enables the agent to handle high-dimensional input spaces like images or sensor data, where traditional Q-tables would be infeasible.

  To train the Q-network, DQN uses the same Q-value update rule as Q-Learning, but with some modifications to improve stability and performance. One of the key innovations in DQN is the **replay buffer**, which stores past experiences (state, action, reward, next state) in a memory buffer. During training, an agent samples random batches from this buffer to break the correlation between consecutive experiences, which stabilizes training. Another important innovation is the use of a **target network**, which is a copy of the Q-network, albeit one that is updated less frequently. This prevents the instability that can arise from using the same network for both action selection and Q-value updates. The Q-network is trained using stochastic gradient descent to minimize the difference between the predicted Q-values and the target Q-values that are based on the Bellman equation.

  DQN has been particularly successful in environments with high-dimensional state spaces, such as Atari video games, where it has achieved human-level performance in many cases. The combination of Q-Learning with deep learning enables DQN to learn policies in environments that were previously too complex for traditional methods. However, training DQNs can be computationally intensive and may require careful tuning of hyperparameters like learning rate, network architecture, and replay buffer size. Furthermore, while DQN is powerful, it can struggle with environments that require long-term planning or thrive in continuous action spaces.

Algorithm Selection and Performance Evaluation

Choosing the right machine learning algorithm is a critical step in solving a problem effectively. The decision depends on several factors like the nature of the data, the specific task at hand, and the performance criteria we prioritize. A few of these considerations are mentioned as follows:

- **Data**: The type of data you have (numerical, categorical, or mixed) significantly influences the algorithm choice. For example, decision trees can handle both numerical and categorical data, while algorithms like linear regression or SVMs may require the data to be transformed or normalized. The size and complexity of the dataset also matter; some algorithms, like K-Nearest Neighbors (K-NN), perform well with small datasets but can struggle with larger, more complex ones. In contrast, deep learning models shine in environments with vast amounts of high-dimensional data (like images or text), but require large datasets to avoid overfitting.
- **Task**: The task you are trying to solve–whether it is classification, regression, clustering, or reinforcement learning–also dictates the choice of algorithm. For example, if the goal is to classify data into distinct categories, algorithms like logistic regression, decision trees, or neural networks might be appropriate. For predicting continuous values (regression tasks), algorithms such as linear regression or support vector regression would be more suitable.
- **Performance Criteria**: Lastly, the metrics you care about–accuracy, speed, interpretability, scalability, and so on–will guide the choice. Some models may offer high accuracy, but are computationally expensive (for example, deep learning). Other models might offer faster predictions but be less accurate (for example, decision trees). Additionally, some tasks may require models that are easy to interpret (for example, linear regression), while others can tolerate more complexity (for example, neural networks).

The algorithm you choose must align with the nature of the data, the type of problem you are solving, and the specific performance requirements.

Bias-Variance Tradeoff: Balancing Model Complexity to Avoid Underfitting or Overfitting

The **bias-variance tradeoff** is a fundamental concept in ML that balances the complexity of a model to achieve the best performance.

- **Bias** refers to the error introduced by simplifying assumptions in the model. High bias typically occurs when a model is too simple, making strong assumptions about the data and unable to capture its underlying patterns effectively. A high-bias model is prone to **underfitting**, as it performs poorly on both the training and test datasets. It is because the model has failed to capture the true relationship in the data. For example, using a linear model to represent a nonlinear relationship between variables will introduce high bias.

- **Variance**, on the other hand, refers to the error introduced by the model's sensitivity to small fluctuations in the training data. High variance occurs when a model is too complex, allowing it to fit the training data very well. However, it ends up making the model overly sensitive to noise or fluctuations in the training set. This leads to **overfitting**, where the model performs well on the training data but performs poorly on unseen test data as it has learned noise or irrelevant patterns that were specific to the training set.

The goal is to find a balance between bias and variance. A model with too much bias will underfit the data and have poor predictive performance, while a model with too much variance will overfit the data and fail to generalize to new, unseen data. Techniques like cross-validation, regularization, and pruning (for decision trees) are used to achieve the optimal bias-variance tradeoff.

Overfitting vs. Underfitting: Ensuring Generalization to Unseen Data

Overfitting and **underfitting** are two common problems encountered during the training of machine learning models, both of which impact a model's ability to generalize to unseen data.

The key to success in machine learning is to find a model that neither overfits nor underfits but instead **generalizes well** to new, unseen data. This can often be achieved by techniques such as cross-validation, tuning hyperparameters, and using appropriate model complexity.

Model Evaluation Metrics

Different tasks in machine learning require different metrics to evaluate how well a model is performing. Below are some of the commonly used metrics for different types of tasks:

Classification Tasks: Accuracy, Precision, Recall, F1-Score

- **Accuracy** is the simplest and most intuitive metric which measures the proportion of correct predictions out of all the predictions made. This refers to the ratio of correctly predicted instances to the total instances. While it is useful, accuracy can be misleading while dealing with imbalanced datasets (where one class is much more frequent than the other), as it might convey a false sense of exceptional model performance.
- **Precision** measures the proportion of true positive predictions among all the positive predictions made. In other words, it tells you how many of the predicted positive instances were actually correct. Precision is especially important in scenarios where false positives (incorrectly predicting a positive

outcome) are costly or undesirable, such as in fraud detection or medical diagnoses.

- **Recall (Sensitivity)** measures the proportion of true positive predictions out of all actual positive instances. It is useful when minimizing false negatives (that is, failing to detect a positive instance) is critical. For instance, in medical testing, it is often more important to catch all positive cases (even at the cost of some false positives) than to miss any.
- **F1-Score** is the harmonic mean of precision and recall, which provides a single metric to balance the other two. It is especially useful when dealing with imbalanced datasets, as it accounts for both false positives and false negatives and gives a more balanced view of model performance than accuracy alone.

Regression Tasks: Mean Squared Error (MSE), R-Squared

- **Mean Squared Error (MSE)** is one of the most common metrics used for regression tasks. It measures the average squared difference between the predicted and actual values. A lower MSE indicates a better fit, as it implies that the model's predictions are closer to the true values. However, MSE is sensitive to outliers since the differences are squared and can disproportionately affect the performance evaluation.
- **R-squared (R^2)** is another widely used regression metric that indicates how well the independent variables explain the variation in the dependent variable. It ranges between 0 to 1, with higher values indicating better model performance. An R^2 value of 1 means the model explains all the variance in the data, while an R^2 value of 0 means the model does not explain any of the variance.

Clustering Performance: Silhouette Score, Dunn Index

- **Silhouette Score** is used to measure how similar each point is to its own cluster compared to other clusters. It combines ideas of cohesion (how close the points in a cluster are to each other) and separation (how far apart different clusters are). A silhouette score close to 1 indicates that the points are well-clustered, while a score leaning towards -1 indicates that the points might have been assigned to the wrong cluster.
- **Dunn Index** measures the ratio of the minimum inter-cluster distance to the maximum intra-cluster distance. A higher Dunn index indicates that the clusters are well-separated and compact. It is especially useful for comparing the quality of different clustering algorithms, and determining the optimal number of clusters.

Real-World Applications of Data Science Algorithms

Data science algorithms play a critical role in transforming raw data into actionable insights across a wide range of industries. By identifying patterns, making predictions, and automating decision-making, these algorithms enable organizations to improve efficiency, reduce risk, and deliver personalized experiences. Their real-world impact is evident in sectors such as healthcare, finance, retail, transportation, and technology.

Healthcare: Disease Prediction, Medical Imaging Analysis

Healthcare generates vast amounts of data from patient records, diagnostic tests, and medical imaging, creating significant opportunities for data-driven innovation. Data science algorithms help transform this complex data into insights that support earlier diagnosis, more accurate predictions, and improved clinical decision-making. The following applications highlight how these techniques are being used to enhance patient care and healthcare outcomes.

- **Disease Prediction**: ML algorithms like **logistic regression**, **decision trees**, and **random forests** are used to predict the likelihood of a patient developing a specific disease. By analyzing historical medical data such as genetic information, lifestyle factors, and previous health conditions, these algorithms can predict diseases such as diabetes, heart disease, or cancer. For example, predictive models can estimate the risk of heart disease based on a patient's age, cholesterol levels, and family history. These predictions allow for early intervention, personalized treatment plans, and better resource allocation in healthcare systems.
- **Medical Imaging Analysis**: In medical imaging, algorithms such as **Convolutional Neural Networks (CNNs)** are widely used to analyze images from X-rays, MRIs, CT scans, and ultrasounds. These deep learning models are capable of identifying patterns in complex medical images, assisting radiologists in detecting anomalies like tumors, fractures, or abnormal growths with high accuracy. For example, CNNs are extensively used in detecting early signs of cancer in mammograms or identifying brain tumors in MRI scans. This improves diagnostic accuracy and helps doctors make faster, more reliable decisions. AI-powered imaging systems can also automate routine tasks, thus allowing healthcare professionals to focus on more complex cases.

Finance: Fraud Detection, Stock Market Prediction

The finance industry relies heavily on data science algorithms to detect fraudulent activities, predict market trends, and optimize investment strategies. By analyzing large datasets in real-time, algorithms can help financial institutions make more accurate predictions, reduce risks, and enhance decision-making.

- **Fraud Detection**: One of the most significant applications of ML in finance is fraud detection. Algorithms such as decision trees, support vector machines (SVMs), and neural networks are used to analyze transaction patterns and detect unusual activities that may indicate fraud. For instance, credit card companies use algorithms to monitor transactions in real-time. When an irregularity (such as a large transaction in an unusual location) is detected, the algorithm flags it for further investigation. These models are trained on historical data, learning what constitutes normal versus suspicious behavior, and improving over time to reduce false positives and enhance detection accuracy.
- **Stock Market Prediction**: Predicting stock prices and market trends is another area where data science plays a pivotal role. Time series forecasting techniques, such as ARIMA (AutoRegressive Integrated Moving Average) or machine learning models like XGBoost and long short-term memory networks (LSTMs), are used to predict the future movement of stock prices based on historical data. These models analyze historical stock prices, trading volume, and macroeconomic indicators to predict short-term and long-term trends. Investors use these predictions to inform trading decisions, helping them identify profitable opportunities or mitigate risks. Algorithmic trading, where computers automatically buy and sell based on pre-defined criteria, has become a multi-billion dollar industry driven by advanced ML models analyzing vast amounts of market data.

E-commerce: Recommendation Systems, Customer Segmentation

In the e-commerce industry, data science algorithms are essential for improving customer experience, increasing sales, and optimizing marketing efforts. The use of data-driven insights helps businesses provide personalized services, anticipate customer needs, and improve product offerings.

- **Recommendation Systems**: Some of the most prominent applications of data science in e-commerce are **recommendation systems**. Platforms like Amazon, Netflix, and Spotify use algorithms to suggest products, movies, or songs based on user behavior, preferences, and interactions. These systems typically use **collaborative filtering** to analyze the preferences of similar users, and **content-based filtering**, which recommends items similar to the ones that the user has interacted with in the past. For example, if a customer frequently purchases sports equipment, the recommendation engine may suggest new products related to fitness or outdoor activities. This personalized shopping experience helps e-commerce platforms increase engagement and drive sales by offering products that match each customer's interests.

- **Customer Segmentation**: Data science algorithms also play a crucial role in **customer segmentation**, which involves grouping customers based on their purchasing behavior, demographics, or preferences. By using clustering algorithms like **K-means** or **hierarchical clustering**, businesses can segment their customers into distinct groups, such as frequent shoppers, budget-conscious consumers, or first-time visitors. This segmentation enables targeted marketing strategies, allowing companies to direct personalized offers, advertisements, and recommendations to different customer groups, thereby increasing conversion rates and improving customer satisfaction.

Social Media: Sentiment Analysis, Trend Prediction

Social media platforms like Twitter, Facebook, Instagram, and LinkedIn generate vast amounts of data every day. Social media platforms generate continuous, high-volume streams of unstructured data that reflect real-time public opinions and behaviors. Data science techniques make it possible to extract meaningful insights from this data, enabling organizations to monitor sentiment, identify emerging trends, and respond proactively to audience needs. The following applications demonstrate how these insights are derived and applied in practice.

- **Sentiment Analysis**: Powered by natural language processing (NLP) techniques, sentiment analysis, allows businesses to analyze social media posts, reviews, and comments to understand public opinion about products, brands, or events. Algorithms such as **support vector machines (SVMs)**, **Naive Bayes**, and deep learning models like **recurrent neural networks (RNNs)** can classify text into categories like positive, negative, or neutral. For example, a company launching a new product may use sentiment analysis to gauge public response and identify potential issues before they escalate. Political campaigns also use sentiment analysis to understand voters' sentiments on social media and adjust their strategies accordingly.
- **Trend Prediction**: Machine learning algorithms are also used to **predict trends** in social media. By analyzing patterns in user interactions, hashtags, and content engagement over time, algorithms can forecast upcoming trends, topics, or viral content. Techniques like **time series forecasting**, **topic modeling**, and **deep learning** are used to identify emerging discussions or shifts in public interest. For example, Twitter may use trend prediction algorithms to surface

popular topics or hashtags that are gaining traction, which can help users discover new content or assist marketers in capitalizing on trending topics. Trend prediction is valuable for businesses looking to align their marketing strategies with current public interests and capitalize on viral moments.

Conclusion

This chapter provided a comprehensive overview of data science algorithms, while exploring their fundamental concepts, types, selection criteria, and real-world applications. Data science algorithms are the backbone of modern computational problem-solving, as they transform raw data into actionable insights across numerous industries. The three main algorithm categories discussed were supervised learning (including linear regression, logistic regression, decision trees, random forest, support vector machines, and neural networks), unsupervised learning (covering clustering techniques like K-Means and dimensionality reduction methods like PCA), and reinforcement learning (including Markov Decision Processes and Q-Learning). Furthermore, the chapter emphasized that selecting the appropriate algorithm requires careful consideration of data characteristics, specific task requirements, and performance criteria, with particular attention to the bias-variance tradeoff to avoid underfitting or overfitting. Performance evaluation metrics vary by task type, with classification typically using accuracy and F1-score, regression employing mean squared error and R-squared, and clustering utilizing the Silhouette Score and Dunn Index. These powerful algorithms enable transformative applications across industries such as healthcare, finance, e-commerce, and social media, as they provide the foundation for solving complex problems and extracting valuable insights from our increasingly data-driven world.

In the next chapter, we will work with some of these algorithms, and explore their power in real time.

CHAPTER 8
Implementing Machine Learning Models

Introduction

Having established the significance of data science algorithms, we will now turn to their practical application. This chapter explores the implementation of these algorithms to construct working models and analyze their performance.

In this chapter, we will tackle regression, classification, and clustering problems via the "Automobile" dataset from the UC Irvine Machine Learning Repository. Through this process, we will demonstrate how algorithms transform raw data into actionable intelligence, driving informed decisions. Please find the link in the references section of this chapter.

Structure

This chapter will address the following topics:

- Loading and Exploring the "*Automobile*" Dataset
- In-Depth Regression Analysis to Predict Fuel Efficiency
- Detailed Classification Analysis to Categorize Vehicles
- Comprehensive Clustering Analysis to Identify Groups of Similar Vehicles
- Further Explorations, Advanced Techniques, and Potential Extensions
- Appendix: Running Regression, Classification, and Clustering in R

Loading and Exploring the "*Automobile*" Dataset

For this chapter, we have selected UCI Machine Learning Repository's "*Automobile*" dataset due to its versatility in demonstrating a spectrum of machine learning problems. Its attributes will allow us to explore both supervised and unsupervised learning: regression models can predict vehicle prices or fuel efficiency, classification techniques can categorize vehicles by body style or price range, and clustering algorithms can identify inherent groupings of cars based on their features. This ability to address multiple problem types with a single dataset will allow us to compare algorithmic approaches side-by-side.

While it is important to acknowledge that this dataset oversimplifies the complexities often encountered in real-world data science, it also provides an effective foundation for laying essential algorithmic groundwork.

You can download the file locally or directly save the **`.data`** file, which can be read as a CSV. We have to add the relevant column names after referring to the documentation from the UCI's Automobile page.

```
import pandas as pd
# URL to the Automobile dataset (data folder)
data_url = "https://archive.ics.uci.edu/ml/machine-learning-data-
bases/autos/imports-85.data"

# Column names from the dataset's documentation

column_names =
["symboling", "normalized_losses", "make", "fuel_type",
"aspiration", "num_doors", "body_style", "drive_wheels",
"engine_location", "wheel_base", "length", "width", "height",
"curb_weight", "engine_type", "num_cylinders", "engine_size",
"fuel_system","bore", "stroke", "compression_ratio",
"horsepower", "peak_rpm", "city_mpg","highway_mpg","price"
]

# Load the dataset into a pandas DataFrame
df = pd.read_csv(data_url, names=column_names, na_values="?")
# Display the first few rows
df.head()
```

There are 205 rows and 26 columns in this dataset. Here is the summary showing column name, data type, and their respective descriptions:

Column Name	Data Type	Example	Description
symboling	int64	3	Insurance risk rating (-3 to +3)
normalized_losses	float64	122	Relative average insurance loss
make	object	toyota	The manufacturer of the car
fuel_type	object	gas	Type of fuel: gas or diesel
aspiration	object	std	Engine air intake type (std or turbo)
num_doors	object	four	Number of doors (two, four)
body_style	object	sedan	Body design: sedan, hatchback, etc.
drive_wheels	object	fwd	Drive type: fwd, rwd, 4wd
engine_location	object	front	Engine position (front, rear)
wheel_base	float64	98.4	Distance between wheels (inches)
length	float64	176.6	Car length (inches)
width	float64	66.2	Car width (inches)
height	float64	54.3	Car height (inches)
curb_weight	int64	2337	Weight of the car without passengers
engine_type	object	ohc	Type of engine configuration
num_cylinders	object	four	Number of engine cylinders
engine_size	int64	97	Size of the engine (cc)
fuel_system	object	2bbl	Type of fuel system
bore	float64	3.15	Diameter of the engine cylinder (inches)
stroke	float64	3.29	Length of piston movement (inches)
compression_ ratio	float64	9	Engine compression ratio
horsepower	float64	69	Engine power
peak_rpm	float64	5200	Revolutions per minute at max horsepower
city_mpg	int64	31	Miles per gallon in city driving
highway_mpg	int64	38	Miles per gallon on highways
price	float64	13495	Price of the vehicle in USD

Table 8.1: *Description of Columns, Examples, and Data Type*

To build a solid initial understanding of a dataset, we will start with Exploratory Data Analysis (EDA). Histograms and boxplots offer a clear view of data distributions, which allows an analyst to identify potential outliers and skewness. Simultaneously, checking for missing values provides crucial intuition about the completeness of the data and the instances where biases might be introduced.

```
# Check missing values in horsepower
print("Missing values in horsepower:", df['horsepower'].isnull().
sum())


plt.figure(figsize=(8, 5))
df['horsepower'].dropna().astype(float).hist(bins=30)
plt.title('Horsepower Distribution')
plt.xlabel('Horsepower')
plt.ylabel('Frequency')
plt.tight_layout()
plt.show()
```

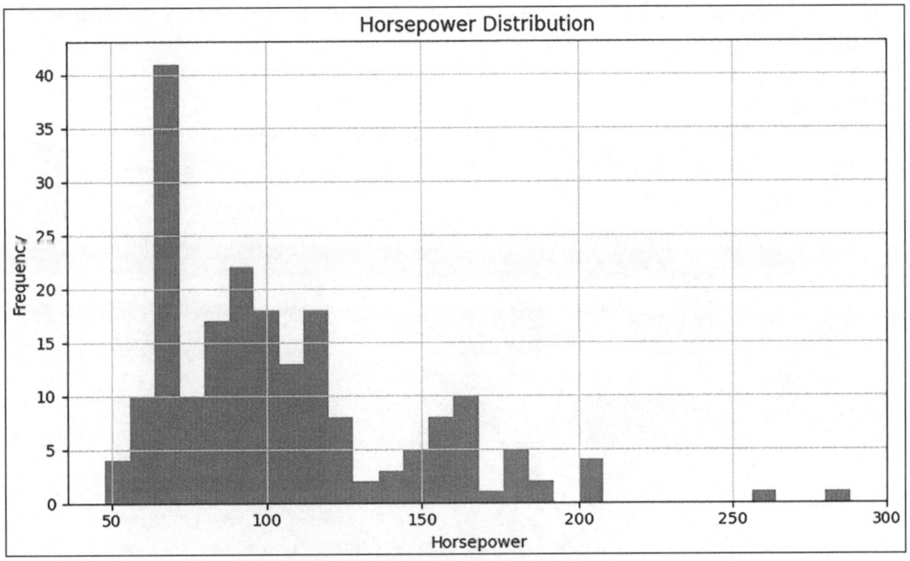

Figure 8.1: *Horsepower Distributions*

`Horsepower` is showing some **outliers** or **long-tailed distributions,** which could potentially affect the analysis.

It is also critical to look at the correlation matrix. Examining the correlation matrix before applying machine learning algorithms is crucial for addressing several potential challenges. Primarily, it helps to identify multicollinearity, which is a condition where predictor variables are highly correlated. Multicollineraity can destabilize regression models and make the individual impact of each predictor obscure. Additionally, the correlation matrix reveals feature redundancy by pinpointing variables that carry similar information. .This enables the removal of unnecessary features and allows users to simplify the model. Beyond these technical considerations, the correlation matrix offers valuable insights into the relationships between variables, which can guide feature engineering and inform us about how to select appropriate machine learning (ML) models.

```
#  Correlation matrix for numeric features
numeric_df = df.select_dtypes(include=['int64', 'float64'])
corr = numeric_df.corr()

# Set diagonal to NaN for better readability
mask = np.eye(len(corr), dtype=bool)
corr_masked = corr.mask(mask)

# Plot larger heatmap for better readability
plt.figure(figsize=(12, 10))
sns.heatmap(corr_masked, annot=True, cmap='coolwarm', fmt='.2f',
square=True, mask=mask)
plt.title('Correlation Matrix of Numeric Features (Diagonal
Hidden)')
plt.tight_layout()
plt.show()
```

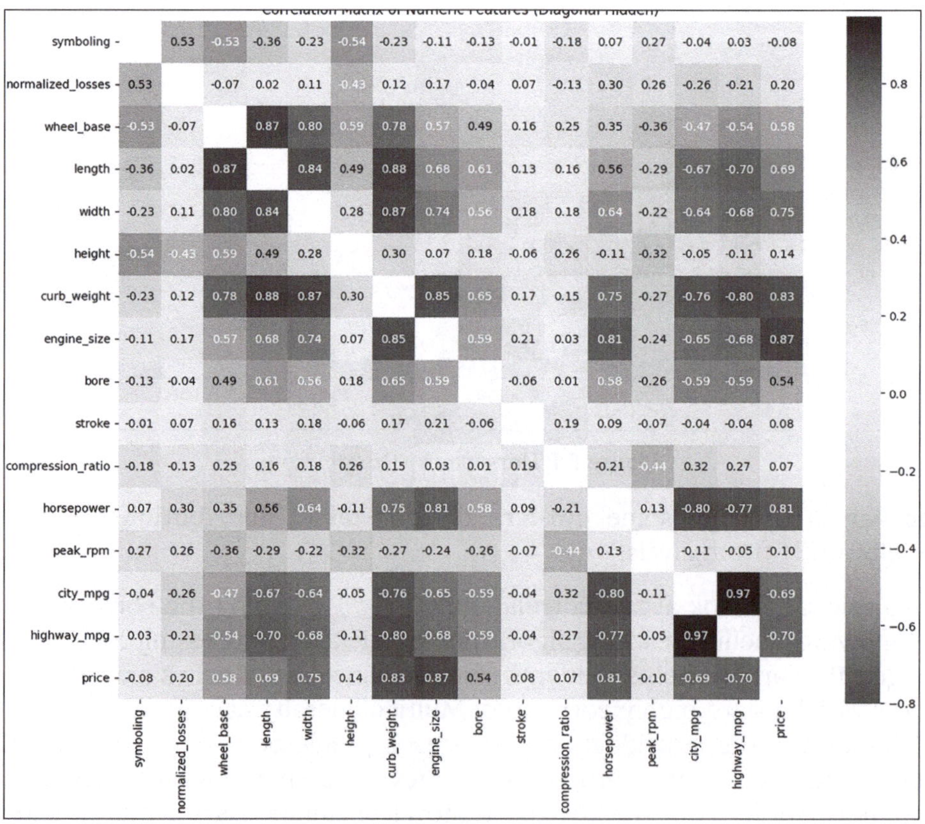

Figure 8.2: *Correlation Analysis*

Here, **curb_weight**, **engine_size**, and **horsepower** are strongly correlated with each other and negatively correlated with **city_mpg**.

In-Depth Regression Analysis to Predict Fuel Efficiency

Regression analysis uncovers relationships between variables to predict a continuous outcome by finding the line (or curve) of best fit. In the context of the "**Automobile**" dataset, predicting fuel efficiency (using **highway_mpg** or **city_mpg**) helps us quantify how car features like engine size or weight impact fuel consumption. This reveals which vehicle characteristics contribute most to fuel economy and ultimately figures while making design and consumer choices.

Before running any analysis, it is critical to think about the features that would make sense intuitively in predicting **city_mpg.**To predict **city_mpg** effectively, engine-related attributes like **engine-size**, **engine-type**, **num-of-cylinders**, and **fuel-system**, performance-related features such as **horsepower** and **curb-weight**, and physical attributes including **body-style** and **drive-wheels** make sense to pick. These factors influence urban fuel consumption. However, it is crucial to address potential feature redundancy and encode categorical variables appropriately during analysis.

Our first step will be to pick features based on domain knowledge or EDA insights. Then, we will convert categorical variables to dummy variables, while dropping one level (**drop_first=True**) to avoid the dummy variable trap. After that, we will handle missing values and outliers before running any model. We have covered this portion in previous sections; hence, to make things simple, we will remove all rows with missing values and accept any outliers in the analysis for now. This is demonstrated as follows:

```
# Select recommended features and the target
selected_features = [
    'curb_weight', 'engine_size', 'horsepower', 'compression_
ratio', 'peak_rpm',
    'wheel_base', 'length', 'width', 'fuel_type', 'aspiration',
'engine_location',
    'drive_wheels', 'num_cylinders', 'body_style'
]
target = 'city_mpg'

# Create a new DataFrame
df_model = df[selected_features + [target]].dropna()

# Convert categorical columns to dummy variables
categorical_features = ['fuel_type', 'aspiration', 'engine_
location', 'drive_wheels', 'num_cylinders', 'body_style']
```

```
df_model = pd.get_dummies(df_model, columns=categorical_features,
drop_first=True)

# Split into features (X) and target (y)
X = df_model.drop(columns=[target])
y = df_model[target]
```

The next step involves running VIF (Variance Inflation Factor) analysis. VIF quantifies multicollinearity by measuring how much the variance of a feature's estimated regression coefficient is "*inflated*" due to its correlation with other predictor features. Generally, a feature with a VIF score below 5 or 10 is considered acceptable, which indicates relatively low multicollinearity. Such features are typically retained as they contribute unique information to the model. However, features with high VIF scores (above the threshold) are strongly correlated. Addressing them requires a combination of understanding the features and employing strategies like combining them into a single representative feature (for example, averaging or using PCA to create a composite), or removing one or more of the highly correlated features. At the end, we prioritize those variables that are not very important theoretically or have weaker correlations with the target variable.

```
# Ensure numeric and clean input for VIF
X = X.apply(lambda col: pd.to_numeric(col, errors='coerce')).
astype(float)
X = X.replace([np.inf, -np.inf], np.nan)
X = X.dropna()

# Compute VIF for each feature
vif_data = pd.DataFrame()
vif_data['Feature'] = X.columns
vif_data['VIF'] = [variance_inflation_factor(X.values, i) for i in
range(X.shape[1])]

print("\nVariance Inflation Factor (VIF):")
print(vif_data.sort_values(by='VIF', ascending=False))
```

This can create a structure for iterating on the features. In the preceding example, we can see which features are highly correlated and then drop them. For this version, we will create a simple model with limited features, which is shown as follows:

```
selected_features = [
    'horsepower',
    'curb_weight',
    'peak_rpm',
    'aspiration'
]

target = 'city_mpg'
```

```
# Create a new DataFrame
df_model = df[selected_features + [target]].dropna()

# Convert categorical columns to dummy variables

categorical_features = [
    'aspiration'
    ]
df_model = pd.get_dummies(df_model, columns=categorical_features,
drop_first=True)

# Split into features (X) and target (y)
X = df_model.drop(columns=[target])
y = df_model[target]
```

Once the relevant features are selected, the next decision is to choose the appropriate regression model. This choice often depends on balancing the need for model explainability against the goal of minimizing prediction errors. When computational resources are sufficient, it will be feasible to run and compare multiple models simultaneously. This is shown in the code below:

```
#importing relevant packages

from sklearn.linear_model import LinearRegression, Ridge, Lasso
from sklearn.tree import DecisionTreeRegressor
from sklearn.ensemble import RandomForestRegressor, Gradient-
BoostingRegressor
from sklearn.neighbors import KNeighborsRegressor
from sklearn.metrics import r2_score, mean_squared_error
from sklearn.model_selection import train_test_split
# Splitting the dataset into 20% Testing and 80% Training

X_train, X_test, y_train, y_test = train_test_split(X, y, test_
size=0.2, random_state=42)

# Dictionary to hold models
models = {
    'LinearRegression': LinearRegression(),
    'Ridge': Ridge(),
    'Lasso': Lasso(),
    'DecisionTree': DecisionTreeRegressor(),
    'RandomForest': RandomForestRegressor(),
    'GradientBoosting': GradientBoostingRegressor(),
    'KNN': KNeighborsRegressor()
}

# DataFrame to store results
```

```
results = pd.DataFrame(columns=['Model', 'R2 Score', 'MSE'])

# Train and evaluate each model
for name, model in models.items():
    model.fit(X_train, y_train)
    y_pred = model.predict(X_test)
    r2 = r2_score(y_test, y_pred)
    mse = mean_squared_error(y_test, y_pred)
    results = pd.concat([results, pd.DataFrame([[name, r2, mse]],
columns=['Model', 'R2 Score', 'MSE'])], ignore_index=True)
```

While evaluating regression models, R-squared (R^2) helps us understand how well the model explains the variability of the target variable, like **city_mpg**. It ranges from 0 to 1, where a higher R^2 indicates that the model is able to better explain the variance in **city_mpg**; it can also be negative, which indicates a poor model fit. In contrast, Mean Squared Error (MSE) measures the average of the squared differences between the actual and predicted values. MSE is always positive, and a lower MSE signifies better predictions. However, it is important to note that MSE is sensitive to outliers because the errors are squared. This will allot larger errors a disproportionately larger weight.

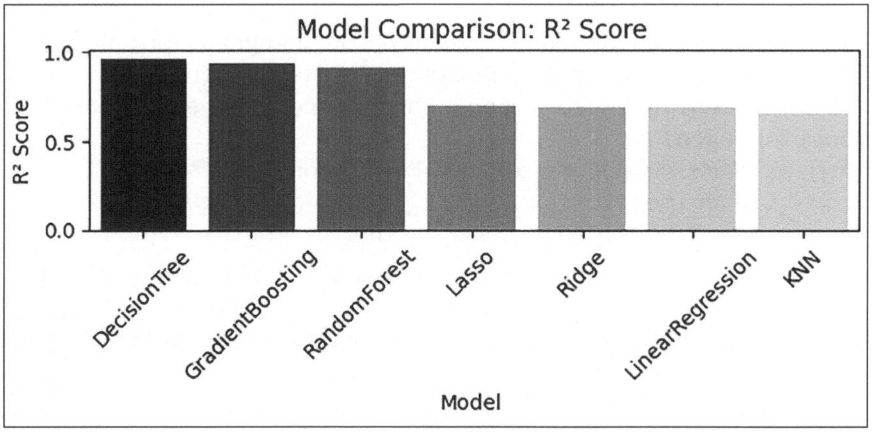

Figure 8.3: *Model Comparison*

An analyst will also have to look at which features are inherently important. This is where linear models are useful, you can learn about the importance of each feature by looking at the corresponding coefficient of regression. This is shown as follows:

```
lr_model = LinearRegression()
lr_model.fit(X_train, y_train)

coeff_df = pd.DataFrame({
    'Feature': X.columns,
    'Coefficient': lr_model.coef_
```

```
}).sort_values(by='Coefficient', ascending=False)

plt.figure(figsize=(10, 6))
sns.barplot(data=coeff_df, x='Coefficient', y='Feature', pal-
ette='coolwarm')
plt.title('Feature Importance (Linear Regression Coefficients)')
plt.axvline(0, color='gray', linestyle='--')
plt.tight_layout()
plt.show()
```

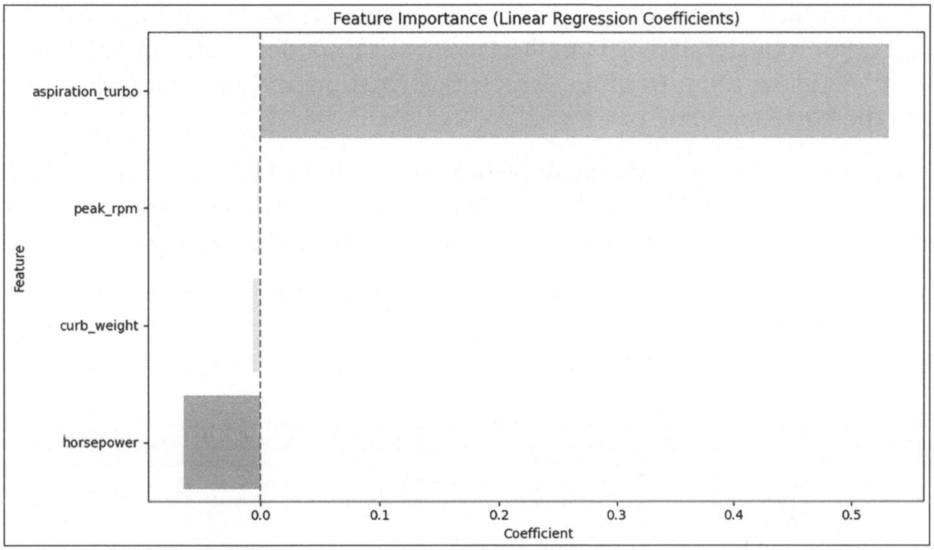

Figure 8.4: *Regression Coefficients from the Linear Model*

This makes sense intuitively as *Ceteris paribus* (Latin phrase that means "*all other things being equal*" or "*keeping other things constant*"), increasing horsepower by 1 unit can decrease mpg by ~0.1 (which is equivalent to the coefficient of horsepower).

Conclusion from the Regression Model

To predict fuel efficiency, we have conducted an in-depth regression analysis using the UCI Automobile dataset. After using exploratory data analysis to understand feature distributions and correlations, we have selected relevant predictors based on domain intuition and statistical validity. Categorical features were transformed using dummy encoding, and multicollinearity was addressed through the Variance Inflation Factor (VIF) analysis, which revealed highly collinear variables such as width and **`wheel_base`**. We have previously evaluated multiple regression models, including Linear, Ridge, Lasso, Decision Trees, Random Forests, and Gradient Boosting, and have compared their performance via R^2 score and Mean Squared Error. The visualizations of feature importance and model metrics have provided further interpretability. This robust pipeline has allowed us to assess the variables that significantly influence city MPG and the ones that help us identify the most effective predictive models.

Detailed Classification Analysis to Categorize Vehicles

Classification involves assigning data points to predefined categories. Before performing analysis, it is crucial to handle categorical features appropriately and address potential class imbalances within the target variable. In the Automobile dataset, creating three price bands (like economy, mid-range, and luxury) offers a mechanism to filter cars for potential buyers, while streamlining their search based on budget. For a dealership, this multiclassification model could serve as a valuable tool, as it will allow them to input vehicle information and automatically categorize cars into the corresponding price level.

For this problem, let us perform data-driven binning of the pricing to decide on economy, mid-range, and luxury bands. We will create quintile bands of 0 to 33% as economy, 33% to 66% as mid-range, and anything above that as luxury.

```
# Let's make a copy of the dataframe df to modify it for
classification
df_copy = df.copy()

# Data-driven price range binning using quantiles

quantile_edges = df_class['price'].quantile([0, 0.33, 0.66,
1.0]).values
price_labels = ['Economy', 'Mid-range', 'Luxury']
df_class['price_range'] = pd.cut(df_class['price'],
bins=quantile_edges, labels=price_labels, include_lowest=True)
```

To begin structuring our model, we will first define the initial set of features. Then, we will prepare the data for analysis by converting categorical variables into dummy variables and splitting the dataset into independent variables (X) and dependent variables (y). It is also a good practice to apply standardization (using **`StandardScaler()`**) to numeric variables. Many classification algorithms (like Support Vector Machines or those using distance-based calculations) are sensitive to the scale of the input features. If a feature has a much larger range of values than others, it can dominate the distance calculations and introduce bias in the model.

```
# Features to use for classification
features_class = [
    'curb_weight', 'engine_size', 'horsepower', 'compression_
ratio', 'peak_rpm',
    'wheel_base', 'length', 'width', 'fuel_type', 'aspiration',
'engine_location',
    'drive_wheels', 'num_cylinders', 'body_style'
]
```

```
df_class = df_class[features_class + ['price_range']].dropna()

# Convert categorical to dummy variables
cat_features_class = ['fuel_type', 'aspiration',
'engine_location', 'drive_wheels', 'num_cylinders', 'body_style']
df_class = pd.get_dummies(df_class, columns=cat_features_class,
drop_first=True)

# Split into X and y
X_class = df_class.drop(columns='price_range')
y_class = df_class['price_range']
```

Just like in regression analysis, various techniques can be used to select the most relevant features for training classification models. One such method is ANOVA (Analysis of Variance), a statistical approach to assess the variance of a numerical variable across different categories. To implement this, **SelectKBest** calculates the ANOVA F-statistic for each numerical feature in the dataset with respect to the categorical target variable.

Each feature is then assigned a score based on its F-statistic and the top "K" features with the highest scores are selected. This process reduces the number of input features, which ultimately speeds up training, simplifies the model, and prevents overfitting.

```
from sklearn.feature_selection import SelectKBest, f_classif
selector = SelectKBest(score_func=f_classif, k=10)
X_selected = selector.fit_transform(X_class, y_class)
selected_features = X_class.columns[selector.get_support()].
tolist()
X_selected_df = pd.DataFrame(X_selected, columns=selected_
features)
```

Once the features are selected, we can decide on the algorithm for the classification problem. Logistic regression is a fundamentally linear model designed for binary classification by using the sigmoid function to estimate probabilities. To extend it to multi-class, we need strategies like One-vs-Rest or Softmax to create multiple binary classifiers or modify the probability estimation. Tree-based methods (like Random Forest or Decision Trees) can inherently handle multiple classes through their structure of splitting data. Hence, **LogisticRegression()** function has additional parameters like **multi_class='multinomial'** and **solver='lbfgs'** to accommodate multiple classes.

```
# Multiple Models with Hyperparameter Tuning and Evaluation
models = {
    'Logistic Regression': LogisticRegression(multi_class
='multinomial', solver='lbfgs', max_iter=5000),
    'Random Forest': RandomForestClassifier(random_state=42),
    'K-Nearest Neighbors': KNeighborsClassifier(),
```

```
    'Gradient Boosting': GradientBoostingClassifier(random_
state=42),
    'Decision Tree': DecisionTreeClassifier(random_state=42)
}

results = []

for name, model in models.items():
    model.fit(X_train_class, y_train_class)
    y_pred = model.predict(X_test_class)
    acc = accuracy_score(y_test_class, y_pred)
    f1 = f1_score(y_test_class, y_pred, average='weighted')
    results.append((name, acc, f1))
    print(f"\n{name} Classification Report:")
    print(classification_report(y_test_class, y_pred))
```

Evaluating a classification model involves using several metrics to understand its performance. The confusion matrix provides a detailed breakdown of correct and incorrect predictions, showing true positives, true negatives, false positives, and false negatives. '**Accuracy**' is the most straightforward metric, as it measures the overall proportion of correct predictions. However, accuracy can be misleading in cases of imbalanced classes. The 'F1 Score' provides a balanced measure of a model's precision and recall, which is especially useful when classes are unevenly distributed. The ROC Curve (Receiver Operating Characteristic Curve) visualizes a model's ability to distinguish between classes across different classification thresholds. This is useful in assessing the trade-off between the true positive rate and the false positive rate.

In our exemplar dataset, accuracy and F1 scores were calculated for each model while it was being run. Often, the best way to understand model performance is to visualize the results in the following way:

```
from sklearn.metrics import ConfusionMatrixDisplay

cm = confusion_matrix(y_test_class, y_pred, labels=price_labels)
disp = ConfusionMatrixDisplay(confusion_matrix=cm, display_
labels=price_labels)
disp.plot(cmap='Blues')
plt.title(f'Confusion Matrix - {name}')
plt.show()
```

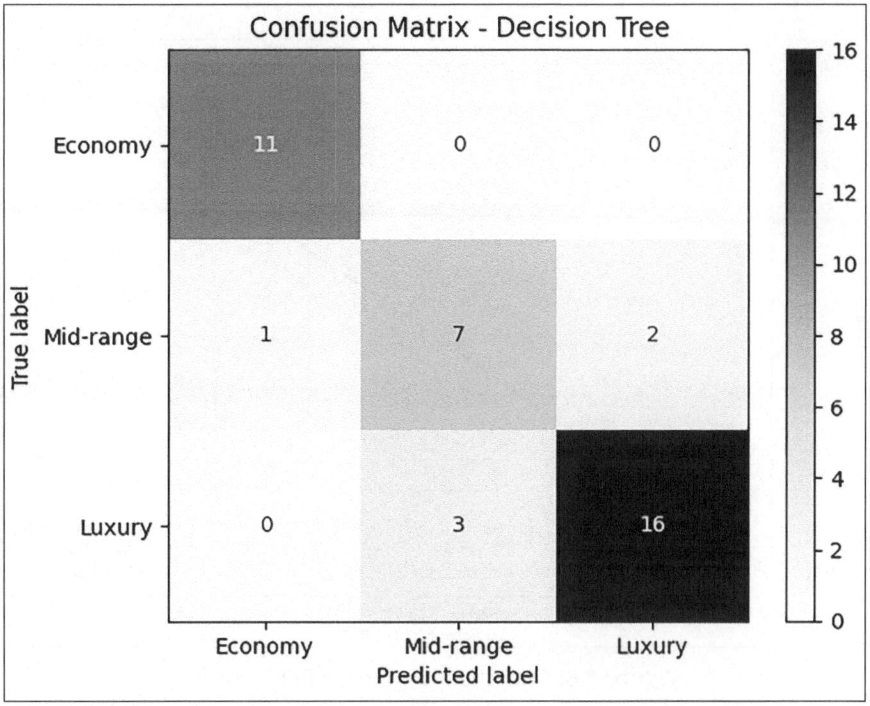

Figure 8.5: *Classification Model: Multilevel Confusion Matrix*

```
# Plot ROC Curve
plt.figure(figsize=(8, 6))
for i in range(y_test_bin.shape[1]):
    fpr, tpr, _ = roc_curve(y_test_bin[:, i], y_proba[:, i])
    plt.plot(fpr, tpr, label=f"Class {price_labels[i]}")
plt.plot([0, 1], [0, 1], 'k--')
plt.title('ROC Curve (Random Forest)')
plt.xlabel('False Positive Rate')
plt.ylabel('True Positive Rate')
plt.legend()
plt.tight_layout()
plt.show()
```

To further visualize the classification results, we can use an ROC curve. As demonstrated by the confusion matrix, the model has achieved 100% accuracy in predicting the Economy class. This means that for the **Economy** class, the model has correctly identified all actual Economy class instances, which has resulted in a True Positive Rate of 1. This value is clearly shown on the ROC curve.

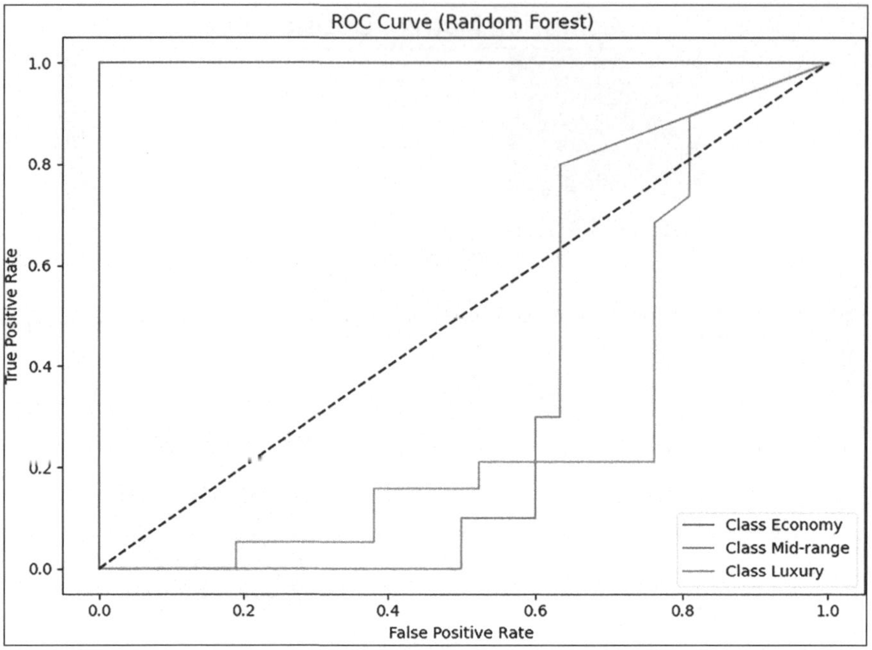

Figure 8.6: *Classification Model: ROC Curve*

Conclusion from the Classification Model

In conclusion, our application of multi-class classification to the "**`Automobile`**" dataset demonstrates a systematic approach to categorizing vehicles. This process carries significant implications for both buyers and sellers. So far, applying this approach to the selected dataset has involved a carefully orchestrated sequence of steps: first is feature selection, where techniques like ANOVA F-statistic helped us identify the most relevant attributes for prediction; second, feature scaling, which used **`StandardScaler`** to ensure equitable contribution of each feature to the model; third, training and comparing various classification models that are suited to tackle different aspects of the dataset; and finally, conducting a thorough evaluation of model performance using a confusion matrix and metrics like accuracy, precision, recall, F1-score, and ROC curves for a holistic understanding of the model's strengths and limitations. By following this methodology, we have transformed raw vehicle data into actionable intelligence. This showcases the power of classification algorithms to streamline decision-making in the automotive domain.

Comprehensive Clustering Analysis to Identify Groups of Similar Vehicles

This section transitions to unsupervised learning, focusing on the application of clustering analysis. Clustering techniques will be employed to identify inherent groupings within the **Automobile** dataset. This approach enables the discovery of structure in the data without relying on predefined labels, while revealing potential relationships and segments among the vehicles based on their attributes.

Unlike supervised learning, which relies on labeled data, unsupervised learning algorithms like K-Means or DBSCAN uncover structure from unlabeled data. These algorithms group data points based on similarity, using distance metrics to determine how close data points are to each other. A crucial aspect of clustering is data preprocessing, which may involve feature scaling and dimensionality reduction to ensure meaningful results. Evaluating the "accuracy" of clustering presents a unique challenge, as there are no "**correct**" labels. Instead, evaluation metrics focus on the quality and separation of the resulting clusters, while assessing how compact clusters are and how well-separated they are from each other.

For clustering analysis, the preprocessing stage involved several key steps to ensure data quality and suitability for the algorithm. Initially, rows containing missing values are removed to avoid introducing bias or errors during the clustering process. To prevent data leakage, where information from a target variable influences the clustering, the **price_range** column is omitted. Numerical features are then scaled using StandardScaler to give them equal weight and prevent features with larger values from dominating the distance calculations in KMeans. Finally, the K-Means algorithm is applied and the optimal number of clusters is determined using a combination of the elbow and silhouette methods. This helps an analyst develop a more informed and robust clustering solution.

```
df_cluster = df_class.drop(columns=['price_range'])
X_cluster_scaled = scaler.fit_transform(df_cluster)
```

The **Elbow** and **Silhouette** Methods are two handy tools for figuring out the optimal number of clusters during clustering analysis:

- **Elbow Method:** Imagine plotting a graph where the X-axis is the number of clusters (k) and the Y-axis is the within-cluster sum of squares (WCSS). WCSS measures the total distance of data points to their respective cluster centroids. Initially, as you increase k, WCSS decreases sharply. However, at some point, adding more clusters provides diminishing returns, and the decrease in WCSS becomes less significant. The "**elbow**" point on the graph, where the rate of decrease changes noticeably, is often considered a good estimate for the optimal k.
- **Silhouette Method:** This method provides a way to assess how well each data point fits within its assigned cluster. For each data point, a silhouette coefficient is calculated, ranging from -1 to 1. A score close to +1 indicates that the point is well-clustered; a score around 0 suggests it is near a cluster boundary, while a negative score implies it might be in the wrong cluster. The average silhouette score across all data points gives an overall measure

of clustering quality. By calculating the average silhouette score for different values of k, you can identify the k that maximizes the score, thereby indicating better-defined clusters.

```
# Elbow and Silhouette Method
inertia = []
silhouette = []
K = range(2, 10)
for k in K:
    model = KMeans(n_clusters=k, random_state=42)
    model.fit(X_cluster_scaled)
    inertia.append(model.inertia_)
    silhouette.append(silhouette_score(X_cluster_scaled, model.
labels_))

plt.figure(figsize=(10, 4))
plt.subplot(1, 2, 1)
plt.plot(K, inertia, marker='o')
plt.title('Elbow Method (Inertia)')
plt.xlabel('Number of clusters')
plt.ylabel('Inertia')

plt.subplot(1, 2, 2)
plt.plot(K, silhouette, marker='o')
plt.title('Silhouette Score')
plt.xlabel('Number of clusters')
plt.ylabel('Score')
plt.tight_layout()
plt.show()
```

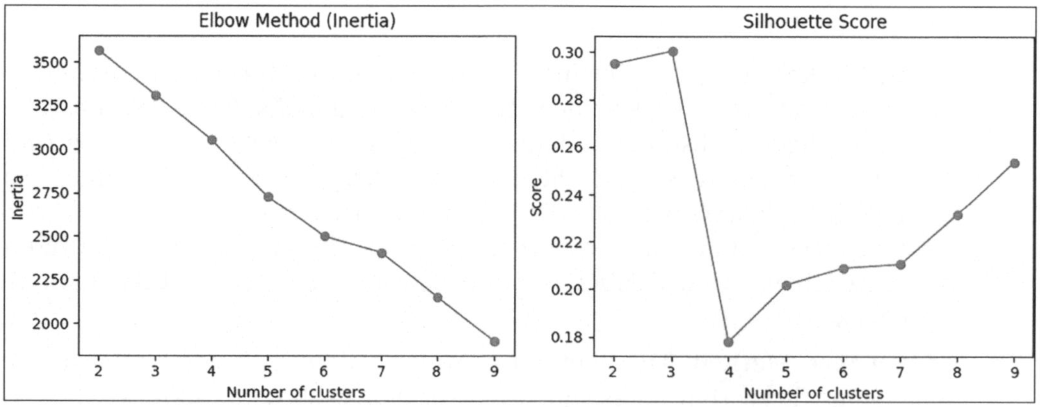

***Figure 8.7**: Elbow Method and Silhouette Score*

Since we ran the classification on the same data set, it will be interesting to view the average of features for each cluster. We can also try to infer and see if we see obvious differences, such as in the exemplar code here:

```
# Join with classification labels to interpret
df_viz = df_class.copy()
df_viz['cluster'] = df_cluster['cluster']

# Select only numeric columns for aggregation
numeric_cols = df_viz.select_dtypes(include=[np.number]).columns
grouped_stats = df_viz.groupby('cluster')[numeric_cols].mean()

styled_output = grouped_stats.style\
    .background_gradient(cmap='YlGnBu')\
    .format(precision=0)\
    .set_caption("Mean Values of Numeric Features per Cluster")

styled_output
```

Mean Values of Numeric Features per Cluster

cluster	curb_weight	engine_size	horsepower	compression_ratio	peak_rpm	wheel_base	length	width	cluster
0	2240	106	90	9	5230	95	165	65	0
1	3180	173	144	10	5019	105	187	68	1
2	3141	154	119	14	5040	106	188	70	2
3	2304	108	85	11	5106	97	171	65	3

***Figure 8.8**: Comparison of Clusters with Classification Features*

While all clusters have differences, clusters 1 and 2 have very similar **curb_weight**, **length**, but a stark difference in **compression_ratio** shows the differences in engine parameters.

Let us compare other parameters for these clusters.

```
# Apply KMeans with chosen k (for example, k=3)
kmeans = KMeans(n_clusters=4, random_state=42)
df_cluster['cluster'] = kmeans.fit_predict(X_cluster_scaled)
# Pairplot of selected features by cluster
sns.pairplot(df_viz[['curb_weight', 'engine_size', 'horsepower',
'cluster']], hue='cluster', palette='Set2')
plt.suptitle("Feature Distributions by Cluster", y=1.02)
plt.show()
```

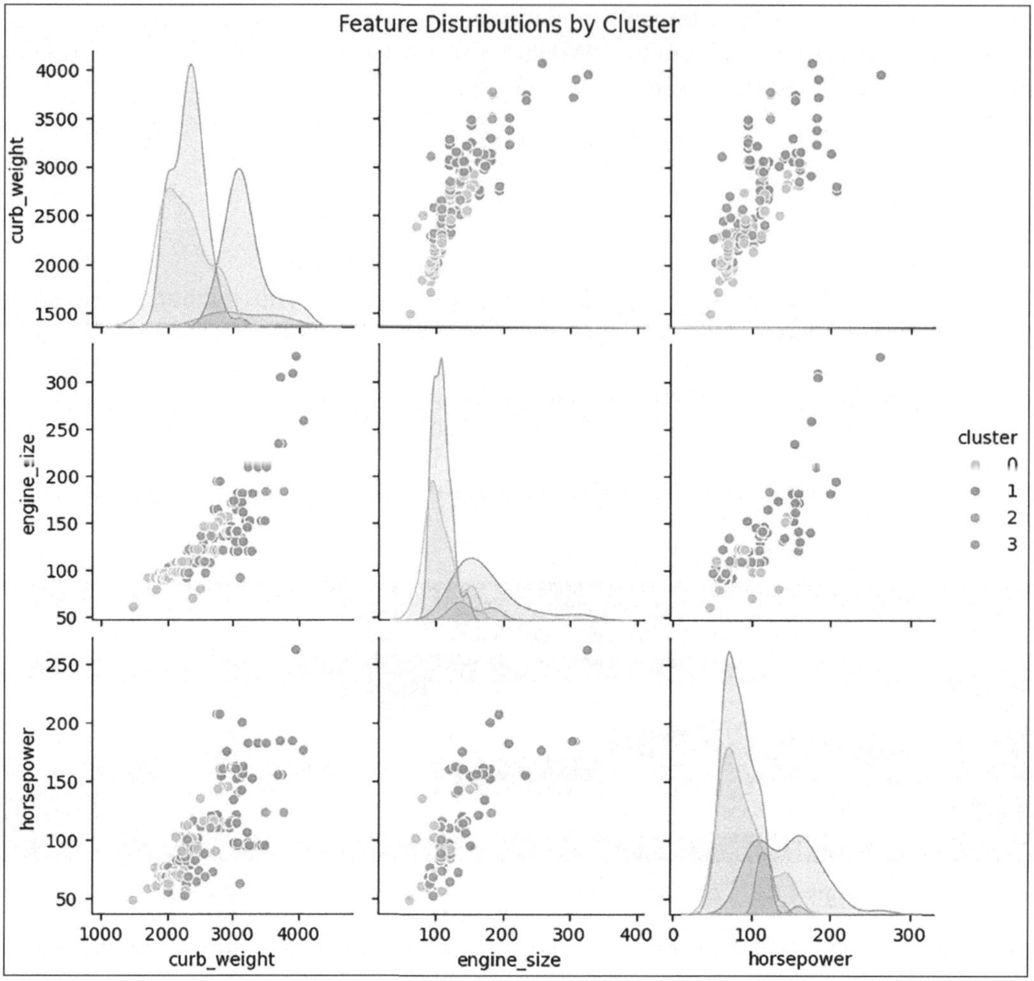

Figure 8.9: *Cluster Distributions and Feature Comparisons*

Visualizing clusters using PCA serves several important purposes. Firstly, PCA reduces the dimensionality of the data from many features to just two or three principal components. This makes it possible to plot the clusters and grasp their structure. This dimensionality reduction is crucial because it is far easier to visualize data in two or three dimensions than in higher-dimensional space. Secondly, PCA strives to preserve the original distances between data points during this reduction, which maintains the separation between clusters that existed in the original data. This means that if the clustering algorithm effectively identified distinct groups, PCA visualization should reflect it. Finally, visualizing with PCA allows for a qualitative assessment of cluster separation: we can directly observe whether clusters are well-defined and clearly distinct or if there is significant overlap, which indicates less effective clustering.

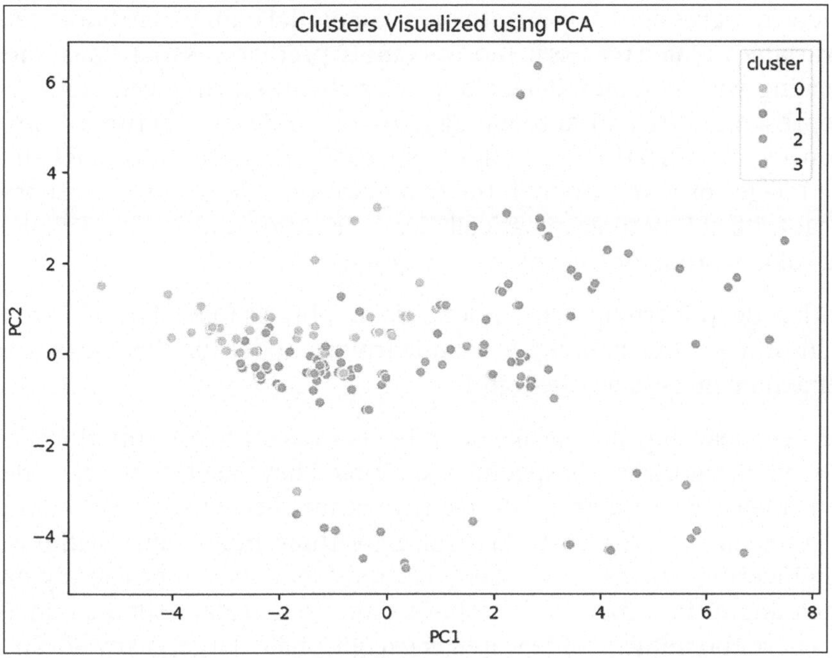

Figure 8.10: *Clusters Comparison with PC1 and PC2*

Conclusion from the Clustering Analysis

In summary, applying clustering techniques to the Automobile dataset allows us to identify inherent groupings within data. Through careful preprocessing and using appropriate evaluation methods, it is possible to derive meaningful segments from a collection of vehicle attributes. This analysis demonstrates the utility of clustering in uncovering underlying data structures. It is therefore valuable for applications such as market analysis, customer segmentation, and product development.

Further Explorations, Advanced Techniques and Potential Extensions

While this chapter has covered fundamental machine learning algorithms, the field continues to evolve with advanced techniques. Deep learning, which is inspired by the structure of the human brain, offers powerful tools to tackle complex problems across various domains. Neural networks, which form the core of deep learning, consist of interconnected layers of nodes that learn intricate patterns from data. These models have achieved remarkable success in areas such as image and speech recognition, natural language processing, and even in enhancing traditional tasks like regression and classification.

For instance, in regression, neural networks can model highly non-linear relationships between variables, which results in more accurate predictions than linear models when we are dealing with complex datasets. In classification, they can learn hierarchical feature representations and automatically extract relevant features from raw data. This improves classification accuracy, especially in tasks with high-dimensional inputs like images or text. Although the computational demands of deep learning can be significant, its ability to automatically learn features and model complex patterns makes it a valuable tool for further exploration in ML.

Implementing deep learning can be done using libraries like *TensorFlow*, *Keras*, and PyTorch. In other words running a deep learning model for this dataset will be like bringing machine guns to a knife fight!

In general, deep learning models like neural networks often are superior than classical machine learning algorithms in specific scenarios. They excel when one is dealing with highly non-linear or intricate relationships within the data. Using them effectively captures complex patterns that classical algorithms might miss without extensive feature engineering. Furthermore, deep learning models can efficiently process and extract meaningful information from high-dimensional data such as images, audio, and text, where the number of features is exceptionally large. A key advantage lies in their ability to automatically learn relevant features from raw data, which simplifies the workflow compared to classical methods that require manual feature engineering. However, it is important to note that deep learning models typically require and benefit from very large datasets to achieve optimal performance and generalization.

Appendix: Running Regression, Classification, and Clustering in R

This section will explore how to implement one of the previously developed ML models using the R programming language. One such illustration is demonstrated as follows:

```
# Required libraries
library(tidyverse)
library(caret)
library(GGally)
library(car)
library(corrplot)
library(data.table)
library(randomForest)
library(gbm)
library(MASS)
library(glmnet)
library(e1071)
```

```
# Load dataset
data_url <- "https://archive.ics.uci.edu/ml/machine-learning-
databases/autos/imports-85.data"
column_names <- c(
  "symboling", "normalized_losses", "make", "fuel_type",
"aspiration", "num_doors",
  "body_style", "drive_wheels", "engine_location", "wheel_base",
"length", "width",
  "height", "curb_weight", "engine_type", "num_cylinders",
"engine_size", "fuel_system",
  "bore", "stroke", "compression_ratio", "horsepower",
"peak_rpm", "city_mpg",
  "highway_mpg", "price"
)

df <- fread(data_url, na.strings = "?", col.names = column_names)

# Exploratory Data Analysis
cat("\nDataset shape:\n")
print(dim(df))

cat("\nData types and non-null values:\n")
print(str(df))

cat("\nSummary statistics:\n")
print(summary(df))

cat("\nMissing values per column:\n")
print(colSums(is.na(df)))

cat("\nUnique values in categorical columns:\n")
categorical_cols <- names(df)[sapply(df, is.character)]
sapply(df[, ..categorical_cols], function(x) length(unique(x)))

# Frequency tables
cat("\nFuel type distribution:\n")
print(table(df$fuel_type))

cat("\nBody style distribution:\n")
print(table(df$body_style))

# Correlation plot
numeric_df <- df %>% select_if(is.numeric)
corr <- cor(na.omit(numeric_df), use = "pairwise.complete.obs")
corrplot(corr, method = "color", type = "upper", tl.cex = 0.7,
number.cex = 0.7)
```

```
# Histograms
df %>% filter(!is.na(price)) %>%
  ggplot(aes(as.numeric(price))) +
  geom_histogram(bins = 30, fill = "skyblue") +
  labs(title = "Price Distribution", x = "Price", y = "Frequency")

df %>% filter(!is.na(horsepower)) %>%
  ggplot(aes(as.numeric(horsepower))) +
  geom_histogram(bins = 30, fill = "lightgreen") +
  labs(title = "Horsepower Distribution", x = "Horsepower", y =
"Frequency")

# Boxplot: Price by Fuel Type
df %>% filter(!is.na(price)) %>%
  ggplot(aes(fuel_type, as.numeric(price))) +
  geom_boxplot(fill = "lightcoral") +
  labs(title = "Price by Fuel Type", x = "Fuel Type", y =
"Price")

# ========================
# Regression Preparation
# ========================

selected_features <- c(
  'curb_weight', 'engine_size', 'horsepower', 'compression_
ratio', 'peak_rpm',
  'wheel_base', 'length', 'width', 'fuel_type', 'aspiration',
'engine_location',
  'drive_wheels', 'num_cylinders', 'body_style'
)
target <- 'city_mpg'

df_model <- df[, c(selected_features, target), with = FALSE] %>%
na.omit()

# Convert categorical variables to dummy variables
df_model <- dummyVars(~ ., data = df_model, fullRank = TRUE) %>%
  predict(newdata = df_model) %>%
  as.data.frame()

# Split data
set.seed(42)
trainIndex <- createDataPartition(df_model[, target], p = 0.8,
list = FALSE)
train <- df_model[trainIndex, ]
test <- df_model[-trainIndex, ]
```

```
X_train <- train[, !names(train) %in% target]
y_train <- train[, target]
X_test <- test[, !names(test) %in% target]
y_test <- test[, target]

# VIF Calculation
vif_model <- lm(city_mpg ~ ., data = train)
vif_vals <- vif(vif_model)
vif_df <- data.frame(Feature = names(vif_vals), VIF = vif_vals)
print(vif_df[order(-vif_df$VIF), ])

# ========================
# Model Training & Testing
# ========================

models <- list(
  LinearRegression = train,
  Ridge = function(...) train(..., method = "ridge"),
  Lasso = function(...) train(..., method = "lasso"),
  DecisionTree = function(...) train(..., method = "rpart"),
  RandomForest = function(...) train(..., method = "rf"),
  GradientBoosting = function(...) train(..., method = "gbm",
verbose = FALSE),
  KNN = function(...) train(..., method = "knn")
)

results <- data.frame(Model = character(), R2 = numeric(), MSE
= numeric(), stringsAsFactors = FALSE)

for (name in names(models)) {
  model <- models[[name]](X_train, y_train, trControl = trainCon-
trol(method = "none"))
  pred <- predict(model, X_test)
  r2 <- R2(pred, y_test)
  mse <- mean((y_test - pred)^2)
  results <- rbind(results, data.frame(Model = name, R2 = r2, MSE
= mse))
}

print(results[order(-results$R2), ])

# ========================
# Visualizations
# ========================

results %>%
  ggplot(aes(reorder(Model, R2), R2)) +
```

```
  geom_col(fill = "steelblue") +
  coord_flip() +
  labs(title = "Model Comparison: R² Score", x = "Model", y
= "R² Score")

results %>%
  ggplot(aes(reorder(Model, -MSE), MSE)) +
  geom_col(fill = "darkorange") +
  coord_flip() +
  labs(title = "Model Comparison: Mean Squared Error", x
= "Model", y = "MSE")

# ========================
# Linear Coefficients Plot
# ========================

linear_model <- lm(city_mpg ~ ., data = train)
coeff_df <- data.frame(
  Feature = names(coef(linear_model))[-1],
  Coefficient = coef(linear_model)[-1]
)

ggplot(coeff_df, aes(x = reorder(Feature, Coefficient), y
= Coefficient)) +
  geom_bar(stat = "identity", fill = "skyblue") +
  coord_flip() +
  labs(title = "Feature Importance (Linear Regression)", x =
"Feature", y = "Coefficient")
```

Code for Classification and Clustering

```
# Load Required Libraries
install.packages(c("tidyverse", "caret", "randomForest", "e1071",
"nnet", "cluster", "factoextra", "pROC", "reshape2", "gridExtra",
"GGally", "RColorBrewer", "NbClust", "glmnet"))
library(tidyverse)
library(caret)
library(randomForest)
library(e1071)
library(pROC)
library(factoextra)
library(cluster)
library(reshape2)
library(GGally)
library(NbClust)
library(glmnet)

# Load Data
```

```
data_url <- "https://archive.ics.uci.edu/ml/machine-learning-
databases/autos/imports-85.data"
column_names <- c("symboling", "normalized_losses", "make",
"fuel_type", "aspiration", "num_doors",
                  "body_style", "drive_wheels", "engine_
location", "wheel_base", "length", "width",
                  "height", "curb_weight", "engine_type",
"num_cylinders", "engine_size", "fuel_system",
                  "bore", "stroke", "compression_ratio",
"horsepower", "peak_rpm", "city_mpg",
                  "highway_mpg", "price")
df <- read.csv(data_url, header = FALSE, na.strings = "?", col.
names = column_names, stringsAsFactors = TRUE)

# Preprocessing
df <- df[complete.cases(df$price), ]
df$price <- as.numeric(as.character(df$price))

# Create price_range based on quantiles
quantiles <- quantile(df$price, probs = c(0, 0.33, 0.66, 1))
df$price_range <- cut(df$price, breaks = quantiles, labels =
c("Economy", "Mid-range", "Luxury"), include.lowest = TRUE)

# Feature Selection
features <- c("curb_weight", "engine_size", "horsepower",
"compression_ratio", "peak_rpm",
              "wheel_base", "length", "width", "fuel_type",
"aspiration", "engine_location",
              "drive_wheels", "num_cylinders", "body_style")
df_model <- df[, c(features, "price_range")]
df_model <- df_model[complete.cases(df_model), ]

# Convert categorical variables
df_model <- dummyVars(price_range ~ ., data = df_model, fullRank
= TRUE) %>%
  predict(newdata = df_model) %>%
  as.data.frame() %>%
  cbind(price_range = df$price_range[complete.cases(df_model)])

# Standardization
scaler <- preProcess(df_model[, -ncol(df_model)], method =
c("center", "scale"))
X_scaled <- predict(scaler, df_model[, -ncol(df_model)])
y <- df_model$price_range

# Feature selection using ANOVA F-test
anova_scores <- apply(X_scaled, 2, function(x) summary(aov(x ~
```

```
y))[[1]][["F value"]][1])
top_features <- names(sort(anova_scores, decreasing = TRUE)
[1:10])
X_selected <- X_scaled[, top_features]

# Train-test split
set.seed(42)
train_index <- createDataPartition(y, p = 0.8, list = FALSE)
X_train <- X_selected[train_index, ]
X_test <- X_selected[-train_index, ]
y_train <- y[train_index]
y_test <- y[-train_index]

# Models
models <- list(
  Logistic = train(x = X_train, y = y_train, method = "multinom",
trace = FALSE),
  RandomForest = train(x = X_train, y = y_train, method = "rf"),
  KNN = train(x = X_train, y = y_train, method = "knn"),
  GradientBoosting = train(x = X_train, y = y_train, method =
"gbm", verbose = FALSE),
  DecisionTree = train(x = X_train, y = y_train, method =
"rpart")
)

# Evaluation
results <- data.frame(Model = character(), Accuracy = numeric(),
F1 = numeric())

for (name in names(models)) {
  pred <- predict(models[[name]], X_test)
  acc <- mean(pred == y_test)
  f1 <- F_meas(data = pred, reference = y_test, relevant
= levels(y_test))
  results <- rbind(results, data.frame(Model = name, Accuracy =
acc, F1 = f1))
  cat("\n", name, "Classification Report\n")
  print(confusionMatrix(pred, y_test))
}

# Accuracy & F1 Plot
results_long <- melt(results, id.vars = "Model")
ggplot(results_long, aes(x = reorder(Model, -value), y = value,
fill = variable)) +
  geom_bar(stat = "identity", position = position_dodge()) +
  labs(title = "Model Accuracy & F1 Score Comparison", y = "", x
= "Model") +
```

```
  theme_minimal()

# ROC Curve for Random Forest
rf_model <- models$RandomForest
rf_probs <- predict(rf_model, X_test, type = "prob")
y_test_bin <- model.matrix(~ y_test - 1)

par(mfrow = c(1, 1))
for (i in 1:ncol(rf_probs)) {
  roc_obj <- roc(y_test_bin[, i], rf_probs[, i])
  plot(roc_obj, col = i + 1, main = "ROC Curves", add = i != 1)
}
legend("bottomright", legend = colnames(rf_probs), col =
2:(ncol(rf_probs) + 1), lwd = 2)

# ====================
# Clustering Analysis
# ====================
# Use full X_scaled for clustering
set.seed(42)
fviz_nbclust(X_scaled, kmeans, method = "wss") + labs(title
= "Elbow Method")
fviz_nbclust(X_scaled, kmeans, method = "silhouette") + labs
(title = "Silhouette Method")

# KMeans with k = 3
kmeans_model <- kmeans(X_scaled, centers = 3, nstart = 25)
df_model$cluster <- factor(kmeans_model$cluster)

# PCA for visualization
pca_res <- prcomp(X_scaled, center = TRUE, scale. = TRUE)
pca_df <- data.frame(pca_res$x[, 1:2], Cluster = df_model$cluster)

ggplot(pca_df, aes(x = PC1, y = PC2, color = Cluster)) +
  geom_point(alpha = 0.7) +
  labs(title = "PCA Cluster Visualization") +
  theme_minimal()
```

Conclusion

In this chapter, we explored the Automobile dataset and demonstrated its application across both supervised and unsupervised learning tasks. Through detailed regression analysis, we predicted vehicle prices and fuel efficiency, while the classification section focused on categorizing cars based on features such as body style and price range. We further employed clustering techniques to uncover natural groupings within the data, while highlighting similarities among vehicles. The chapter concluded with advanced explorations and an R-based appendix that reinforced concepts through cross-language implementation. These exercises provided a comprehensive, hands-on understanding of core ML techniques.

In the next chapter, we will focus on exercising Version Control using Git, which is an essential tool for managing code, collaboration, and project tracking in data science workflows.

References

https://archive.ics.uci.edu/dataset/10/automobile

Schlimmer, J. (1985). Automobile [Dataset]. UCI Machine Learning Repository. https://doi.org/10.24432/C5B01C.

Chapter 9
Version Control with Git

Introduction

Imagine that you are writing a Python application, and your code evolves with the passage of time. You add new features, fix bugs, and re-factor sections to optimize performance. But what if you make a mistake or break something in the process? Version control is the solution to this problem.

Version control is a system that tracks changes to your code, so that you can:

- View the history of your project.
- Undo changes if something breaks.
- Collaborate with others without worrying about losing work.

In Python development (or any software development), version control is essential as it allows you to track, manage, and share changes efficiently. In this chapter, we are going to focus on version control with one Git, which is a specific system that you will use extensively in your data science journey going forward.

Structure

This chapter will address the following topics:

- Understanding Git
- GitHub
- Getting Started with GitHub
- Using PyCharm to Manage Git and GitHub
- Understanding Branching
- Merging Changes
- Pull Requests on GitHub

- Resolving Merge Conflicts
- Rebasing: Cleaning Up Your Commit History

Understanding Git

Git is one of the most popular version control systems. It was created by Linus Torvalds, the creator of Linux, in 2005. Git is specifically useful for developers and data scientists who need to keep track of the history of their code–whether it is a simple Python script or a large project.

Git is an essential tool in data science workflows, offering several key features that support collaborative, iterative, and reproducible research. One of its most valuable capabilities is maintaining a local history, which allows data scientists to track the evolution of their code, notebooks, and datasets over time. Since Git locally stores the entire project history, it enables offline access to past versions, which makes it easier to experiment without the risk of losing previous work.

A critical aspect of data science is trying different models, parameters, or data preprocessing strategies. Git is branching and merging features support this by letting users create separate branches for testing new algorithms, feature engineering, or visualization approaches. These branches can be merged back into the main workflow once validated, thereby maintaining a clean and organized project structure.

Git also enhances collaboration, which is especially important in data science teams that often include data engineers, analysts, and domain experts. Git tracks each contributor's changes to code, notebooks, and documentation, making it easier to coordinate and avoid overwriting one another's work. Tools like GitHub and GitLab further streamline this process with features like pull requests and code reviews.

Finally, Git is distributed architecture gives every team member a full copy of the repository, including its entire history. This supports independent work and ensures that all experiments and analyses are reproducible and well-documented. In data science, where reproducibility is a cornerstone of credible results, Git provides a robust foundation for managing evolving codebases and collaborative research efforts.

GitHub

GitHub is a web-based platform built around Git. It provides a cloud-based repository to host your Git projects. It allows you to store your code, track issues, and collaborate with other developers on your Python projects. GitHub also adds extra features like wikis, discussions, and project boards to enhance collaboration.

GitHub is a powerful platform that extends Git is capabilities and offers features specifically designed to enhance collaboration, transparency, and project management in software and data science projects. At the heart of GitHub are **repositories**, which serve as centralized spaces to store and manage Python scripts, Jupyter Notebooks, datasets, and documentation. These repositories act as hubs for your entire data science project, where you can host and perform version control on your code, besides tracking progress and collaborating with team members.

One of GitHub's standout features is the **Pull Request (PR)** system, which enables structured and peer-reviewed development. After implementing a new feature, running an analysis, or cleaning a dataset, a data scientist can open a pull request to propose their changes. This invites team members to review the code, suggest improvements, and approve or request modifications before merging it into the main branch, thereby maintaining code quality and reproducibility.

Issues play a vital role in managing the various tasks within a data science project. Whether it is logging a bug in a data pipeline, planning a new visualization, or tracking the progress of a machine learning model, GitHub's issue tracker keeps all project tasks organized and visible. You can label, assign, and comment on issues, which will help you prioritize work and stay aligned with project goals.

Finally, GitHub is built for collaboration, which is fundamental in data science. Here, teams often span across disciplines and geographies. GitHub handles version control, conflict resolution, and team notifications, and makes it easier for multiple contributors to work together without stepping on each other's toes. By integrating seamlessly with tools like Git, Jupyter, and CI/CD platforms, GitHub becomes a central workspace for building, sharing, and maintaining robust data science workflows.

Getting Started with GitHub

Now that we know what version control, Git, GitHub, and PyCharm are, let us set them up and integrate them into a Python development workflow.

Step 1. Installing Git

You need to install Git on your system in order to use it. Here is how to do that:

a. **Downloading Git**: Visit https://git-scm.com/downloads and choose the version for your operating system (Windows, macOS, or Linux).

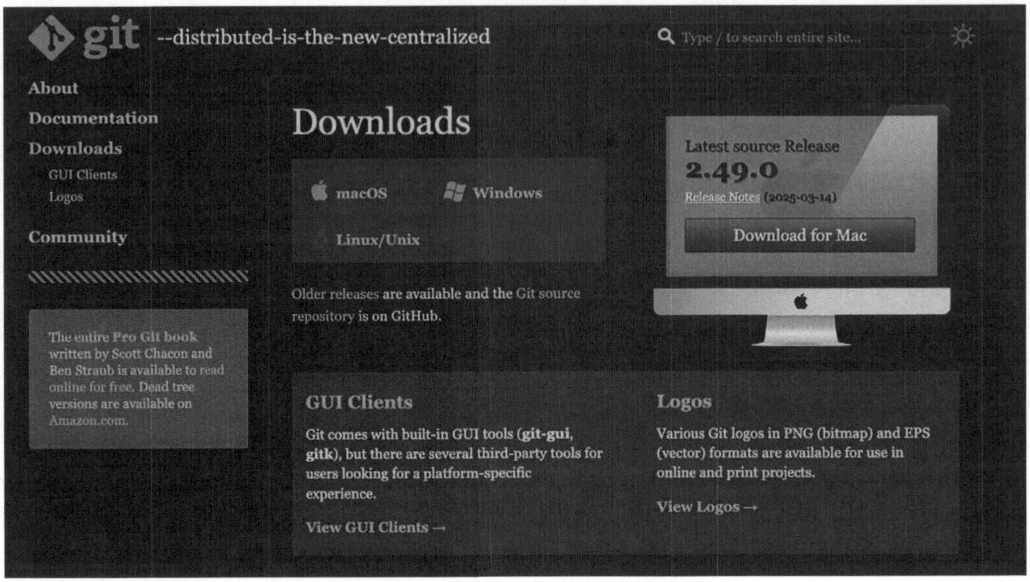

***Figure 9.1**: Git Download Page*

b. **Installing Git**: Follow the installation instructions. For most users, the default settings will be sufficient.

   Verify Installation: Once installed, open your terminal (or Git Bash on Windows) and check that Git is installed by typing:

   ```
   git --version
   ```

c. This should return the installed Git version.

***Figure 9.2**: Git Version*

Step 2. Configuring Git

Once Git is installed, configure it to use your name and email. This is a way to identify you in your project's history.

In your terminal, type the following commands:

```
git config --global user.name "Your Name"
git config --global user.email "your.email@example.com"
```

This sets your name and email for all Git repositories on your machine.

Step 3. Setting Up a Python Project with Git

Let us create a Python project and set it up with Git for version control.

a. **Create a Python Project**: Open your terminal, create a directory for your Python project, and navigate to it:

```
mkdir my_python_project
cd my_python_project
```

b. **Create a Python File**: Inside your project folder, create a simple Python file, for example, **`main.py`**, and write code like:

```
print("Hello, Git and GitHub!")
```

c. **Initialize Git**: Now, initialize Git to start tracking this project through:

```
git init
```

d. **Add the Python File to Git**: Tell Git to start tracking the **`main.py`** file:

```
git add main.py
```

e. **Commit the Changes**: After adding the file, commit the changes to your local repository:

```
git commit -m "Initial commit with main.py"
```

Step 4. Creating a GitHub Repository

Now that your project is set up locally, let us push it to GitHub.

a. **Create a new repository on GitHub**: Go to GitHub (https://github.com/) and sign in (or create an account).

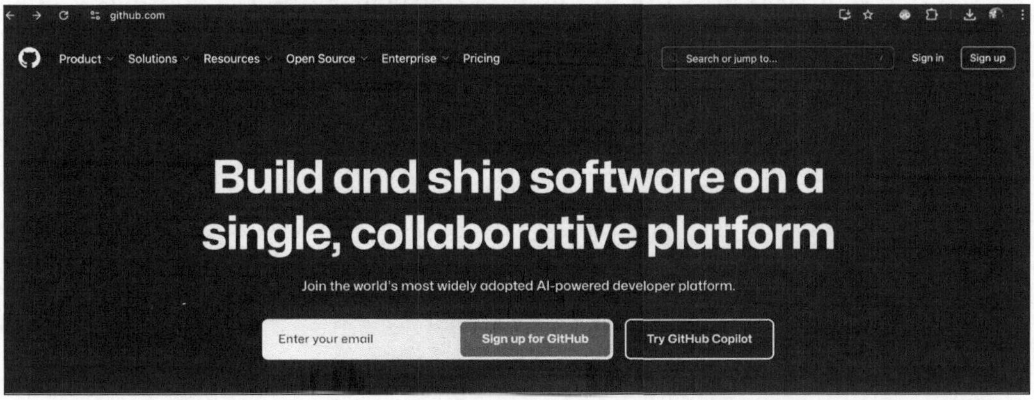

Figure 9.3: *githib.com Landing Page*

b. Click the **+** in the top-right corner and choose **`New repository`**.

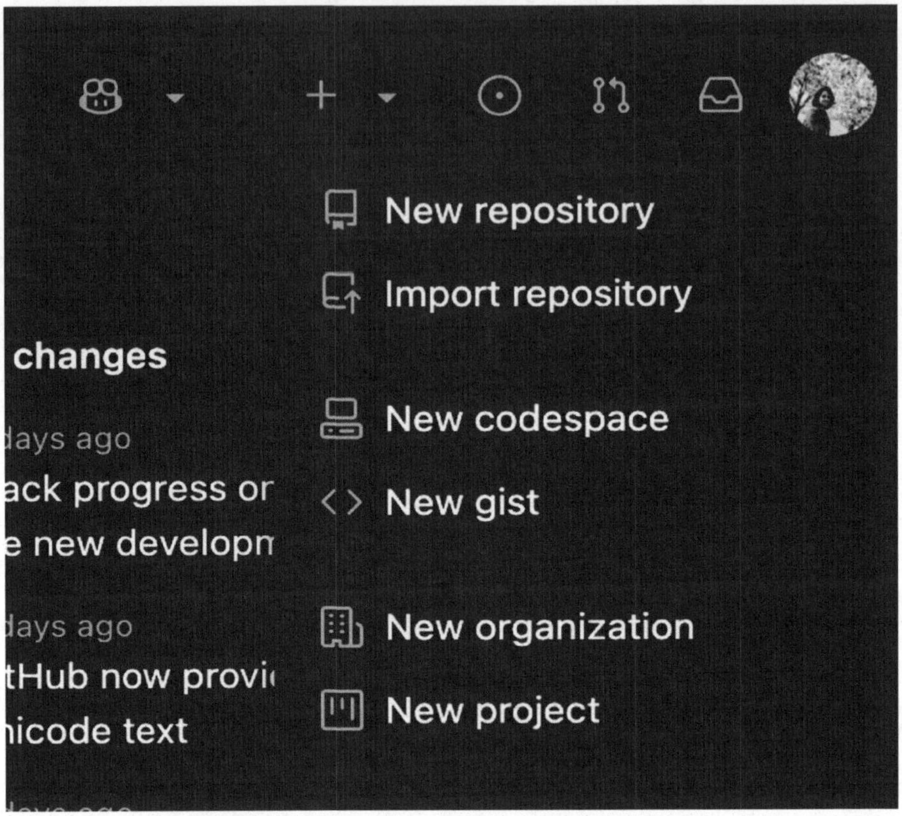

Figure 9.4: *Creating a New Repository in Github*

c. Name your repository (for example, **`my-python-project`**), choose its visibility (public or private), and click on **`Create repository`**.

c. **Push Changes**: After committing, you can push your changes to GitHub by going to **`Git > Push`** or pressing *Ctrl* + *Shift* + K (Windows/Linux) or *Cmd* + *Shift* + K (macOS). PyCharm will upload your changes to the GitHub repository.

Pulling Changes from GitHub

To fetch the latest changes from the GitHub repository, go to **`Git > Pull`** or press *Ctrl* + T (Windows/Linux) or *Cmd* + T (macOS). This will update your local copy with any changes made by collaborators.

Understanding Branching

When working on a Python project, it is common to add new features, fix bugs, or experiment with different approaches. **Branching** allows you to do this in an organized way.

A **branch** is essentially a parallel version of your project. Each branch contains the code you are working on, and you can switch between branches to work on different tasks. The advantage of branching is that it keeps your main project, typically called master or main, intact while you work on other things.

Why Use Branching?

Branching is a fundamental concept in version control systems like Git and is especially valuable in data science projects where experimentation, collaboration, and version stability are critical. One key benefit of using branches is **isolation**. When working on a new feature, such as implementing a new machine learning algorithm, testing a data preprocessing method, or improving a visualization, you can do so in a separate branch. This ensures that the main or stable version of your project remains unaffected and a working baseline is preserved while you explore new ideas.

Branching also significantly enhances **collaboration**. In a typical data science team, different members might be responsible for different aspects of a project, such as data cleaning, model development, or dashboard creation. With branching, each team member can work in their own isolated environment without interfering with others. Once their work is ready and reviewed, it can be merged into the main branch, streamlining teamwork and reducing the risk of conflicts.

Additionally, branching encourages **experimentation**. Data science thrives on iteration and testing, regardless of you trying out new features, testing model hyperparameters, or experimenting with alternative data sources. By creating a branch, you can test these ideas freely, knowing that any mistakes or failed attempts will not disrupt the primary codebase. This makes the development process more flexible, creative, and resilient, ultimately leading to better outcomes.

Creating a Branch in Git

To create a new branch in Git, use the following command:

```
git branch <branch-name>
```

This creates the branch but does not switch to it. To switch to the new branch, use:

```
git checkout <branch-name>
```

Alternatively, you can combine both commands using the following:

```
git checkout -b <branch-name>
```

Viewing Branches

To see a list of all branches in your Git project, run:

```
git branch
```

The current branch you are working on will be highlighted with an asterisk.

Example: Working on a New Feature

Let us say you are adding a new feature to your Python project. For instance, a function that returns the Fibonacci sequence. To work on this, follow these steps:

1. **Create a branch** for the new feature:

   ```
   git checkout -b fibonacci-feature
   ```

2. **Write the code** for the Fibonacci function in fibonacci.py:

   ```
   def fibonacci(n):
       a, b = 0, 1
       for _ in range(n):
           a, b = b, a + b
       return a
   ```

3. **Commit your changes**:

   ```
   git add fibonacci.py
   git commit -m "Add Fibonacci function"
   ```

Once you are happy with the feature, **merge** it back into the main branch.

Merging Changes

Once you have finished working on a branch, you will want to bring those changes back into the main project. This process is called **merging**.

Imagine you are working on a data science project with a team. You have one main version of your project (this is the main branch) that contains things like your cleaned dataset, analysis notebooks, or model code. Now, let us say you want to try a new experiment–maybe you are testing a different machine learning model or feature engineering approach. Instead of changing the main version directly, you create a new branch where you can work freely without messing up the main project.

Once you are happy with your experiment and want to keep it, you can use Git merge to integrate changes from your experiment branch into the main branch. Git will try to automatically combine the code, data, or notebooks. If there are no conflicting changes, it is done! However, if another user also made changes to the same part of a file (like a Jupyter Notebook), Git will ask you to fix the conflict manually before finishing the merge.

So, merging helps you safely try out new ideas (like testing a new model or cleaning data differently), and then combine them into the main project once you are ready. It is a way to collaborate without overwriting each other's work.

Merging in Git

To merge your branch into `main` (or `master`), follow these steps:

1. **Switch back to the main branch**:

   ```
   git checkout main
   ```
2. **Merge the feature branch** into main:

   ```
   git merge fibonacci-feature
   ```
3. **Push the changes** to GitHub:

   ```
   git push origin main
   ```

Merging combines the changes from the `fibonacci-feature` branch into `main`.

Once your branch is merged, you can delete it to keep your repository clean:

```
git branch -d fibonacci-feature
```

Pull Requests on GitHub

When working with a team, you often do not merge directly into the main branch yourself. Instead, you use **Pull Requests (PRs)** on GitHub to propose changes. A PR lets you show your changes, get feedback, and discuss the code before merging it into the main project.

A pull request (PR) is a way to propose changes to a project, typically used in collaborative environments like GitHub. It allows you to notify others that you have made changes to a branch (such as a new machine learning model or data cleaning process) and want those changes to be reviewed and merged into the main project.

When you create a pull request, you are essentially asking your team to "**`pull`**" your changes into their version of the project. Your team can then review the changes, leave comments, suggest improvements, and approve the merge. This process ensures that code is thoroughly checked before it becomes part of the main branch, which prevents errors and improves the overall quality of the project. For example, in a data science project, if you have added a new feature to a Jupyter Notebook, you would create a pull request to let your teammates review your code and results before integrating it into the main version. Once everyone is happy with the changes, the pull request is merged, and the updates are officially added to the project. This process helps maintain a smooth and organized workflow, especially when multiple people are contributing to the same project.

Creating a Pull Request

Here is how to create a pull request:

Push your branch to GitHub:

```
git push origin fibonacci-feature
```

1. Go to the **`GitHub repository`** in your browser.
2. GitHub will often prompt you with a message like "**`Compare & pull request`**" once you have pushed a branch. Click on that button.
3. Fill in the details for your pull request and click on **`Create pull request`**.

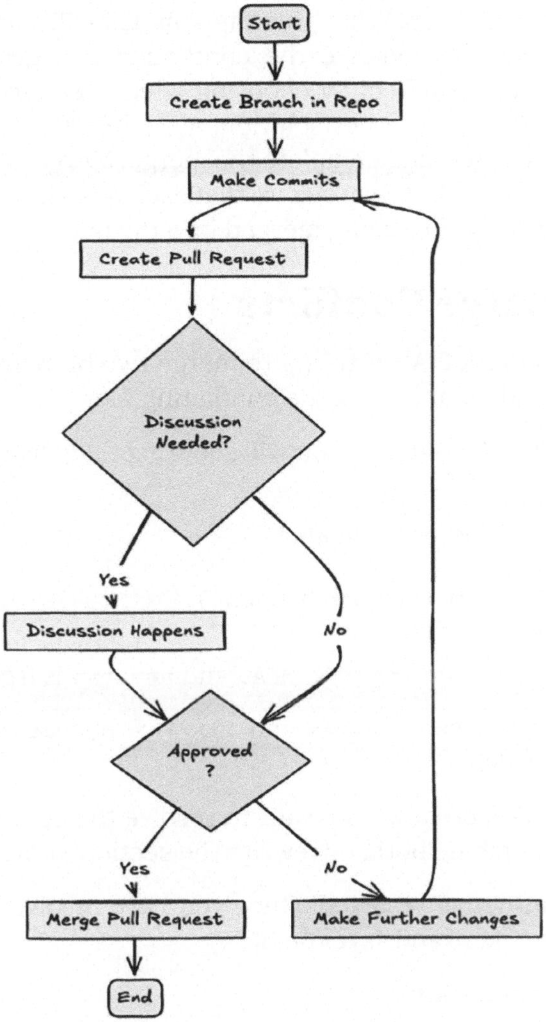

Figure 9.6: *Typical Workflow on GitHub*

You can now review the code, discuss changes, and once everyone is satisfied with it, you can **merge the pull request** into the main branch.

Resolving Merge Conflicts

A **merge conflict** occurs when Git is unable to automatically combine changes from two branches due to conflicting edits that are made to the same part of a file. This often happens in collaborative projects, such as data science work, when multiple people modify the same file (like a Jupyter Notebook) simultaneously. For example, if you and a teammate both change the same cell in a notebook—perhaps one person alters a data cleaning step while the other updates a machine learning model—Git will not know which version to keep. When this happens, Git will mark the file as conflicted and add special markers to indicate the conflicting changes. You must manually review and resolve these conflicts by choosing which version to keep, merging the changes together, or finding another solution. After resolving the conflict, you stage the file, commit the changes, and complete the merge. Merge conflicts are common in collaborative environments, but they ensure that each team member's work is properly integrated and reviewed before being merged into the main project.

How to Fix Merge Conflicts

1. **Identify the conflict**: After trying to merge two branches, Git will inform you if there is a conflict and mark the conflicting files.
2. **Open the file** with conflicts. You will see something like this:

   ```
   <<<<<<< HEAD
   print("Hello from main branch")
   =======
   print("Hello from feature branch")
   >>>>>>> fibonacci-feature
   ```

   a. The code between **`<<<<<<< HEAD`** and **`=======`** is from the **`main`** branch.

   b. The code between **`=======`** and **`>>>>>>> fibonacci-feature`** is from the feature branch.
3. **Edit the file**: Decide how you want to resolve the conflict. You might choose one version, combine both, or rewrite the section entirely.
4. **Mark the conflict as resolved**: Once you have resolved the conflict, remove the conflict markers and save the file.
5. **Commit the resolution**:

   ```
   git add <file-name>
   git commit -m "Resolve merge conflict in <file-name>"
   ```
6. **Push the changes**: Finally, push the resolved merge to GitHub:

   ```
   git push
   ```

Rebasing: Clean Up Your Commit History

Rebasing is a way to rewrite your Git history to make it cleaner and more linear. While **merging** creates a commit that combines the changes from two branches, **rebasing** re-applies your changes on top of another branch, which can make your project history easier to follow.

Example of Rebasing

Let us say you have been working on a feature and want to update it with the latest changes from **`main`** before merging:

1. **Switch to your feature branch**:

   ```
   git checkout fibonacci-feature
   ```

2. **Rebase your branch onto `main`**:

   ```
   git rebase main
   ```

   Git will re-apply your changes on top of **`main`**. If there are conflicts, resolve them in the manner described earlier.

3. **Push the changes** (with the **`--force`** flag, because you have rewritten history):

   ```
   git push origin fibonacci-feature --force
   ```

Before Rebase

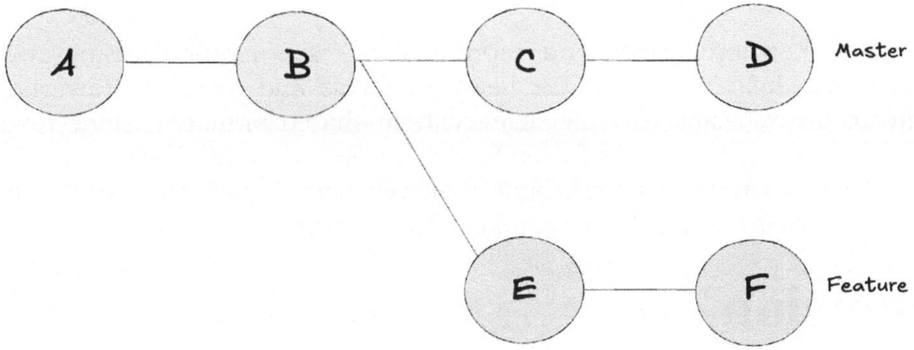

Figure 9.7: *A Different Feature Being Worked On*

After Rebase

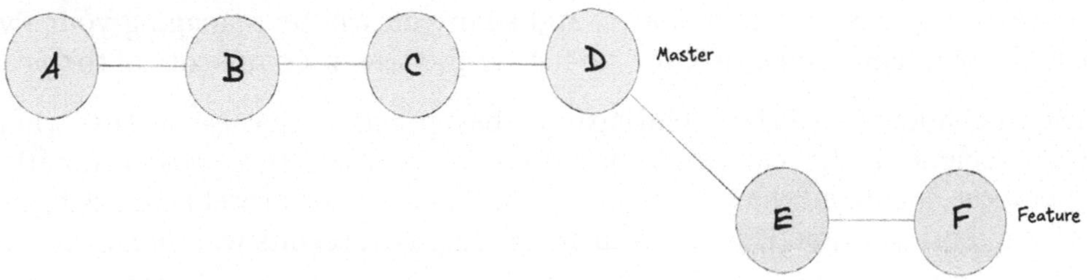

Figure 9.8: *Changes Reapplied on Top of Main*

When to Use Rebasing

Rebasing is a Git feature that can be particularly useful in data science projects when you want to maintain a streamlined and easy-to-follow project history. One of the main reasons to use rebasing is to create a **cleaner history**. Unlike merging, which combines changes from different branches and often results in merge commits, rebasing re-applies your changes directly onto the tip of another branch. This results in a linear, chronological history that is easier to read and understand. It is especially useful when reviewing the evolution of your data pipeline evolved or tracking the progression of a model over time.

Rebasing is especially effective in **small teams** or solo projects, where coordination overhead is lower. In these settings, rebasing allows you to continuously integrate your work with the latest changes from the main branch without cluttering the commit history with merge commits. For example, if you are working on a new analysis or training a model and want to stay up-to-date with the latest data or utility functions from the main branch, you can rebase your work to incorporate those updates seamlessly.

In data science, where clarity and reproducibility are essential, using rebasing strategically can help keep your Git history concise and focused. However, it is important to use rebasing carefully, especially in shared branches, since rewriting history can cause conflicts or confusion for others. For example, if you are working in a larger team, be cautious when rebasing. Avoid rebasing shared branches that others are working on, as it rewrites history and can lead to coordination problems.

Conclusion

In this chapter, you have learned some advanced Git features that are essential for managing larger Python projects and collaborating with others. By mastering branching, merging, pull requests, resolving merge conflicts, and rebasing, you can handle complex workflows and maintain a clean, organized Git history.

Keep practicing these Git techniques, and soon you will be managing your Python code with confidence and efficiency, no matter the size or complexity of the project!

In the next chapter, we will be exploring more best practices that you will use when you apply data science in the real world. You will learn how to organize projects for effective collaboration, document work clearly for reproducibility, and protect data using proper security and privacy practices. You will also ensure that results will remain consistent across different environments. In addition, you will be introduced to Deployment and MLOps, where production systems will rely on continuous monitoring, explainability, automation, and scalable infrastructure for reliable performance.

CHAPTER 10
Data Science and Analytics in Industry

Introduction

Pursuing a career in data science is rarely a solitary pursuit of discovery. It is a fast-paced, goal-driven practice deeply embedded in real-world constraints and collaborative environments. Unlike academic projects that may prioritize novelty or depth, industrial data science must deliver value quickly, repeatedly, and often under ambiguous requirements. This chapter aims to bridge the gap between technical skills and professional practice by outlining how to structure, document, secure, and share data science projects in ways that align with business goals and organizational workflows. By adopting these practices early, beginners can position themselves to contribute meaningfully to team-based data efforts and avoid common pitfalls in professional settings.

Structure

This chapter will address the following topics:

- Structuring Your Data Science Project
- Documentation and Commenting
- Data Security and Privacy
- Reproducibility in Data Science
- Deployment and MLOps

Structuring Your Data Science Project

In industrial settings, data science projects are rarely one-off explorations; they are part of a broader system where multiple people, tools, and business goals intersect. A well-structured project is essential for maintainability, collaboration, and long-term value. Without a clear structure, even the most insightful analysis can become difficult to interpret, reproduce, or scale.

This section outlines practical strategies to structure your data science project in a way that supports productivity, transparency, and team alignment from day one.

Start with Clear Objectives

Before writing any code, make sure you understand the purpose of the project. This can include the following questions:

- What business question are you trying to answer?
- What decisions will your results influence?

Clear objectives help keep the work focused and prevent unnecessary detours. Collaborate with stakeholders to define measurable goals and key performance indicators (KPIs). Instead of "*Improve sales,*" a better problem statement will be "*Predict which customers are most likely to churn in the next quarter.*" This helps you pack in more focus in your tasks.

It is critical to define success metrics for any project. The choice of metric will depend on the problem you are trying to solve. For example, how will you know if your model is successful? Define specific, quantifiable metrics such as accuracy, F1-score, or a business metric such as '*reducing customer churn by 5%*'. This will anchor the project to tangible outcomes.

Scope and Plan Your Work

Time and resources are limited in any business environment. Create a Minimum Viable Product (MVP) and define its simplest possible version that still provides value. This will clear your path to a quick win and provides a foundation for future iterations. For example, an MVP might be a simple linear regression model, which can later be improved with more complex algorithms.

Break your project into manageable phases or milestones. This will not only help you track progress, but also make it easier to pivot if your priorities shift down the line. Many teams use lightweight Agile or Kanban-style boards to track tasks and deliverables.

Using a Consistent Folder Structure

Organizing your files makes your project easier to navigate for yourself and others. A typical folder structure might look like:

```
project-name/
├── data/           # Raw and processed data
├── notebooks/      # Exploratory analysis and experimentation
├── src/            # Source code (functions, models)
├── models/         # Saved model artifacts
├── outputs/        # Plots, reports, results
├── config/        # Parameter and settings files
├── docs/           # Documentation
└── README.md       # Project overview and instructions
```

Version Control Integration

Version control is the practice of tracking and managing changes to code, data, and configuration files over time, which enables teams to collaborate without overwriting each other's work. Git is the most widely used distributed version control system in the industry, which allows developers to create branches, merge changes, and roll back to previous states when needed.

Popular repository hosting services such as GitHub, GitLab, and Bitbucket provide cloud-based Git repositories along with collaboration tools such as pull requests, issue tracking, and CI/CD integration. While Git dominates modern development, other systems such as Subversion (SVN), Mercurial, and Perforce are still used in certain enterprises, especially where large binary files or specialized workflows are involved.

Documentation and Commenting

Documentation and commenting are essential for the success and maintainability of any data science project. They ensure that your work is understandable, reproducible, and easy to collaborate on, both for your current team and for anyone who might work on the project in the future.

Project-Level Documentation

This type of documentation provides a high-level overview of the project. It is the "*what*" and "*why*" of the project, not just the "*how*."

- **README File:** This is the first file anyone sees in your project repository. A good `README.md` should include:
    - The project title and a brief description.
    - **Problem Statement**: The specific business problem the project aims to solve.
    - **Data Description**: Information about the datasets used, including sources and schemas.

- **Installation Instructions**: A guide on how to set up the project environment and install dependencies.
- **Usage**: How to run the code and reproduce the results.
- **File Structure**: A simple explanation of the project's directory layout.

- **Jupyter Notebooks:** While often used for exploratory analysis, well-structured Jupyter Notebooks can serve as excellent documentation. They combine code, visualizations, and markdown text to tell the story of your analysis, thus making the entire process transparent.
- **requirements.txt:** This file lists all the Python libraries and their versions required to run the project. It is crucial for ensuring reproducibility across different environments. You can generate it using **`pip freeze`** > **`requirements.txt`**.
- **CONTRIBUTING.md:** In collaborative or enterprise environments, this file outlines how others can contribute to the project. It includes coding conventions, branch-naming guidelines, testing requirements, and the preferred workflow for submitting pull requests. Well-written contribution guidelines promote consistency, improve code quality, and allow teams to collaborate more smoothly.
- **LICENSE File:** Every open-source or shared enterprise project should include a license file that specifies how the project can be used, modified, or distributed. Common licenses like MIT, Apache 2.0, or GPL define the rights and limitations for users and contributors. Including a **`LICENSE`** file upfront protects both the developers and the organization legally and ethically.

Code Comments

Code comments explain the "*why*" behind your code, not the "*what*." The code itself should be self-explanatory for the most part. However, comments can elaborate upon the following aspects:

- **Explain Complex Logic:** Use comments to clarify tricky or non-obvious sections of code. For example, if you are using a specific statistical method or a complex algorithm, a comment can explain its purpose and any assumptions you are making.
- **Document Functions and Classes:** Write docstrings (multi-line comments at the beginning of a function or class) that explain what the code does, its parameters, and what it returns. This best practice is particularly helpful while dealing with auto-documentation tools.

```
def calculate_kpi(data):
    """
    Calculate business KPI from sales data.
    Parameters:
```

```
        data (DataFrame): Sales records with dates and values.
    Returns:
        float: KPI score.
    """
```

- **Avoid Redundant Comments:** Do not comment on every line of code. A comment like # Add 1 to x is useless. Focus on explaining the intent and logic.

Process Documentation

This covers the workflow and procedures used during the project. It is especially useful for handing over a project or for team collaboration.

- **Data Dictionary**: This document provides detailed information about each variable in your dataset, including its name, data type, and description.
- **Methodology Section**: This document explains the data cleaning steps, feature engineering techniques, and modeling approach used. This could be part of a final report or a separate markdown file.

During process documentation, it is crucial to document the decisions taken, assumptions made, and data sources used throughout the project lifecycle. This creates a transparent record of the project's evolution. For example, documenting a decision to use a specific model architecture, such as a random forest over a neural network, along with the reasoning (for example, interpretability needs or dataset size), helps future team members understand the choices you have made.

Similarly, clearly stating assumptions, like "*the distribution of customer behavior will remain stable over the next year*," is vital because if it is proved to be false, it will directly impacts the model's performance and highlights where the project might need to be re-evaluated. Finally, listing all data sources, including URLs for public datasets, database queries, or names of internal APIs, is essential for data lineage. This ensures that the data used can be traced, validated, and, updated. The latter is especially fundamental for reproducibility and auditing purposes. Even on the methodology and business decisions, maintain a changelog for major updates.

Tools for Documentation, Process Flow and Project Management

Documentation and commenting are necessary for a data science project's success. While code comments explain complex logic, documentation provides a higher-level view of the project's purpose, methodology, and reproducibility. Effective use of the right tools can streamline this process, and keep a project organized.

- **Sphinx:** It is a powerful and popular tool within the Python community that generates high-quality documentation from source code and

`ReStructuredText` files. Sphinx can automatically extract docstrings from your Python functions and classes, which eliminates the need to write separate documentation for your code. It is highly customizable and the de facto standard for Python library documentation.

- **MkDocs:** It is a simpler alternative to Sphinx that builds static websites from Markdown files. It is very easy to set up and use.
- **Jupyter Notebooks:** While it is primarily a development environment, a well-structured Jupyter Notebook serves as a form of documentation itself. By combining code, visualizations, and explanatory text in Markdown cells, you can create a living document that tells the story of your analysis from start to finish. You can easily share and version-control these notebooks.
- **Doxygen:** A cross-platform documentation generator that is widely used in software development, but also supports Python. Doxygen can parse your source code and generate documentation in various formats like HTML, PDF, and RTF. It is particularly good at generating diagrams that show the relationships between different classes and functions.

Tools for Project Management

Effective project management is essential for keeping data science projects on track. These tools help you organize tasks, track progress, and manage collaboration. Some of these tools are mentioned as follows:

- **Trello:** A simple, visual project management tool that uses a Kanban board system. You organize tasks into "*cards*" and move them across "*lists*" (for example, "*To Do*," "*In Progress*," "*Done*"). Trello's visual nature is intuitive and great for managing smaller teams and projects, as well as for tracking the different stages of a machine learning pipeline.

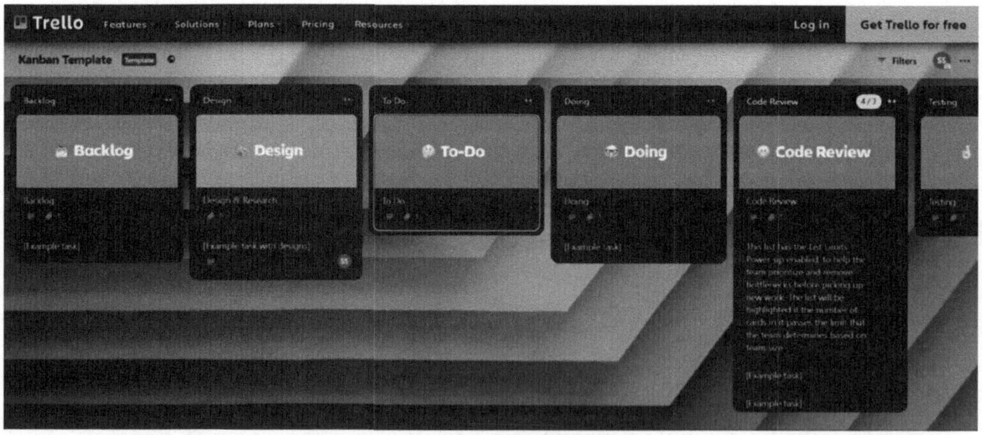

Figure 10.1: *Kanban Template from trello.com/templates/engineering/kanban-template-LGHXvZNL*

- **Jira:** A more robust and powerful tool, which is also owned by Atlassian. Jira is designed for agile development and is ideal for managing complex projects with many moving parts. You can create user stories, bug reports, and a variety of other task types using Jira. Moreover, its advanced reporting and customization options are well-suited for larger, more formal data science projects.
- **Asana:** A flexible project management platform that allows teams to organize, track, and manage their work. Asana provides multiple views (list, board, timeline, calendar) and powerful automation features, which makes it easy to create repeatable workflows and keep everyone aligned on project goals and deadlines.
- **GitHub Projects and GitLab Issues/Boards:** Many data science teams prefer to keep project tracking integrated with their version control system. GitHub Projects and GitLab Boards combine code and task management in one place. Teams can link pull requests or merge requests directly to issues, track model development progress alongside commits, and automate workflows using CI/CD pipelines. This integration ensures transparency between code changes and project status, which is a critical aspect in enterprise and collaborative environments.

Visualizing your workflow is crucial for clear communication and identifying bottlenecks. These tools help create flowcharts and diagrams that document your data and model pipelines. This is where platforms like Miro come into play. Miro is a collaborative online whiteboard that is perfect for creating visual representations of your project's process flow. You can easily create flowcharts, data flow diagrams, and swimlane diagrams, and then collaborate with your team in real time. Miro can be integrated with popular tools such as Jira and Asana, which makes it a powerful addition to your toolkit.

Data Security and Privacy

Industry projects often involve sensitive or proprietary data; protection is both a legal and ethical responsibility. Protecting sensitive information from breaches and misuse is not just a technical challenge; it is a legal and ethical imperative that can impact a company's reputation and bottom line. A data-driven organization must embed security and privacy from the project's inception, and not feature them as a mere afterthought. This involves crafting a multi-layered strategy that addresses the data itself, the systems that process it, and the people who interact with it.

Data Classification

The first step to craft a robust security strategy is to know the data you have and understand how sensitive it is. Data classification is the process of categorizing data based on its level of confidentiality and the risks it is vulnerable to. You might deal with data categories such as:

- **Public:** Data that can be shared freely without any security concerns.
- **Internal:** Data that is for internal business use only (for example, employee contact lists).
- **Confidential:** Data that, if disclosed, could cause harm to the organization or individuals (for example, financial records, and customer email addresses).
- **Highly Confidential:** The most sensitive data, such as Personally Identifiable Information (PII), Protected Health Information (PHI), or intellectual property, which often requires the highest level of protection.

Proper classification dictates the security measures, storage methods, and access controls that must be applied to the data.

Secure Storage and Transfer

Once the data is classified, it must be protected throughout its lifecycle. To safeguard sensitive data, you must use encrypted storage for cloud-based data science projects. Major cloud providers like AWS and Azure offer built-in, server-side encryption to protect data.

With Amazon S3, you can use Server-Side Encryption (SSE) with S3-managed keys (SSE-S3) or AWS Key Management Service (SSE-KMS). SSE-S3 is the default for all new S3 objects and encrypts data automatically using AES-256, with AWS handling key management. SSE-KMS provides more control, which allows you to manage encryption keys through the KMS service.

Similarly, Azure Blob storage also offers server-side encryption that automatically encrypts all data using 256-bit AES encryption. These methods can be enabled simply with both the platforms and ensure that the data is encrypted while it is stored in the cloud. This also meets security and compliance requirements without requiring you to manage the encryption process yourself.

Secure Transfer: Data must also be encrypted in transit. In other words, it should be encrypted while being moved across networks. Protocols like HTTPS for web traffic and Secure Shell (SSH) for file transfers ensure that data remains confidential even if intercepted.

Access Controls

Access control mechanisms ensure that only authorized individuals can view or modify data. The principle of least privilege is paramount here: users should only be granted the minimum level of access required to perform their jobs.

- **Role-Based Access Control (RBAC):** This is a common method where access is granted based on a user's role within the organization. For example, a data analyst might have read-only access to customer data, while a database administrator will have full administrative privileges.
- **Attribute-Based Access Control (ABAC):** Some modern cloud platforms extend RBAC with ABAC, where access decisions are made dynamically based on attributes rather than fixed roles. These attributes can include user characteristics (for example, department, job title), resource types (for example, database, model, dataset), or environmental factors (for example, time of access, location, device security). ABAC provides finer-grained control and flexibility, particularly in environments like **AWS IAM**, **Google Cloud IAM**, or **Azure Active Directory**, where policies can automatically adapt to context and scale across large, complex systems.
- **Multi-Factor Authentication (MFA):** Requiring users to provide more than one form of verification (for example, a password and a code from a mobile app) significantly reduces the risk of unauthorized access.

Anonymization and De-Identification

Data privacy is not just about security; it is about safeguarding the anonymity of individuals in certain cases. Hence, it is important to institute the following mechanisms:

- **Anonymization:** This involves removing all identifying information from a dataset so that individuals can no longer be linked to it. For example, a dataset might replace names and addresses with unique identifiers.
- **De-identification:** A slightly less strict approach, where some identifiers are removed, but the data is still potentially re-identifiable. The goal is to reduce the risk of re-identification to an acceptable level. Techniques include masking, shuffling, or generalizing data (for example, replacing a specific age with an age range).
- **Differential Privacy:** An advanced technique that adds a controlled amount of random noise to data in order to protect individual privacy while still allowing for meaningful analysis.

Compliance Frameworks

The regulatory landscape for data privacy is complex and constantly evolving. Adhering to these frameworks is not optional, but a necessity. The following compliance frameworks should be factored in while planning for data privacy:

- **General Data Protection Regulation (GDPR):** This European Union (EU) regulation is one of the strictest privacy laws in the world. It mandates strict rules for collecting, processing, and storing the personal data of EU citizens.
- **California Consumer Privacy Act (CCPA):** This landmark law grants California residents more control over their personal information.
- **Health Insurance Portability and Accountability Act (HIPAA):** This US law protects the privacy and security of a person's medical information.

Organizations must understand which frameworks are applicable to their business and ensure their data science practices are compliant to avoid hefty fines and legal action.

Reproducibility in Data Science

Reproducibility in data science is the ability to obtain the same results from a given analysis using the same data, code, and computational environment. It is a cornerstone of scientific rigor and project reliability, ensuring that findings can be verified, models can be redeployed, and projects can be easily allotted to others.

Environment Management

A key challenge in reproducibility is managing the software dependencies and their specific versions. Different versions of libraries can produce different results.

Python:

- **`requirements.txt`**: This is a text file that lists all the Python packages and their versions needed for a project. It is the most common method for managing dependencies. You can create one by running **`pip freeze > requirements.txt`** and installing dependencies with **`pip install -r requirements.txt`**.
- **Pipenv**: This tool combines the functionality of **`pip`** and **`virtualenv`**. It creates a virtual environment for your project and generates a **`Pipfile`** and **`Pipfile.lock`** to manage dependencies. **`Pipfile.lock`** ensures that every user gets the same package versions.
- **Conda**: For projects with complex dependencies, including non-Python libraries, Conda is an excellent choice. You can export a snapshot of your environment with **`conda env export > environment.yml`** and recreate it on another machine with **`conda env create -f environment.yml`**.

R:

- `renv`: This package provides a robust solution for managing project-specific R libraries. It creates a private library for your project, while ensuring that it remains isolated from your global R environment. It automatically tracks the R packages you use and stores all their versions, which you can save in a lockfile (`renv.lock`) to share with others.

Reproducibility in data science is the ability to obtain the same results from a given analysis using the same data, code, and computational environment. It is a cornerstone of scientific rigor and project reliability, ensuring that findings can be verified, models can be redeployed, and projects can be easily handed off to others.

Random Seeds

Many data science tasks like model training involve random processes. To ensure these processes are consistent, you must set a random seed at the beginning of your code. This gives the random number generator a starting point, so it produces the same sequence of numbers every time. For example, in Python, you might set seeds for `numpy`, `tensorflow`, and `torch` to control randomness across your entire pipeline.

Data Versioning

Just as code changes over time, so do datasets. Using an old version of a dataset with your code can lead to different results. Data versioning ensures that you are always using the correct data.

- **Data Version Control (DVC):** This is a popular open-source tool that works with Git. It tracks large data files and models by storing pointers to them in Git while the actual data resides in a remote location (for example, S3, Google Cloud Storage). This allows you to easily switch between different versions of your data and models.
- **Immutable Dataset Snapshots:** Another approach is to store immutable copies of your datasets. Whenever you make changes to a dataset (for example, clean, filter, or augment it), you save a new version with a unique identifier or timestamp. This ensures that a specific version of your code is always linked to a specific, unchanging version of the data.

Pipeline Automation

Manual, ad-hoc execution of a data science workflow is an error-prone process. Automating your pipeline ensures that the entire process, from data ingestion to model deployment, runs consistently.

Make

This classic tool is great for defining a sequence of commands in a **`Makefile`**. It is lightweight and works well for small to medium-sized projects, ensuring that all steps (for example, data preprocessing, feature engineering, or model training) are executed in the correct order.

Then there are more powerful tools like Airflow for building, scheduling, and monitoring complex workflows. Airflow allows you to define Directed Acyclic Graphs (DAGs) that represent your pipeline. These tools are ideal for production-level systems and provide robust logging and error-handling features. A DAG is a collection of tasks that you want to run and is organized in a way that shows their relationships and dependencies.

The term "*Directed*" means there is a clear direction of flow, where tasks move from upstream to downstream. "*Acyclic*" means that there are no loops, so a task cannot depend on itself or on a task that eventually depends on it. "*Graph*" refers to the structure of nodes (tasks) and edges (dependencies), which helps you visualize the entire workflow. Airflow uses Python code to define DAGs, which makes it easy to create, maintain, and test complex pipelines. Here, each node represents a task and the edges define dependencies between them. *Figure 10.2* illustrates a simple DAG example showing branching and task dependencies in Apache Airflow.

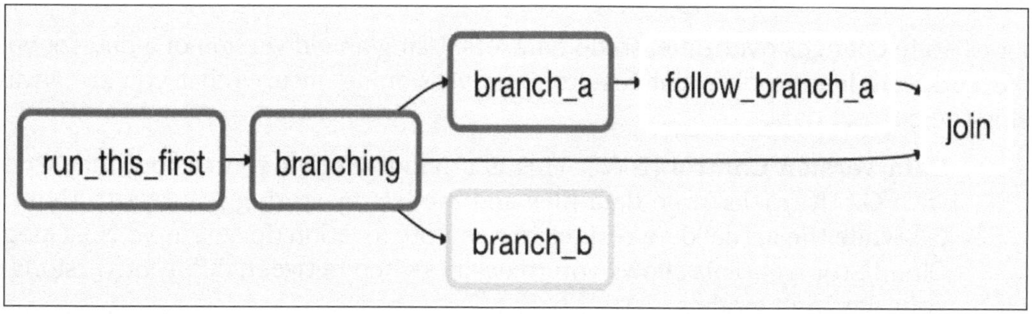

Figure 10.2: *DAG Concept and Tutorial. Source: airflow.apache.org/docs/apache-airflow/1.10.9/concepts.html*

targets (R)

This R package is designed specifically for pipeline automation in data science. It automatically tracks changes, and runs only the parts of the pipeline that need to be updated, making your workflows more efficient.

Testing

Testing ensures that your code and data are behaving as expected, which is a key part of reproducibility. Here are some features you can integrate in testing processes to make them more robust:

- **Unit tests:** Use a framework such as `pytest` (Python) or `testthat` (R) to write tests for individual functions. This confirms that the preprocessing and feature engineering code is working as intended, regardless of the data it is applied to.
- **Data Validation Checks:** Implement checks to ensure your data is in the correct format and range. For example, you might assert that a column contains only positive values or that a specific column exists in your dataset. Frameworks like pandera (for Python) or validate (for R) extend this idea to formal data unit testing, where schemas define expected data types, ranges, and constraints. These tools integrate seamlessly into pipelines and automatically validate datasets at each . They also help in detecting schema drift or corrupted inputs early on in production workflows.

Deployment and MLOps

In an industrial setting, building an accurate machine learning model is only a part of a lengthy journey. The real challenge lies in deploying the model into production, keeping it healthy over time, and ensuring it scales to meet business needs. This is where Deployment and Machine Learning Operations (MLOps) come into play. MLOps extends traditional DevOps principles to the ML lifecycle, covering deployment, monitoring, scalability, and automation of workflows.

Model Deployment

Deploying a model into production requires more than just a trained algorithm–it involves creating a reliable, reproducible environment where the model can be served to users or integrated with other systems. In modern machine learning workflows, this typically starts with **Dockerization**, which is a process where the model, its dependencies, and runtime environment are packaged into a lightweight, portable container. Containers ensure that the model behaves consistently across different stages–from a developer's local machine to testing and production clusters–regardless of the variations in system configurations.

Once built, these containers are stored in container registries, which act as centralized repositories for deployment-ready images. Popular registries include Docker Hub, Amazon Elastic Container Registry (ECR), and Google Container Registry (GCR). These services allow teams to manage container versions, enforce access control, and seamlessly deploy models to production environments using orchestration platforms such as Kubernetes, AWS ECS, or Google Cloud Run.

The method of deployment depends heavily on the use case. For real-time applications, models are often exposed as APIs using frameworks such as Flask, FastAPI, or Django in Python. For larger-scale, production-grade deployments, specialized serving tools such as TorchServe, TensorFlow Serving, or managed endpoints on AWS SageMaker, Google Vertex AI, or Azure ML are common choices.

Batch processing workflows, where predictions are generated on a schedule, can be managed using orchestration tools like Apache Airflow or Prefect. For low-latency streaming use cases such as fraud detection or recommendation systems, integration with Apache Kafka Streams or Spark Structured Streaming enables real-time inference. In edge computing scenarios, models can be optimized and deployed on devices via TensorFlow Lite or ONNX Runtime.

Before deployment, models are typically serialized into a portable format such as **`Pickle`** or **`joblib`** (for scikit-learn), SavedModel (for TensorFlow), or **`.pt`** files (for PyTorch). These artifacts are stored in repositories like MLflow, DVC, or cloud storage (for example, S3) for version control and traceability.

Monitoring and Maintenance

Once deployed, a model's work environment will inevitably change. Data distributions evolve, user behavior shifts, and new external factors emerge. Without continuous monitoring, a once-accurate model can quickly become obsolete. Effective monitoring involves tracking both model performance metrics (for example, accuracy, precision, recall, F1-score, RMSE) and data drift indicators that signal when the statistical properties of incoming data differ from the training set.

Tools such as Evidently AI, WhyLabs, and Fiddler AI can automate drift detection and provide visual dashboards. Performance monitoring can be integrated with Prometheus for metric collection and Grafana for visualization. Automated alerts ensure that data science teams are notified whenever thresholds are breached.

In addition to performance tracking, model explainability is increasingly becoming a production requirement, especially in regulated industries such as healthcare, finance, and insurance. Explainability tools like SHAP (SHapley Additive exPlanations) and LIME (Local Interpretable Model-agnostic Explanations) help teams understand how input features influence model predictions. These tools can be integrated into production monitoring dashboards to provide real-time insights into model decision logic, detect unexpected feature behavior, and build stakeholder trust.

Maintenance often involves retraining models on fresh data. This can be scheduled periodically (for example, monthly retraining) or triggered automatically when drift or performance degradation exceeds a predefined threshold. Over time, retraining pipelines become as important as the initial deployment process, ensuring that models remain relevant, explainable, and aligned with evolving business conditions.

Scalability

As adoption grows, a deployed model must handle increased workloads without compromising performance. Scalability is often addressed through horizontal scaling, where additional instances of a model service are created and orchestrated using Kubernetes or AWS ECS. Think of horizontal scaling as adding more machines or instances to handle increased workload, rather than making a single machine more powerful. Auto-scaling policies can dynamically adjust resources to match demand, while NGINX or cloud load balancers distribute requests evenly.

Model optimization techniques like quantization, pruning, and knowledge distillation can reduce computational load and improve inference speed. Frameworks such as TensorRT (NVIDIA), ONNX Runtime, or TF-TRT provide production-ready optimizations.

TensorRT provides high-performance optimizations for deep learning models on NVIDIA GPUs, enabling faster throughput and lower latency. ONNX Runtime is an open-source inference engine that supports multiple hardware backends, thus allowing you to deploy a single model format across diverse environments. TF-TRT, a TensorFlow integration with TensorRT, combines TensorFlow's flexibility with NVIDIA's GPU optimizations, which makes it ideal for accelerating TensorFlow models in production. These frameworks are especially valuable in high-traffic or low-latency scenarios where every millisecond matters.

In some cases, caching predictions for frequently repeated queries can significantly reduce system load.

CI/CD for Machine Learning

Continuous Integration and Continuous Deployment (CI/CD) make an ML workflow automated and reliable. Unlike traditional software, ML pipelines must handle not just code but also data, models, and configurations. A typical MLOps CI/CD process begins with data validation, ensuring that incoming data conforms to expected formats and ranges. Tools such as Great Expectations or TensorFlow Data Validation can automate this step.

Once data is validated, the pipeline triggers model training using frameworks like Kubeflow Pipelines, Vertex AI Pipelines, or orchestration with MLflow. Unit and integration tests validate both preprocessing scripts and inference APIs. Deployment can be automated through GitOps workflows with ArgoCD or CI/CD services like GitHub Actions, GitLab CI, or Jenkins.

Safe rollout strategies are deployment methods designed to reduce risk when introducing a new model version in the production phase. Instead of replacing the old model all at once, these strategies let you test the new version in a controlled way. This allows you to roll back quickly if issues arise. Strategies like canary deployments or blue-green deployments allow teams to monitor new models in production before fully adopting them.

In a canary deployment, the new model is released to a small subset of users or traffic first, for example, 5-10% of incoming requests. The majority of users can still interact with the stable, existing model. Performance metrics and error rates are closely monitored. If the new model behaves as expected, the traffic is gradually increased until it fully replaces the old version. If problems occur, you can easily switch the traffic to the old model.

In a blue-green deployment, you can maintain two identical production environments. 'Blue' is the current, active environment running the old model and 'green' is the new environment with the updated model. Once the green environment is fully tested and ready, you can simply switch the traffic from blue to green. This is usually done by changing a load balancer's routing. If issues appear, you can immediately switch back to the blue environment. This approach minimizes downtime, and simplifies rollback.

Best Practices for Sustainable MLOps

Beyond the technical steps, sustainable MLOps requires thoughtful infrastructure and governance. Infrastructure-as-Code (IaC) tools allow you to define and manage infrastructure using version-controlled configuration files rather than manual setup. This ensures that your environments are reproducible, consistent, and easy to deploy.

Terraform is a cloud-agnostic IaC tool that uses a declarative language (HCL) to provision resources across providers like AWS, Azure, and GCP. Pulumi offers similar capabilities but allows you to define infrastructure in general-purpose programming languages like Python, TypeScript, or Go, which makes it more flexible for development teams.

AWS CloudFormation is a native AWS service that uses JSON or YAML templates to create and manage AWS resources predictably. By committing these configuration files to source control, teams can track infrastructure changes alongside code, roll back to previous states, and replicate the same environment for testing, staging, and production. This reduces configuration drift and eliminates the guesswork of manual deployments.

Security best practices include API authentication (OAuth2), encrypted storage of model artifacts, and secure endpoints with SSL/TLS. Detailed runbooks and deployment playbooks help teams respond quickly to incidents and reduce operational downtime.

By embedding MLOps principles into your project workflow, you can create a sustainable ecosystem where models are not just built, but are maintained, improved, and trusted over time. This shift from a "one-off delivery" mindset to a "continuous service" mindset is what truly differentiates experimental data science from production-grade machine learning.

Conclusion

In this chapter, we explored how data science moves from experimentation to structured, industry-ready practice. So far, you have learned how to organize projects for collaboration, document work for clarity and reproducibility, protect data through proper security and privacy measures, and ensure reproducibility across environments. We also introduced Deployment and MLOps, while emphasizing how production systems rely on continuous monitoring, explainability, automation, and scalable infrastructure.

Mastering these professional practices can transform a data scientist from an individual contributor into a reliable team player capable of delivering production-grade, value-driven solutions. The ability to structure, document, secure, and operationalize your work bridges the gap between academic experimentation and real-world impact. This skill is a remarkable characteristic of strong practitioners in today's data-driven organizations.

In the next chapter, we will move beyond foundational environments and explore how modern data science operates at scale. You will learn how models evolve into full-fledged products, how teams handle data at scale, and how AI-assisted development tools streamline workflows. We will also touch on orchestration frameworks, collaborative platforms, and governance practices that support large, distributed data science initiatives. Finally, we will chart your growth roadmap, while helping you understand how to continue advancing your technical and professional journey in the field of data science.

CHAPTER 11
Advanced Topics and Next Steps

Introduction

As you have reached the final pages of this book, take a moment to reflect on how far you have come. You have laid a solid foundation for your journey into data science, which includes hands-on experience in setting up your development environment, working confidently within Jupyter Notebooks, using Pandas for data exploration and manipulation, and even running your first simple models. These fundamental skills are the building blocks for everything that will follow.

Throughout the book, you have not only installed and configured essential tools, but also begun to develop a data scientist's mindset by asking questions, seeking patterns in data, and using code as a tool for discovery. Now, with these core competencies under your belt, you will be ready to venture beyond the basics.

This final chapter takes a broader view. It offers a high-level survey of more advanced topics and areas of specialization within data science. You will gain insight into where the field is headed, the skills that are in demand, and how to keep growing through real-world projects, continuous learning, and community involvement.

Consider this chapter a roadmap for your next steps. Whether your interest lies in becoming an ML engineer, a data analyst, or a research scientist, the tools and concepts you have learned here are just the beginning. Let us take a look at the paths ahead and how you can continue building on the solid groundwork you have established.

Structure

This chapter will address the following topics:

- From Models to Products
- Moving Beyond the Basic Environments
- Data at Scale

- AI-Assisted Coding and Development
- Orchestrating Complex Workflows
- Collaborative Environments
- Specialized Environments for Advanced Analytics
- Governance, Security and Compliance
- Your Growth Roadmap

From Models to Products

In real-world scenarios, building a model is only a part of the whole equation. A perfectly tuned model sitting on your laptop is not going anywhere. To truly deliver value, your model must be integrated into applications, products, and systems that end-users can actually interact with. This is where model deployment comes into play.

At its core, deployment means taking your trained ML model and making it accessible for consumption by other systems or users. A common starting point is to wrap the model inside a web service. Frameworks such as Flask (https://flask.palletsprojects.com/en/stable/installation/) and FastAPI (https://fastapi.tiangolo.com/) make this process approachable: you define an API endpoint, load your model, and expose it over HTTP. Once these are in place, other applications can send requests and receive predictions in return.

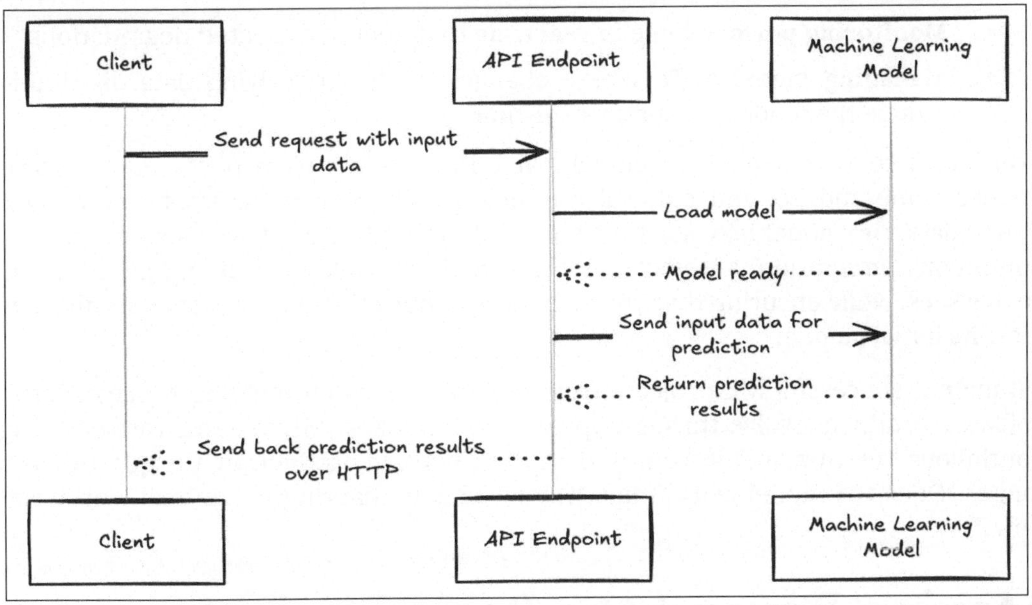

Figure 11.1: *Real-Time Client to Model Communication Flow*

This pattern enables a wide range of use cases such as:

- **Real-time predictions** in a web or mobile app (for example, fraud detection in financial transactions)
- **Conversational agents** or chatbots that respond intelligently to user queries
- **Recommendation engines** that dynamically suggest products, movies, or articles

For projects that demand higher scalability, fault tolerance, or global reach, cloud platforms step in. Services like AWS SageMaker (https://aws.amazon.com/sagemaker/), Google Cloud AI Platform (https://cloud.google.com/products/ai), and Azure Machine Learning (https://azure.microsoft.com/en-us/products/machine-learning) provide managed ML infrastructure. With these platforms, you deploy models and handle training, version control, autoscaling, and monitoring. This frees you from the complexities of setting up servers, managing container orchestration, or worrying about uptime. Eventually, it allows you to focus on the core data science work.

However, deployment is not the finish line, but the starting point of a continuous lifecycle. Once a model is in production, it enters the domain of MLOps (Machine Learning Operations). MLOps adapts the principles of DevOps to the unique challenges of ML workflows, which include:

- **Automating retraining pipelines** to keep models fresh as new data arrives
- **Tracking data and model versions** to ensure reproducibility and compliance
- **Monitoring performance in real time** to detect unexpected degradations
- **Managing model drift**, where changes in the underlying data distribution reduce the model's accuracy over time

Consider a sentiment analysis model trained on social media posts. Slang evolves, memes come and go, and cultural references shift rapidly. Without retraining on newer data, the model may start misinterpreting the language. MLOps practices like continuous integration, automated testing, and scheduled retraining guard against such issues, while ensuring that your model continues to deliver reliable insights even after its initial launch.

Ultimately, successful ML projects treat deployment as an ongoing process. Just as software products evolve through updates and patches, ML systems thrive through continuous iteration, monitoring, and improvement. In production, the question is no longer "Does the model work?", but "How well is it adapting to the real world, right now?"

Moving Beyond the Basic Environments

Previously, you have worked in familiar, self-contained setups like Jupyter Notebooks,

RStudio, and so on. This works beautifully for learning, experimenting, and running small projects.

However, professional data science rarely fits neatly into a single machine. As your work grows in scope and complexity, so will your computational needs. You may find yourself juggling larger datasets, more complex models, and collaborations across time zones. All of these demand a more flexible and scalable environment.

Scaling from Local to Cloud

The cloud offers something your laptop simply cannot: elastic computing power. With the cloud, you can scale resources up or down in minutes, add memory, increase CPU cores, or tap into GPUs and TPUs without buying any hardware. Beyond raw power, the cloud enables global collaboration, where team members can access the same data, notebooks, and code without emailing files or worrying about version mismatches. It also provides consistent environments, which means that everyone can run their work in the same preconfigured setup. This eliminates the classic "*it works/does not work on my machine*" problem. With on-demand resources, you can spin up a powerful instance when needed and shut it down when you are done.

When to Make the Move

Moving to the cloud is not about following a trend; it is a practical step to execute when your local setup becomes a bottleneck. You might find that your datasets are too large for your laptop's memory, which might force you to constantly downsample and limit your analysis. Long model training times are another clear signal. What takes eight hours locally could finish in under thirty minutes on a cloud GPU cluster. Team projects also become far easier in the cloud, as shared workspaces remove the need for ad-hoc file sharing and keep everyone in sync. Finally, if you are constantly wrestling with multiple Python environments or library conflicts, moving to a managed cloud environment can significantly reduce friction.

Popular Cloud Environment Options

There is no one-size-fits-all cloud platform. Your choice will depend on budget, project size, and the technical expertise of your team. Here are some popular cloud environments to consider:

- **Google Colab Pro (https://colab.research.google.com/signup)**: Great for individuals or small teams experimenting with deep learning or GPU-intensive work; offers upgraded GPU/TPU access and integration with Google Drive
- **AWS SageMaker (https://aws.amazon.com/sagemaker/)**: A fully managed environment for training, tuning, and deploying ML models; is a strong choice for enterprise use with integrated data pipelines and monitoring

- **Azure ML Studio (https://learn.microsoft.com/en-us/shows/ai-show/azure-machine-learning-studio)**: Flexible for both drag-and-drop users and code-first workflows; plays well with Microsoft's ecosystem
- **Databricks (https://www.databricks.com/)**: Optimized for large-scale data engineering, spark processing, and collaborative analytics across big data

Hybrid Setups

Moving to the cloud does not have to be an all-or-nothing shift. Many data scientists use hybrid setups to balance flexibility, familiarity, and cost. Some continue coding locally in their preferred IDE like PyCharm, VS Code, or RStudio, while executing the heavy lifting on remote cloud servers. Others mount cloud storage such as AWS S3, Azure Blob Storage, or Google Cloud Storage, so that it appears as a local folder. This will further allow professionals to work with large datasets without straining their laptop's disk space.

A hybrid approach also allows for compute bursts. Training or analysis can be done locally for quick iterations and then shifted to the cloud when a large-scale run is needed.

If you are considering moving to the cloud, start small. Experiment with free tiers or trial credits to get a feel for the tools and the cost structures before committing. Always keep an eye on costs, as unused cloud resources can quickly drain your budget if left running. You must also be mindful of data transfer strategies. Uploading large datasets can be slow and expensive, therefore, you must learn to use command-line tools or direct ingestion methods to move data efficiently.

Scaling your environment is not just about speed, it is about enabling new possibilities. By moving beyond a single machine, you will be able to work with richer datasets, collaborate seamlessly, and deliver more ambitious projects.

Data at Scale

As you progress from exploratory, small-scale projects into the realm of enterprise-level data science, the nature of your work changes fundamentally. You are no longer dealing with CSV files that can be comfortably loaded into memory and manipulated with pandas on your laptop. Instead, you will be faced with datasets that span terabytes or petabytes of information, often arriving continuously from multiple sources. At this scale, the constraints shift from "*Can I analyze this data?*" to "*How can I store, retrieve, and process this data efficiently and cost-effectively?*"

Moving Beyond In-Memory Processing

Traditional tools like pandas are invaluable for rapid prototyping and exploratory analysis, but they operate entirely in memory, which quickly becomes a bottleneck when data sizes exceed a machine's RAM. Scaling up requires distributed computation, breaking your workload into smaller chunks, and executing them in parallel across multiple machines.

One of the most widely adopted solutions for this is Apache Spark (https://spark.apache.org/). Spark's architecture is built around the idea of resilient distributed datasets (RDDs), which allow you to operate on large-scale data across a cluster without having to manually manage how it is split or replicated. Spark shines in scenarios involving massive batch processing, complex transformations, and iterative algorithms. It also supports real-time stream processing via Spark Streaming or Structured Streaming. Its ability to integrate with numerous storage systems, from HDFS to cloud object stores like Amazon S3, makes it a cornerstone of modern big data infrastructure.

Bridging the Gap with Dask

If Spark feels like a huge transition from your current Python-based workflow, Dask (https://www.dask.org/) might be a gentler option. Designed with a familiar Pandas- and NumPy-like API, Dask lets you scale your existing code to larger-than-memory datasets with minimal rewrites. It intelligently chunks data, parallelizes operations, and manages memory under the hood, so that you can work with data that exceeds your machine's RAM. This makes it an excellent option for teams that want to incrementally adopt big data practices without overhauling their tech stack.

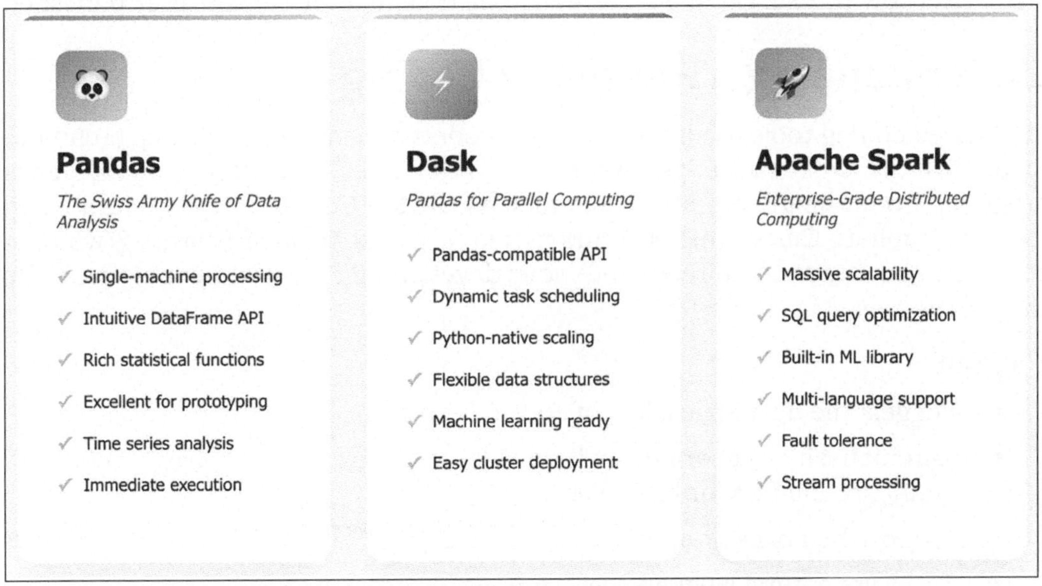

***Figure 11.2**: Comparison of Pandas, Dask, and Spark*

Scaling Storage and Querying

Processing power is only half of the equation. Storing and retrieving massive datasets also demands specialized tools. Cloud-native data warehouses such as Google BigQuery and Amazon Redshift are optimized for analytical workloads over vast datasets. They allow you to run complex SQL queries over billions of rows in seconds, without needing you to manually manage underlying hardware or storage.

For organizations requiring a balance of performance, scalability, and security, Snowflake offers a compelling approach. Its architecture separates compute and storage, allowing workloads to scale independently. It also supports features like secure data sharing and automated scaling, which are essential for enterprise environments.

Perhaps the most subtle challenge in working with data at scale is the cultural shift it demands. Small-scale analysis is often an individual activity. Large-scale data work is inherently collaborative. You will work closely with data engineers, DevOps teams, and stakeholders to design architectures, establish governance policies, and ensure compliance with regulations.

AI-Assisted Coding and Development

Artificial Intelligence (AI) is no longer confined to research labs or data science projects. It is now showing up as an active collaborator in software development. Think of AI-assisted coding as having a junior developer that has memorized every Stack Overflow thread, GitHub issue, and code documentation page ever published.

Understanding AI-Assisted Coding

AI-assisted coding tools use large language models and machine learning techniques to predict the code you might write next, offer fixes, and even generate entire programs from a single prompt. Tools such as GitHub Copilot (https://github.com/features/copilot), Cursor (https://cursor.com/en), and Windsurf (https://windsurf.com/) can be integrated directly into your development environment to streamline the process.

They can:

- Suggest the next logical line of code as you type.
- Automatically generate boilerplate structures like class definitions, configuration files, or test cases.
- Propose bug fixes or optimization strategies.
- Translate natural language descriptions into runnable code.

In data science workflows, where speed, iteration, and reproducibility are essential, AI-assisted coding can be a powerful force multiplier. It enables faster prototyping by auto-generating repetitive setup tasks such as data loading, cleaning, and plotting. For example, you could simply type "Load a CSV from a URL, drop null values, and plot a histogram" and have the code ready in seconds. It also reduces context switching by keeping you focused within your IDE instead of bouncing between your editor, documentation, and the browser, which preserves valuable mental energy. In addition, AI often introduces alternative ideas by suggesting different libraries or approaches you might not have considered. For example, if you typically use **`matplotlib`**, an AI assistant might recommend **`plotly`** for creating interactive visualizations.

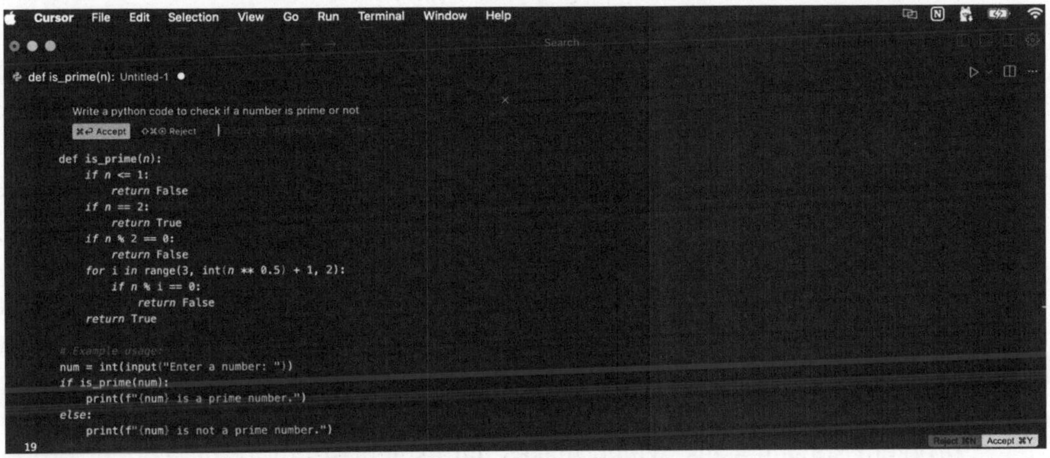

Figure 11.3: *Sample Code on Cursor*

In the preceding image you can see a Cursor window where we interact with text "Write a python code to check if a number is prime or not". The code is completely AI-generated and on the bottom right, the user gets an option to accept or reject the code. The UI and functionality of different AI assisted tools will vary. However, this example is just for illustration purposes.

AI coding assistants are powerful, but they are not infallible. To use them effectively, you must:

1. **Treat AI as a co-pilot, not an autopilot**: The AI's suggestions are only as good as its training data and your review process. Always verify correctness, performance, and security before deploying AI-written code.
2. **Maintain reproducibility**: Document when and how the AI-generated code was produced. Include prompts, comments, and any manual adjustments, so that others (or you, in future) can understand the origins.
3. **Integrate into familiar tools**: AI assistants are the most effective when they blend into your existing workflow such as PyCharm, VS Code, or JupyterLab, rather than forcing you to switch environments.

4. **Know the limits**: AI can hallucinate nonexistent functions or misuse libraries. Do not trust them blindly. You must test, log, and validate them.

AI-assisted coding isn't about replacing developers but about amplifying their capabilities. It can write the scaffolding, handle repetitive chores, and spark new ideas, leaving you free to focus on problem-solving, creativity, and the parts of coding that actually require human judgment.

Potential Risks and Pitfalls

While the promise of AI-assisted coding is exciting, data scientists need to be aware of its limitations and possible downsides such as:

- **Hallucinations and Subtle Bugs**: AI can generate code that looks plausible but is logically flawed, insecure, or even unusable. These errors can be harder to spot than obvious syntax issues.
- **Security Vulnerabilities**: AI models may unknowingly suggest insecure patterns (for example, unsafe SQL queries, weak encryption) because they have learned from public code that includes such flaws.
- **Intellectual Property Concerns**: Some AI-generated code may resemble copyrighted material from its training data. This raises legal and ethical questions about ownership and licensing.
- **Skill Atrophy**: Over-reliance on AI for routine coding could erode fundamental problem-solving skills, which makes data scientists more dependent on the tool over time.
- **Context Misunderstandings**: AI works best with complete, clear prompts. Without proper context, it might generate code that fits the syntax but not the intent.

The safest approach is to treat AI as a fast, helpful assistant, but one that occasionally needs supervision, correction, and sometimes a complete overhaul. As with any powerful tool, its impact depends on the skill and judgment of the person using it.

Orchestrating Complex Workflows

In real-world data science and ML projects, work rarely consists of running a single script in isolation. Instead, projects typically involve a sequence of dependent steps, where each feeds into the next. A typical pipeline might look like this:

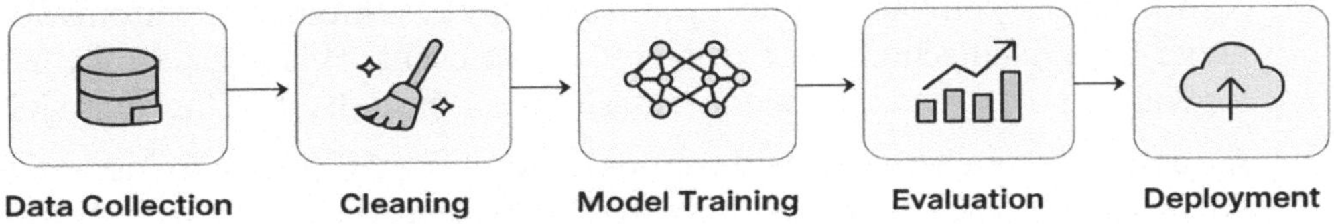

Figure 11.4: *A Typical Pipeline*

These stages must be executed in the right order, often on a regular schedule, and sometimes with conditional branching depending on the results. Managing all this manually can be time-consuming, error-prone, and difficult to scale. That is where workflow orchestration tools come in.

Workflow Orchestration Tools

These tools allow you to define workflows as directed acyclic graphs (DAGs), where each node represents a task and the edges define dependencies. They handle tasks like scheduling, retries, logging, and monitoring effectively, which helps you focus on the data and logic rather than manual coordination.

- **Apache Airflow (https://airflow.apache.org/):** Often considered the industry standard for orchestrating data pipelines, Airflow lets you define workflows in Python code and schedule them to run at precise intervals. It provides a powerful UI for visualizing DAGs, checking task status, and troubleshooting failures. Airflow shines in large, complex pipelines with many interdependent steps.
- **Prefect (https://www.prefect.io/):** A more lightweight alternative to Airflow, Prefect focuses on making workflows easy to write, test, and run. It removes much of Airflow's boilerplate and offers a hybrid execution model. Tasks can run locally or in the cloud, while orchestration happens centrally. This makes Prefect great for smaller teams or those looking for a gentle learning curve without sacrificing flexibility.
- **Dagster (https://dagster.io/):** Dagster emphasizes data quality and observability. It treats your pipeline as a software engineering artifact, with built-in tools for testing, type checking, and versioning. Dagster's asset-based approach makes it easy to track which data assets are up to date and which need to be recomputed making it ideal for data-centric organizations where reproducibility and trust are paramount.

Not all orchestration happens in heavy-duty pipeline frameworks. Sometimes automation means running code at the right time without manual intervention. Hee are a few services that allow you to do so:

- **Scheduled Notebook Runs:** Platforms like Deepnote (https://deepnote.com/), Databricks (https://www.databricks.com/), and Papermill (https://papermill.

readthedocs.io/en/latest/) let you run Jupyter Notebooks automatically, either on a fixed schedule or triggered by an event. This is especially useful for daily reports, recurring model retraining, or periodic data ingestion jobs.

- **AutoML Services:** Services such as Google Cloud AutoML (https://cloud.google.com/automl), H2O.ai (https://h2o.ai/), and Amazon SageMaker Autopilot (https://aws.amazon.com/sagemaker/ai/autopilot/) can automatically select algorithms, tune hyperparameters, and compare models. You supply the dataset, while they handle majority of the modeling work. While not a replacement for human judgment, AutoML can accelerate the early stages of experimentation.

Experiment Tracking

Automation in ML is not just about making things faster. We also need to be making results reliable, explainable, and repeatable. A model that performs well today is only truly valuable if you can reproduce it tomorrow and explain how it got there. That is where experiment tracking comes in.

In practice, ML involves running many experiments, tweaking hyperparameters, swapping architectures, using slightly different datasets, or changing preprocessing steps. Without a system to track these variations, you might lose valuable insights or worse, to will not be able to reproduce a promising result.

Modern experiment tracking tools such as MLflow (https://mlflow.org/), Weights & Biases (https://wandb.ai/site/), and Neptune.ai (https://neptune.ai/) bring structure and visibility to this process. These platforms help you with functions such as:

- **Tracking dataset versions**: Through this, you can know which version of your dataset was used for each run, including transformations or filtering steps.
- **Recording model parameters and hyperparameters**: Capture every choice, from learning rates to optimizer types, so that you can trace how each decision impacted performance.
- **Logging metrics over time**: Monitor accuracy, loss, precision, recall, or custom KPIs, and see how they evolve during training.
- **Comparing runs side by side**: Visually inspect differences between experiments to quickly identify what worked and what did not.

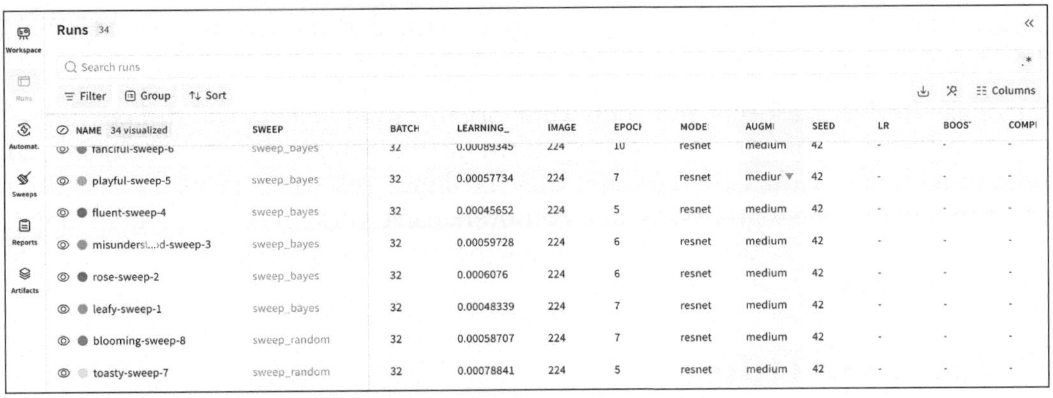

Figure 11.5: *Experiment Tracking Dashboard*

The above figure shows a sample experiment tracking dashboard of Weights and Biases, where you can organize your ML experiments and compare results. This kind of tracking pays dividends in both the short and long term. A well-maintained experiment history enables you to revisit a model later, retrain it with confidence, and verify results under different conditions. It also strengthens your ability to defend findings to stakeholders, auditors, or regulatory bodies by showing a complete and transparent record of the modeling process. Experiment tracking transforms machine learning from trial-and-error into a disciplined, auditable practice.

In a mature ML workflow, orchestration, automation, and tracking work together as shown in the following figure:

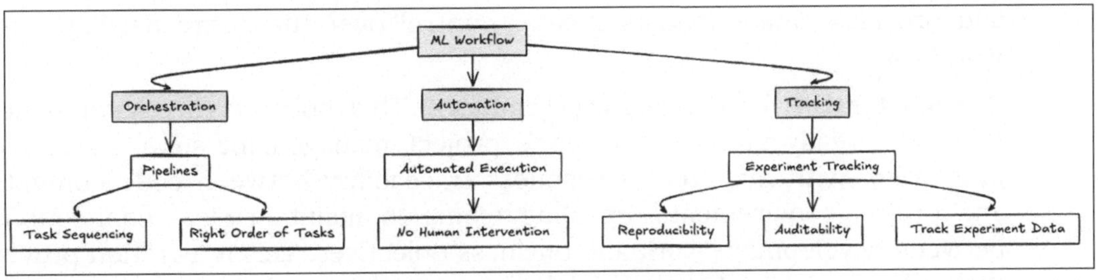

Figure 11.6: *A Mature ML Workflow*

By combining these elements, teams can move faster, reduce human error, and scale projects from prototypes to production systems with confidence.

Collaborative Environments

Data science requires effective collaboration across multiple disciplines and skill sets. While individual expertise in algorithms or data processing is valuable, success depends on establishing robust shared infrastructure for coordinated work. This infrastructure encompasses more than just computational resources. It includes the integrated environment where research, code, data, and models are developed and maintained systematically.

The collaborative platforms and tools your organization selects will directly impact project velocity, output quality, and long-term maintainability. Effective collaboration tools provide more than file storage; they facilitate real-time problem resolution, structured peer review processes, and comprehensive version control. The following sections examine the critical areas where collaborative frameworks prove essential for data science teams:

Beyond GitHub

GitHub is the default choice for collaborative software development as it offers widespread adoption, comprehensive documentation, and is the world's largest open-source ecosystem. However, alternative platforms may better serve specific organizational requirements, regulatory constraints, or workflow preferences.

- **GitLab (https://about.gitlab.com/why-gitlab/)**: This is comparable to GitHub and offers distinct advantages for enterprise environments. GitLab includes integrated continuous integration and continuous deployment (CI/CD) pipelines, comprehensive issue tracking, and project management capabilities within a single interface. GitLab's self-hosting options make it particularly suitable for organizations with stringent security requirements, regulatory compliance needs, or data sovereignty concerns. The platform's built-in DevOps lifecycle management reduces the need for third-party integrations and provides data scientists greater control over the entire development workflow.
- **Bitbucket (https://bitbucket.org/product/)**: This tool excels in environments that are already utilizing Atlassian's project management suite. Its native integration with Jira creates seamless traceability between code commits and project requirements, enabling teams to maintain clear connections between development work and business objectives. This integration proves particularly valuable for organizations managing complex project timelines, sprint planning, and cross-functional collaboration. Bitbucket's branch permissions and pull request workflows provide robust code review processes and maintain alignment with established project management practices.
- **DagsHub (https://dagshub.com/)**: This addresses specific challenges inherent in data science collaboration by treating datasets and machine learning models as first-class repository objects. Unlike traditional version control systems that struggle with large binary files, DagsHub provides native versioning for training datasets, model artifacts, and experiment results. This approach eliminates the common practice of storing critical data assets in separate cloud storage systems, which often leads to version misalignment

and reproducibility issues. The platform's data lineage tracking enables teams to trace model performance back to specific dataset versions and ends up facilitating more rigorous experiment management, while bringing about model governance.

These specialized features become particularly important as data science teams scale and require more sophisticated collaboration patterns around data assets, model lifecycle management, and regulatory compliance requirements.

Shared Notebooks

Interactive notebooks are the primary medium for exploratory data analysis, rapid prototyping, and iterative model development. However, traditional approaches involving standalone .ipynb files distributed through email or messaging platforms create significant collaboration challenges, including version conflicts, lost work, and difficulties in maintaining synchronized development environments. Shared notebook platforms address these limitations by providing real-time, multi-user collaboration capabilities that mirror the collaborative editing experience found in document sharing platforms. Some of these platforms are mentioned as follows:

Google Colab Teams

It extends the widely-adopted Colab environment to support collaborative workflows within shared workspaces. The platform enables simultaneous editing by multiple team members, while eliminating the version control issues inherent in file-based collaboration. Its cloud-hosted architecture standardizes the computational environment across all users, eliminates compatibility issues, ensures consistent package versions and system configurations. This approach reduces onboarding time for new team members and does away with the common "works on my machine" problems that plague local development environments. Integration with Google Drive provides seamless file sharing and organizational capabilities, while built-in access to GPU and TPU resources supports computationally intensive ML workflows without requiring local hardware investments.

Deepnote

This platform focuses specifically on collaborative data analysis workflows, while providing sophisticated commenting and review capabilities that integrate directly with code execution. Users can attach contextual comments to specific cells, provide inline feedback on analysis approaches, and review codc changes without losing execution context. Deepnote maintains a complete history of cell outputs and execution states, which enables team members to understand the evolution of analysis without re-running computationally expensive operations. This asynchronous collaboration model proves particularly valuable for distributed teams working across different time zones and for complex projects requiring extensive peer review.

Hex

This platform combines traditional notebook functionality with interactive dashboard creation capabilities, which enables analysts to develop analytical code and simultaneously create polished presentation materials within a single environment. This integrated approach eliminates the typical workflow fragmentation where analysts must transfer results between Jupyter Notebooks, visualization tools, and presentation software. Hex's dual-mode interface allows technical team members to work directly with code while providing business stakeholders with interactive visualizations and reports. The platform supports SQL, Python, and R, while accommodating diverse technical backgrounds within data teams, and maintaining a unified collaborative environment.

Versioning Data and Models

While software engineers routinely implement rigorous version control practices for source code, data science teams often struggle with equivalent versioning approaches for datasets and trained models. These assets frequently represent the most valuable and computationally expensive components of machine learning projects, yet they are commonly managed through ad-hoc file naming conventions or cloud storage folders. Proper versioning of data and models is thus essential for reproducibility, compliance, and systematic experimentation.

DVC/Data Version Control (https://dvc.org/)

This implements Git-compatible workflows specifically designed for large binary files that are typically found in ML projects. Rather than storing actual data files within Git repositories, DVC maintains lightweight pointers to data stored in external systems such as Amazon S3, Google Cloud Storage, or network-attached storage. This approach preserves Git's branching and merging capabilities while avoiding repository bloat from large datasets. DVC tracks the complete lineage of data transformations and model training processes, enabling teams to reproduce any historical experiment by checking out the corresponding Git commit, and automatically retrieving the associated data snapshots.

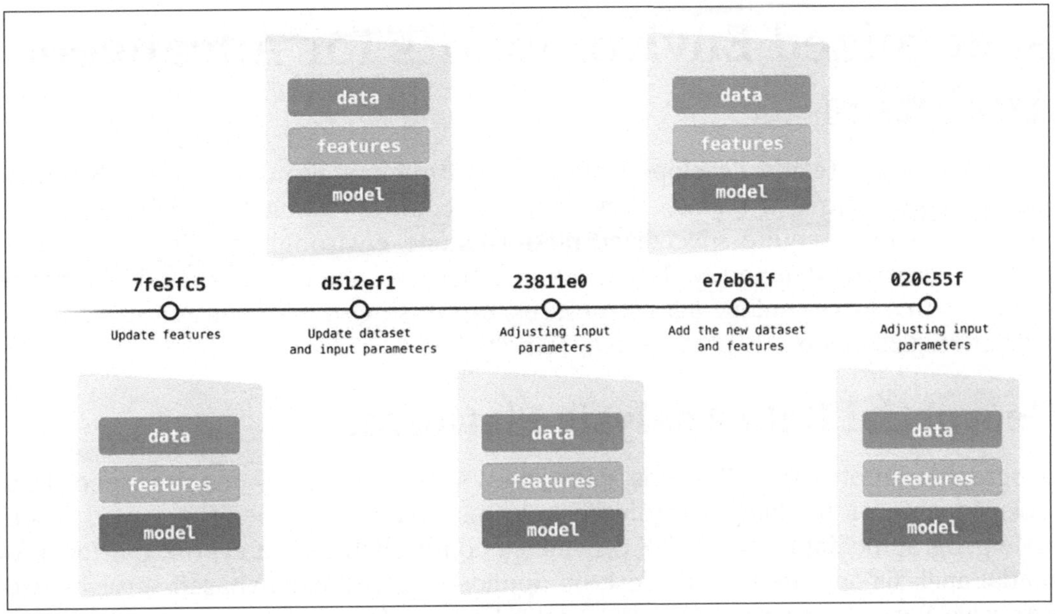

Figure 11.7: *DVC for ML Workflow*

The system integrates with existing CI/CD pipelines and supports collaborative workflows through shared remote storage. It also ensures that all team members are able to access identical datasets for any given project version.

Pachyderm (https://docs.pachyderm.com/)

It provides enterprise-scale data versioning with automatic lineage tracking for complex data processing pipelines. The platform treats data transformations as immutable operations, while creating a complete audit trail from raw input data through all intermediate processing steps, which leads up to final model outputs. This approach enables teams to trace any result back to its exact inputs and transformation logic, supporting both debugging efforts and compliance requirements. Pachyderm's container-based processing model ensures that execution environments stay reproducible and can be scaled to handle petabyte-scale datasets spread across distributed computing infrastructure. The platform's automatic parallelization and incremental processing capabilities optimize computational efficiency by processing only changed data portions rather than recomputing entire pipelines for minor updates.

These versioning systems become increasingly critical as data science teams mature and face requirements for regulatory compliance, model governance, and systematic experimentation practices that demand rigorous reproducibility standards.

Specialized Environments for Advanced Analytics

As data science teams develop proficiency with foundational collaborative tools and version control systems, they often encounter domain-specific analytical challenges which require specialized platforms and environments. These advanced analytics domains demand tools that extend beyond general-purpose data science platforms to address unique data structures, processing requirements, and analytical methodologies inherently present in specific fields.

Geospatial Data Analysis Platforms

Geographic Information Systems (GIS) and spatial analytics require specialized tools capable of handling coordinate systems, geometric operations, and large-scale geographic datasets. ArcGIS provides a comprehensive enterprise platform for spatial analysis and offers both desktop applications and cloud-based services with extensive Python integration via the ArcPy library. The platform supports complex spatial modeling, network analysis, and 3D visualization and provides collaborative capabilities through ArcGIS Online portals. Teams can share maps, datasets, and analytical models while maintaining version control through ArcGIS's built-in revision tracking systems.

QGIS offers an open-source alternative with robust Python bindings through the PyQGIS library, which enables programmatic spatial analysis and automates geographic workflows. The platform's plugin architecture allows teams to develop custom analytical tools and helps them leverage extensive community-contributed functionality. QGIS Server enables web-based map publishing and collaborative editing, while integration with PostGIS databases provides scalable storage for large spatial datasets. The combination of QGIS with Python libraries such as GeoPandas, Shapely, and Folium creates powerful workflows for spatial data science that can be version-controlled and shared through standard collaborative platforms.

Cloud-native geospatial platforms like Google Earth Engine and Microsoft Planetary Computer provide access to petabyte-scale satellite imagery and environmental datasets with built-in distributed processing capabilities. These platforms eliminate the need for local storage of massive geographic datasets while providing collaborative analysis environments and API access for integration with existing data science workflows.

Real-Time Streaming Data Processing

Streaming analytics environments address the unique challenges of processing continuous data flows, requiring tools that handle high-velocity ingestion, real-time transformation, and low-latency response capabilities.

Apache Kafka is the fundamental messaging platform for most streaming architectures. It also provides distributed, fault-tolerant data ingestion with exactly-once processing guarantees. Kafka's ecosystem includes Kafka Streams for lightweight stream processing and Kafka Connect for integrating with external data systems, creating comprehensive data pipeline solutions.

Apache Flink provides advanced stream processing capabilities with support for complex event processing, stateful computations, and exactly-once processing semantics. Flink's unified batch and stream processing model allows teams to develop analytical code that works across both historical and real-time data, while reducing the complexity of maintaining separate systems. The platform's checkpoint and savepoint mechanisms support collaborative development as teams can pause, modify, and resume long-running streaming applications without losing on data. The example use case shown as follows demonstrates an event driven application using Apache Flink. Event-driven applications exemplify real-time streaming data processing by continuously ingesting and reacting to event streams. They maintain state locally alongside computation, while enabling immediate processing and low-latency responses. Fault tolerance is ensured through periodic checkpoints to remote storage, which distinguishes them from traditional, batch-oriented architectures.

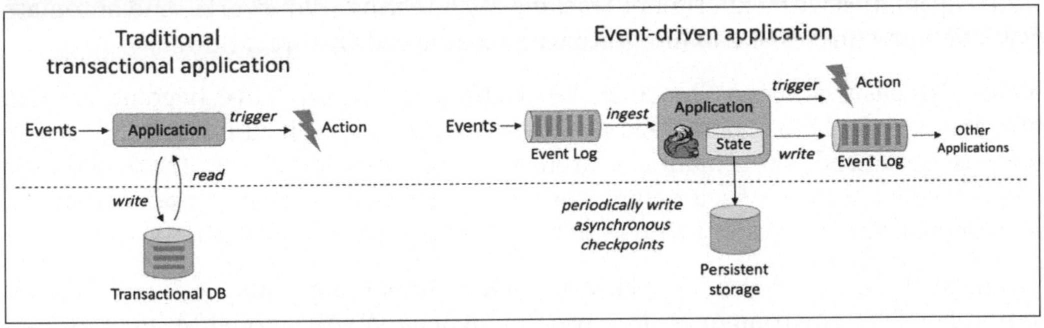

Figure 11.8: *Transactional vs Event-Driven Application Workflow*

Cloud-native streaming platforms such as AWS Kinesis, Google Cloud Dataflow, and Azure Stream Analytics provide managed streaming services with built-in scaling, monitoring, and integration capabilities. These platforms reduce operational overhead and provide collaborative development environments through infrastructure-as-code approaches and integrated version control systems. Advanced platforms like Databricks Structured Streaming combine the collaborative notebook environment with distributed stream processing, which allows teams to develop and deploy streaming analytics using familiar Python and SQL interfaces.

Large Language Model Integration Environments

The emergence of Large Language Models (LLMs) and generative AI has created new requirements for specialized development environments that can handle prompt engineering, model chaining, and integrate with existing data workflows. LangChain provides a comprehensive framework for building applications that combine multiple language models, external data sources, and business logic into coherent workflows. The platform's modular architecture enables teams to develop reusable components for document processing, question answering, and code generation. These abilities unfold as teams maintain version control over prompt templates and model configurations.

LlamaIndex specializes in connecting language models with private data sources, which results in sophisticated indexing and retrieval mechanisms that enable models to access and reason across organizational knowledge bases. The platform supports multiple data formats and storage systems. It also provides evaluation frameworks for measuring retrieval quality and response accuracy. Teams can collaborate on index configurations and query patterns while governing access to sensitive data.

OpenAI Playground and similar model-specific development environments provide interactive interfaces for prompt engineering and model evaluation, while supporting collaborative prompt development through sharing mechanisms and version history. More sophisticated platforms like Weights and Biases Prompts and MLflow extend these capabilities with experiment tracking, A/B testing frameworks, and automated evaluation pipelines that can integrate with existing MLOps workflows.

Vector databases such as Pinecone, Weaviate, and Chroma have become essential infrastructure for LLM applications, as they come with specialized storage and retrieval systems optimized for semantic search and similarity matching. These platforms support collaborative development through API-based access, version control of embeddings, and integration with popular machine learning frameworks.

Advanced LLM development platforms like Humanloop and Helicone provide comprehensive environments for prompt management, model evaluation, and production monitoring, enabling teams to collaboratively develop and deploy language model applications, while they maintain visibility into model performance and cost optimization.

These specialized environments reflect the maturation of data science from general-purpose analytics into domain-specific expertise areas. Each of these environments requires tailored collaborative tools and workflows that can address unique technical and business requirements.

Governance, Security, and Compliance

Governance, security, and compliance refer to the policies, controls, and practices that ensure data science activities are conducted responsibly, securely, and in accordance with legal and organizational standards. Governance defines how data and models are managed, accessed, and maintained; security focuses on protecting data, systems, and intellectual property from unauthorized access or breaches; and compliance ensures adherence to regulations, ethical guidelines, and industry standards. Together, these principles help organizations build trustworthy, scalable, and accountable data science solutions.

Governance, Security, and Compliance Frameworks for Data Science

The transition to cloud-based analytics platforms and the integration of AI-assisted development tools introduces complex governance challenges that extend far beyond traditional software development concerns. Data science environments handle sensitive datasets, proprietary algorithms, and often operate under strict regulatory requirements that demand comprehensive security and compliance frameworks. Organizations must implement robust governance structures that balance collaborative accessibility with stringent security controls, while ensuring compliance with evolving regulatory landscapes.

Role-Based Access Control (RBAC) Systems

Implementing effective access control in data science environments requires sophisticated permission models that address the unique challenges of collaborative analytics and protect sensitive data assets. Role-Based Access Control systems must accommodate the diverse roles within data science teams that might require broad exploratory access or restricted access to specific datasets and visualizations.

Modern RBAC implementations extend beyond simple read/write permissions as they include granular controls over data access patterns, computational resources, and model deployment capabilities. Attribute-Based Access Control (ABAC) systems provide even finer granularity by incorporating contextual factors such as time of access, geographic location, data sensitivity levels, and project classifications into permission decisions. For example, a data scientist might have full access to anonymized customer data during business hours, but will have restricted access to Personally Identifiable Information (PII) outside designated secure environments.

Data classification schemes form the foundation of effective access control, as they require organizations to systematically categorize datasets based on sensitivity levels, regulatory requirements, and business impact. Automated classification tools can scan datasets for PII, financial information, or proprietary content and automatically apply appropriate access restrictions and handling requirements. Integration with data lineage tracking ensures that access controls propagate through derived datasets and model outputs. This prevents inadvertently exposing sensitive information through analytical transformations.

Multi-factor Authentication (MFA) and Single Sign-on (SSO) integration provide additional security layers, while maintaining user experience across diverse analytical platforms. Modern identity providers support conditional access policies that adjust authentication requirements based on risk assessments, requiring additional verification for access to highly sensitive datasets or from unusual locations.

Encryption and Data Protection Standards

Comprehensive data protection requires encryption strategies that address data security throughout its entire lifecycle, from initial ingestion through analytical processing to final output and archival. Encryption in transit protects data movement between systems using protocols like TLS 1.3, while ensuring that analytical queries, model training data, and results remain secure during network transmission. This becomes particularly critical in distributed computing environments where data moves between multiple processing nodes and cloud services.

Encryption at rest presents unique challenges in analytical environments where traditional database encryption might interfere with performance-critical operations like large-scale ML training or real-time analytics queries. Modern solutions include transparent data encryption (TDE) that operates at the storage layer without impacting application performance, and application-layer encryption that selectively protects specific data fields while maintaining query capabilities over non-sensitive attributes.

Key management systems must support the complex key rotation and access patterns inherent in collaborative analytics environments. Hardware Security Modules (HSMs) and cloud-native key management services provide centralized key storage and also offer audit trails and automated rotation capabilities. Envelope encryption techniques can efficiently encrypt large datasets via data encryption keys (DEKs) that are themselves encrypted with key encryption keys (KEKs) stored in secure key management systems.

Field-level encryption and tokenization techniques allow organizations to protect sensitive data elements and maintain analytical utility. For example, customer identifiers can be tokenized to enable cohort analysis and model training, while preventing direct identification of individuals. Format-preserving encryption maintains data structure and relationships necessary for certain analytical techniques, while providing for cryptographic protection.

AI Code Generation Audit and Accountability

The integration of AI-assisted development tools like GitHub Copilot, TabNine, or custom code generation models introduces novel governance challenges that require specialized audit and accountability frameworks. Therefore, AI suggestion logging systems must capture code suggestions provided by AI models as well as developer acceptance patterns, modification history, and ultimate deployment decisions.

Provenance tracking for AI-generated code requires maintaining detailed records of the specific portions of analytical code that have originated from AI suggestions, including the specific model versions and training data used to generate recommendations. This information later becomes critical for security audits, intellectual property assessments, and debugging efforts when AI-suggested code produces unexpected results or exposes security vulnerabilities.

Thus, code review processes must evolve to address AI-generated content. Reviewers must evaluate the functional correctness of code as well as its alignment with organizational security policies and coding standards. Automated scanning tools can detect potential security vulnerabilities or compliance violations in AI-generated code, while flagging issues such as hardcoded credentials, insecure API usage, or data handling practices that violate privacy regulations.

Bias and fairness auditing becomes particularly important when AI tools assist in developing ML models or analytical workflows. Organizations must implement systematic evaluation processes to assess whether AI-generated code introduces algorithmic bias or perpetuates unfair treatment of protected groups. This includes reviewing training data sources for AI coding assistants and continuously monitor model outputs developed with AI assistance.

License compliance tracking for AI-generated code presents complex challenges, particularly when AI models have been trained on open-source code with varying license requirements. Therefore, organizations must implement systems to identify potential license conflicts and ensure compliance with both proprietary and open-source licensing terms in AI-suggested code.

Privacy Regulation Compliance

Global privacy regulations create complex compliance requirements that affect every aspect of data science operations, from initial data collection through model development to result dissemination and data retention. General Data Protection Regulation (GDPR) compliance requires implementing comprehensive frameworks for data subject rights, including the right to access, rectify, port, and erase personal data.

Data minimization principles under GDPR require organizations to collect and process only personal data that is necessary for specified analytical purposes. This necessitates systematic evaluation of dataset requirements, implementation of data reduction techniques, and regular auditing of data retention practices. Purpose limitation requirements mandate that personal data collected for one analytical purpose cannot be used for incompatible purposes without additional legal basis and subject consent.

California Consumer Privacy Act (CCPA) and its successor, the California Privacy Rights Act (CPRA), establish additional requirements for businesses operating in California, including mandatory disclosure of personal information sales, opt-out mechanisms, and enhanced rights for sensitive personal information. These regulations affect data science teams working with California resident data regardless of the organization's physical location.

Data localization requirements in various jurisdictions may restrict where personal data can be processed or stored, affecting cloud provider selection and data pipeline architecture. Regulations such as Russia's Federal Law on Personal Data, China's Cybersecurity Law, and India's Personal Data Protection Bill create complex compliance matrices that data science teams must navigate, while working with international datasets.

Anonymization and pseudonymization techniques provide mechanisms for compliance with privacy regulations while maintaining analytical utility. Differential privacy implementations add mathematical noise to datasets in ways that provide provable privacy guarantees and also enable statistical analysis. k-anonymity, l-diversity, and t-closeness techniques provide alternative approaches for protecting individual privacy in analytical datasets.

Consent management systems must track and enforce data subject consent across complex analytical workflows, ensuring that personal data is only used for purposes covered by valid consent. This includes implementing mechanisms to withdraw consent retroactively and remove associated data from ongoing analytical processes and trained models.

Cross-border data transfer mechanisms such as Standard Contractual Clauses (SCCs), Binding Corporate Rules (BCRs), and adequacy decisions must be properly implemented when data science operations span multiple jurisdictions. Recent legal developments, including the Schrems II decision, have created additional requirements for supplementary measures to ensure adequate protection for international data transfers.

These frameworks represent the essential infrastructure for mature data science operations and require ongoing investment and specialized expertise for data scientists to navigate the regulatory landscape while maintaining operational efficiency and collaborative capabilities.

Your Growth Roadmap

The rapidly evolving landscape of data science tools, methodologies, and regulatory requirements demands a structured approach to continuous professional development. Therefore, organizations and individual practitioners must establish systematic learning frameworks that balance technical skill development with emerging domain knowledge, while fostering collaborative learning within teams and broader professional communities.

Industry Certification Programs

Professional certifications provide structured learning paths and validated credentials that demonstrate proficiency across specific technology stacks and analytical domains. These programs offer both individual career advancement opportunities and organizational benefits through standardized skill development and vendor-specific expertise.

The **AWS Certified Data Analytics-Specialty** certification covers the comprehensive Amazon Web Services data analytics ecosystem, including data ingestion through Amazon Kinesis and AWS Glue, storage optimization using Amazon S3 and data lakes, processing with Amazon EMR and AWS Lambda, and visualization through Amazon QuickSight. The certification exam encompasses advanced topics such as real-time streaming analytics, ML integration with Amazon SageMaker, and cost optimization strategies for large-scale data processing workloads. Preparing for the exam involves having hands-on experience with AWS data pipeline architectures, security configurations, and performance tuning across distributed computing environments.

Another certification is the Google Cloud Professional Data Engineer, which focuses on Google Cloud Platform's data analytics and ML capabilities. The exam syllabus covers BigQuery for petabyte-scale analytics, Cloud Dataflow for stream and batch processing, Cloud AI Platform for ML operations, and Cloud Composer for workflow orchestration. The certification addresses advanced topics including data governance, privacy compliance, and integration with Google's AI and ML services. Candidates must demonstrate proficiency in designing scalable data processing systems, implementing security controls, and optimizing query performance across Google Cloud's analytics stack.

The Microsoft Azure AI Engineer Associate certification encompasses Azure's artificial intelligence and ML services, including Azure Machine Learning for model development and deployment, Cognitive Services for pre-built AI capabilities, and Azure Bot Framework for conversational AI applications. The program covers MLOps practices, responsible AI principles, and integration with Azure's broader cloud ecosystem. Advanced topics include custom model development, automated machine learning workflows, and production deployment strategies enacted across Azure's container and serverless platforms.

Emerging certification programs address specialized domains and emerging technologies. The Certified Analytics Professional (CAP) provides a vendor-neutral validation of analytical skills across the entire analytics lifecycle. Databricks Certified Data Engineer and Certified Machine Learning Professional certifications focus on unified analytics platforms that combine data engineering and ML workflows. Kubernetes certifications such as Certified Kubernetes Administrator (CKA) and Certified Kubernetes Application Developer (CKAD) address container orchestration skills that are increasingly important for deploying scalable analytics workloads.

Professional Community Engagement

Active participation in professional communities provides access to emerging best practices, collaborative problem-solving opportunities, and networking relationships that accelerate both individual and organizational learning. These communities offer diverse engagement models from passive information consumption to active contribution and leadership roles.

Databricks Community provides a comprehensive platform for unified analytics practitioners, while offering discussion forums for data engineering and ML topics, shared notebooks and code repositories, and regular webinars featuring industry experts and product developments. The community includes specialized groups for specific use cases such as healthcare analytics, financial services, and retail applications, enabling domain-specific knowledge sharing and collaboration.

Prefect Slack community focuses on modern workflow orchestration and data pipeline management, providing real-time collaboration opportunities with workflow automation experts and Prefect development team members. The community addresses practical challenges in production workflow deployment, error handling strategies, and integration with various data platforms and cloud services.

GitHub Discussions across major open-source data science projects offer opportunities to engage with tool maintainers and power users, contribute to project roadmaps, and access cutting-edge developments before general availability. Key repositories include scikit-learn for ML algorithms, pandas for data manipulation, and Apache Airflow for workflow management. Participation ranges from bug reporting and feature requests, to contributing code improvements and documentation updates.

Professional organizations such as the International Association for Statistical Computing (IASC), Association for Computing Machinery's Special Interest Group on Knowledge Discovery and Data Mining (ACM SIGKDD), and Institute for Operations Research and the Management Sciences (INFORMS) provide access to academic research, industry best practices, and professional networking opportunities through conferences, workshops, and publications.

Local meetups and chapters of organizations like PyData, and R User Groups offer in-person networking and learning opportunities tailored to specific geographic regions and technology stacks. These groups often feature presentations from local practitioners and provide opportunities for collaborative projects and mentorship relationships.

Continuous Learning and Industry Intelligence

Being aware of rapidly evolving technologies, methodologies, and industry trends requires systematic approaches to information consumption and knowledge synthesis. Effective learning strategies balance depth and breadth and filter signal from noise in crowded information landscapes.

Specialized Newsletters and Publications provide curated content tailored for data science practitioners. Data Science Weekly aggregates significant developments in machine learning research, industry applications, and tool announcements with editorial commentary on implications for practitioners. Import AI focuses specifically on artificial intelligence developments with emphasis on research breakthroughs, policy implications, and ethical considerations. The Batch by deeplearning.ai provides weekly summaries of AI industry news along with educational context for understanding broader implications.

Academic and Industry Publications include Journal of Machine Learning Research (JMLR), Proceedings of Machine Learning Research (PMLR), and Nature Machine Intelligence for accessing cutting-edge research developments. Industry publications such as Harvard Business Review's Analytics and AI section and MIT Technology Review provide strategic perspectives on technology adoption and business impact. arXiv preprint server offers early access to research developments before formal publication with RSS feeds and email alerts for specific subject areas.

Podcast and Video Content platforms provide learning opportunities during commutes and exercise routines. Data Skeptic, Linear Digressions, and The TWIML AI Podcast offer regular content that covers both technical developments and industry applications. YouTube channels such as 3Blue1Brown for mathematical concepts, Two Minute Papers for research summaries, and vendor-specific channels from Google Cloud, AWS, and Microsoft Azure for platform-specific developments.

Conference and Workshop Attendance provides access to both announced developments and informal networking opportunities. Major conferences include Neural Information Processing Systems (NeurIPS), International Conference on Machine Learning (ICML), Knowledge Discovery and Data Mining (KDD), and Strata Data Conference. Virtual attendance options have expanded access while in-person events continue to provide valuable networking opportunities and hands-on workshops.

Industry Analyst Research from organizations such as Gartner, Forrester, and IDC provides strategic perspectives on technology trends, vendor evaluations, and market forecasts that inform long-term technology investment decisions. Many organizations provide complimentary access to research summaries and webinars that offer valuable insights without full subscription costs.

Internal Learning Programs within organizations can amplify individual learning efforts through knowledge sharing, internal conferences, and collaborative learning initiatives. Journal clubs for reviewing and discussing recent research papers, internal tech talks for sharing project experiences and lessons learned, and hackathons for exploring new technologies provide structured learning opportunities within organizational contexts.

This comprehensive approach to professional development ensures that data science practitioners maintain current knowledge while developing deep expertise in areas most relevant to their career objectives and organizational needs. The combination of formal certification programs, community engagement, practical project experience, and systematic information consumption creates a foundation for sustained professional growth in the rapidly evolving data science landscape.

Conclusion

The transformation from foundational data science skills to professional expertise represents more than technical growth. It requires a fundamental shift in perspective from individual analysis to collaborative, production-ready systems that deliver measurable business value. This chapter has outlined the essential pathways that bridge the gap between learning data science and practicing it at scale in real-world environments.

The core theme throughout these advanced topics is integration: models that integrate into products, local environments that integrate with cloud infrastructure, individual workflows that integrate into orchestrated pipelines, and isolated work that integrates into collaborative team processes. This integration mindset separates hobbyist data science from professional practice, where success depends not only on analytical skills but on the ability to build reliable, scalable, and maintainable systems.

Equally important is the recognition that modern data science operates within increasingly complex governance frameworks. Security, compliance, and ethical considerations are not afterthoughts but fundamental design requirements that shape every aspect of professional practice. The most successful data scientists are those who can navigate these constraints while maintaining innovation and analytical rigor.

Perhaps most critically, this chapter emphasizes that data science has evolved into a collaborative discipline requiring diverse skills, continuous learning, and active community engagement. The days of the isolated analyst working alone with static datasets are rapidly disappearing and are replaced by cross-functional teams managing dynamic, large-scale systems that serve real users.

Your journey from this point forward will be defined by your ability to synthesize technical expertise with systems thinking, individual skills with collaborative capabilities, and analytical insights with business impact. The tools and frameworks discussed here provide the foundation, but your success will ultimately depend on your ability to adapt, learn continuously, and contribute meaningfully to the evolving data science ecosystem.

The future belongs to data scientists who can think beyond models to entire systems and weave technical solutions into human-centered impact. With the solid roadmap outlined in this chapter, you are well-positioned to meet these challenges, and contribute to the next phase of evolution in data science practice.

Index

D

S

U

V

W